Praise for *Black Politics in Transition*

Candis Smith and Christina Greer have filled a significant void. This is the first book to examine how Black migratory patterns within metropolitan regions, urban neighborhoods, and across state boundaries—combined with the influx of Blacks from Africa and the Caribbean—have transformed Black Politics. *Black Politics in Transition* adds new insights and theories about African American political life.

Marion Orr, *Frederick Lippitt Professor of*
Public Policy & Professor of Political Science,
Brown University, author of Black Social Capital

Transitions are exciting, intimidating, hopeful, sad—and transformative. This book's focus on immigration, suburbanization, and gentrification is right on the front edge of scholarship, racial and ethnic politics, and individual choice or constraint. It sets us up for the next few decades of research on race in America.

Jennifer Hochschild, *Henry LaBarre Jayne*
Professor of Government, and Professor of African and
African American Studies, Harvard University

BLACK POLITICS IN TRANSITION

Black Politics in Transition considers the impact of three transformative forces—immigration, suburbanization, and gentrification—on Black politics today. Demographic changes resulting from immigration and ethnic blending are dramatically affecting the character and identity of Black populations throughout the US. Black Americans are becoming more ethnically diverse at the same time that they are sharing space with newcomers from near and far. In addition, the movement of Black populations out of the cities to which they migrated a generation ago—a reverse migration to the American South, in some cases, and in other cases a movement from cities to suburbs shifts the locus of Black politics. At the same time, middle class and white populations are returning to cities, displacing low income Blacks and immigrants alike in a renewal of gentrification. All this makes for an important laboratory of discovery among social scientists, including the diverse range of authors represented here. Drawing on a wide array of disciplinary perspectives and methodological strategies, original chapters analyze the geography of opportunity for Black Americans and Black politics in accessible, jargon-free language. Moving beyond the Black–white binary, this book explores the tri-part relationship among Blacks, whites, and Latinos as well. Some of the most important developments in Black politics are happening at state and local levels today, and this book captures that for students, scholars, and citizens engaged in this dynamic milieu.

Candis Watts Smith is Assistant Professor of Public Policy at the University of North Carolina–Chapel Hill. She also has affiliations with the Department of African and African American Diaspora Studies and Department of Political Science.

Christina M. Greer is Associate Professor of Political Science and American Studies at Fordham University. She also has affiliations with the Urban Studies Program and American Studies Department.

Race, Ethnicity, and Gender in Politics and Policy

In collaboration with the Center for the Study of Race, Ethnicity, and Gender in the Social Sciences at Duke University

Series Editors: Kerry L. Haynie and Paula D. McClain

This series is devoted to publishing studies that examine and explain the dramatic transformations in race, ethnicity, and gender politics over the past decade. We welcome work that highlights and analyzes the ways that race, ethnicity, and gender—and especially, their various intersections—interact to shape political institutions, individual attitudes and behaviors, social norms, and the policy-making process. Books in the series will include original scholarly research, core textbooks, supplementary topical books, and reference works.

Titles in the Series

African American LGBTQ Politics
Jerome Hunt and Shameka Nicole Cathey

Black Politics in Transition
Immigration, Suburbanization, and Gentrification
Edited by Candis Watts Smith and Christina M. Greer

https://www.routledge.com/Race-Ethnicity-and-Gender-in-Politics-and-Policy/book-series/REGPP

BLACK POLITICS IN TRANSITION

Immigration, Suburbanization, and Gentrification

Edited by Candis Watts Smith

University of North Carolina-Chapel Hill

Christina M. Greer

Fordham University

Routledge
Taylor & Francis Group

NEW YORK AND LONDON

Published 2019
by Routledge
711 Third Avenue, New York, NY 10017

and by Routledge
2 Park Square, Milton Park, Abingdon, Oxon, OX14 4RN

Routledge is an imprint of the Taylor & Francis Group, an informa business

© 2019 Taylor & Francis

The right of Candis Watts Smith and Christina M. Greer to be
identified as the author of the editorial material, and of the authors for
their individual chapters, has been asserted in accordance with sections
77 and 78 of the Copyright, Designs and Patents Act 1988.

Library of Congress Cataloging-in-Publication Data
A catalog record has been requested for this book

ISBN: 978-1-138-05848-4 (hbk)
ISBN: 978-1-138-05850-7 (pbk)
ISBN: 978-1-315-16423-6 (ebk)

Typeset in Bembo
by codeMantra

To the people who have moved or
have had to move for their families,
or because of natural disasters,
man-made disasters, empty-nest syndrome,
terrible housemates, political oppression,
condemned homes, post-incarceration,
new opportunities, upward mobility,
climate change, downsizing, foreclosure,
bad water, famine, eviction, school, love,
war, jobs, abusive relationships, to start over,
to close the long-distance relationship gap,
or because the rent has just gotten too damn high.

CONTENTS

CONTRIBUTORS

Sharon D. Wright Austin is Director of the African American Studies Program and Professor of Political Science at the University of Florida. She received a doctorate in Political Science from the University of Tennessee at Knoxville. She is the author of three books—*Race, Power, and Political Emergence in Memphis* (Routledge, 1999); *The Transformation of Plantation Politics in the Mississippi Delta: Black Politics, Concentrated Poverty, and Social Capital in the Mississippi Delta* (SUNY Press 2007); and *The Caribbeanization of Black Politics: Race, Group Consciousness, and Political Participation in America* (SUNY Press, 2018). She is also the author of several scholarly articles.

Andrea Benjamin is Assistant Professor at the University of Missouri-Columbia. She earned her PhD in Political Science from the University of Michigan. She is the author of *Racial Coalition Building in Local Elections: Elite Cues and Cross-Ethnic Voting* (Cambridge University Press, 2017).

Niambi M. Carter is Assistant Professor of Political Science at Howard University. She earned her PhD in Political Science from Duke University and her work has appeared in numerous journals such as *Political Psychology; Politics, Groups, and Identities; The Journal of Politics; Journal of African American Studies*; and many other outlets.

Cory Charles Gooding is Assistant Professor of Political Science at the University of San Diego. He earned his PhD in Political Science from the University of California, Los Angeles. His work focuses on race, ethnicity, and citizenship and has appeared in several edited volumes and journals.

Christina M. Greer is Associate Professor of Political Science at Fordham University in New York City. She has an affiliation with Urban Studies and American Studies. She earned her PhD in Political Science from Columbia University and is the author of *Black Ethnics: Race, Immigration, and the Pursuit of the American Dream* (Oxford University Press, 2013).

Sarah Mayorga-Gallo is Assistant Professor of Sociology at the University of Massachusetts-Boston. She earned her PhD in Sociology from Duke University and is the author of *Behind the White Picket Fence: Power and Privilege in a Multiethnic Neighborhood* (UNC Press, 2014), which won the Distinguished Contribution to Research Book Award from the American Sociological Association's Latino/a Sociology Section in 2015.

Ernest B. McGowen III is Associate Professor of Political Science at the University of Richmond. His specialties include race and ethnicity, political behavior, and social networks. He is the author of *African Americans in White Suburbia* (University Press of Kansas, 2017).

Reuel R. Rogers is Associate Professor of Political Science at Northwestern University, where he also is affiliated with the Department of African American Studies and the Latin American and Caribbean Studies Program. He earned his PhD in Politics from Princeton University. He is the author of *Afro-Caribbean Immigrants and the Politics of Incorporation: Ethnicity, Exception, or Exit* (Cambridge University Press, 2006).

Candis Watts Smith is Assistant Professor of Public Policy at the University of North Carolina-Chapel Hill. She has affiliations with the Department of Political Science and Department of African and African American Diaspora Studies. She earned her PhD in Political Science from Duke University and is the author of *Black Mosaic: The Politics of Black Pan-Ethnic Diversity* (NYU Press, 2014).

Jessica Lynn Stewart is a post-doctoral fellow of the Anna Julia Cooper Center in the Department of Politics and International Affairs at Wake Forest University. Following her fellowship, she will join the faculty of Emory University as assistant professor of African American Studies, focusing on Political Economy of Race. She is a former Mayo Clinic Administrative Fellow and POSSE Foundation alumna. Her published works can be found in edited volumes and in journals such as the *National Political Science Review.*

INTRODUCTION

Black Flight

Candis Watts Smith

Old tropes are often rooted in partial truths, and they tend to die very slow deaths.[1] Persistent, negative stereotypes and inaccurate, taken-for-granted narratives of Black communities, Black politics, and Black people provide illustrative examples of this observation. For instance, during the 2016 presidential campaign, then-candidate Donald J. Trump traded the racial dog whistle for a bullhorn to address his overwhelmingly white audience:

> Look how much African American communities have suffered under Democratic control. To those, I say the following, "What do you have to lose by trying something new like Trump? What do you have to lose?... I'll say it again, what do you have to lose? Look, what do you have to lose? You're living in poverty, your schools are no good, you have no jobs, fifty-eight percent of your youth is unemployed. What the hell do you have to lose?... And at the end of four years, I guarantee you that I will get over 95 per cent of the African American vote. I promise you."

These familiar images and narratives, though "completely void of details about the serious economic and political challenges" Black people face, are taken as fact. Partial truths are convenient because they do not "need irrefutable evidence to be effective," and they are powerful because they "justify the public's instinctive biases about certain groups" (Cohen, 2010, pp. 28–30). Throughout his campaign, the candidate often relied on coded racial appeals, asserting the necessity of "law and order" policies in "inner-cities," such as Chicago, Illinois, and Ferguson, Missouri (which is actually a suburb); his suggestions also included expanding the use of stop-and-frisk and other aggressive police tactics to tame Black communities. Though many on the left argue that Trump, his politics, and his rhetoric are not "who we are as Americans," we cannot ignore that approximately 62,979,879 American citizens voted him into office.

Trump is by no means the only person to believe that Black communities are homogeneous spaces best characterized by chaos and violence; his supporters are not alone in ignoring the diversity and vitality of Black communities. It is true that if we delve into a nuanced assessment of Black life in America, we would find that Black people *do* face enduring inequalities brought on by policymakers—both Democratic and Republican. Many cities *have* lost populations due to white and Black middle-class flight. Dilapidation and social blight *have* become commonplace in many cities, and in far too many locales, there *is* evidence of financial mismanagement and overall failures in executive leadership. The notion that the overwhelming majority of Black people live in impoverished inner cities is enduring but inaccurate, and the suggestion that Black people have no real political agency or choice in the American political environment is asinine.

Since the mid-1960s a set of watershed changes in American politics and policy has broadened the geography of opportunity for Black people but also presented new challenges to Black politics. For instance, we have seen a change in the porousness of the color-line, though not a wholesale elimination. Mary Pattillo explains, "The color-line is a metaphor for the mechanisms and practices that maintain racial inequality as well as a more literal description of the many places and systems in which blacks are on one side and whites are on another side of a visible or invisible line. Blacks live on one side of the city, whites on another…" (as cited in Drake & Cayton, 1945/2015, p. xvi). The 1964 Civil Rights Act, the Voting Rights Act of 1965, and the Fair Housing Act enacted in 1968 made it illegal to discriminate in many (but not all) realms of American society, and opened up the chances for Black Americans to employ the power of the ballot in order to elect leaders of their choice.

Another policy that broadened the borders of opportunity for Black folks (across the Diaspora) was the Immigration and Nationality Act of 1965. This policy abolished the national quota systems, outlined by the Johnson-Reed Act four decades prior. Though people usually associate the policy with increasing the number of Latinx and Asian immigrants to the United States, this policy also served to change the ethnic composition of Blacks in this country. The movement of Latinx, Asian, and Black immigrants to the United States shifted the points of focus of Black politics across an array of American communities. Finally, and perhaps due in part to the aforementioned policies, not only have Black Americans taken the opportunity to cross the physical color-line, moving into predominately white neighborhoods or into historically white suburbs, but they have also reversed the trend of the Great Migration. Rather than moving away from the South to the West, Midwest, and Northeast, many Blacks across the national and international Diaspora have found the South to be a welcoming home (Frey, 2004; Pendergrass, 2013; Tavernier, 2015; Wilkerson, 2010).

The tremendous movement of people—this "Black flight" we are seeing sweep across neighborhoods, cities, states, regions, and countries in the first decades of the twenty-first century—is not inconsequential, and although demographic change is not destiny, it can send reverberations across social, economic, and political landscapes. Through this collection of new works, the contributors of *Black Politics in Transition* provide us with a better understanding of the ways in which three important mechanisms of demographic change— immigration, gentrification, and suburbanization—are influencing Black politics across the United States. The contributors ask and seek to answer the following questions: How have these mechanisms influenced Black political behavior? Black policy preferences? Black identities? What new complexities arise in the face of increasing ethnic diversity among Blacks? How has (racialized) neighborhood change, such as gentrification, influenced Blacks' political power, efficacy, and ability to enact important policy changes? Taken together, this volume sets the record straight by providing a set of nuanced assessments of twenty-first-century Black politics, grounded within the dynamics of local contexts.

Black Metropolises

In 1945, sociologists St. Clair Drake and Horace R. Cayton published *Black Metropolis: A Study of Negro Life in a Northern City*. There, they meticulously articulated the life, challenges, and vitality of African Americans in Chicago's Black Metropolis, or the "eight square miles" of Bronzeville. The Black Metropolis can be thought of as not just a physical space where Black people reside, but a psychological space where "Black people strive for liberty" (Pattillo, 2017). When Drake and Cayton were writing in the 1930s and the 1940s (and even later, when they updated and expanded their study in the 1950s and 1960s), Black citizens were in the process of escaping the South's racial terrorism by moving to the Midwest, West, and Northeast regions of the United States to find better lives; they encountered fewer but also newer racial restrictions, including where they were allowed to live. As such, the physical and the psychological Black Metropolis were one in the same, highly centralized and geographically constrained. To be clear, there were multiple Black Metropolises cropping up across the country due to the Great Migration, and even within these areas, there was incredible class and ideological heterogeneity (Dawson, 2001; Drake & Cayton, 1945/2015; Frazier, 1957).

What happens when Black people have a greater range of latitude to move from one country to another, from one state to another, from city to suburbs, or to just move on up? Between World War I and the 1970s, Blacks moved from places like Louisiana to California, from Mississippi to Chicago, and from North Carolina to New York. This mass exodus, the Great Migration, both shifted and boosted Black political, social, and economic capital

(Boyd, 2012). After World War II, some Blacks were able to gain access to federal resources to attend college, gain vocational training, or purchase a home through programs outlined by the Serviceman's Readjustment Act of 1944, better known as the GI Bill (Katznelson, 2005). These changes and new policies in combination with Supreme Court decisions like *Shelley vs. Kraemer*[2] that chipped away at *de jure* racial discrimination meant Blacks were presented with a greater range of opportunities[3] to purchase homes and to do so in (what would oftentimes become *formerly*) white suburbs (Hayward & Swanstrom, 2011). Hayward and Swanstrom note that around the 1950s, "African Americans had gained access to places from which they had previously been excluded. But that gain proved a weak foundation for equalizing resources and opportunities" (Hayward & Swanstrom, 2011, p. 2). Without romanticizing racial segregation, we can still remember the ways in which Black folk were able to thrive by leveraging systemic inequalities to their economic and social advantage. Blacks were able to develop their own businesses, insurance companies, medical and law practices, as examples. Taken together, we see that with the growth of the Black middle class and new civil rights guarantees, Blacks were able to move out of the confines of the ghetto, thus expanding the boundaries of the Black Metropolis.

Moreover, Blacks leveraged their resources in the domain of politics as well; indeed, it is in the political domain where Black folks have been able to reinforce that historically weak foundation for future opportunities. The Black counterpublic—"the network of all-Black institutions that historically has served as a staging ground for collective action and a site for opinion formation, debate, and consensus-building among African Americans" (Rogers, this volume)—was able to flourish due to the fact that Blacks were able to congregate and discuss strategies for Black uplift (Cohen, 1999; Dawson, 1994, 2001; Harris-Lacewell, 2004). Over time, Black voters were able to elect members of their own group to represent them in city councils or as mayor. Later and still due to the structural constraints of residential segregation, Blacks would be able to shift their efforts from protest to employing the franchise to elect more Black representatives to Congress (Haynie, 2001; Tate, 1994).

Since the 1970s, we have seen yet another shift in the geography of the Black Metropolis—indeed, the physical and psychological do not align as closely as they once did in part due to the fact that Blacks are increasingly enjoying and employing their rights of liberty and freedom of movement. Some Black folks have been able to take their social and economic capital and voluntarily migrate across the country, or for some Blacks in the Diaspora, emigrate (Austin, Middleton, & Yon, 2012; Greer, 2013; Rogers, 2006; Smith, 2014). Meanwhile, others have been pushed out of their cities and neighborhoods due to reasons ranging from white and middle-class gentrification to, perhaps ironically, the implementation of neoliberal governance by Black political leaders (Cohen, 2010; Spence, McClerking, & Brown, 2009). And still, other longtime

Black residents find their neighbors and neighborhoods are changing around them due to Central and Latin American immigration patterns (Frey, 1999; Mayorga-Gallo, 2014; McClain, Carter, DeFrancesco Soto, & Lyle, 2006; Telles, Sawyer, & Rivera-Salgado, 2011). Black flight has expanded the geography of Black Metropolises. Below we outline some of the noteworthy dynamics in contemporary geographic and demographic change, with a special emphasis on Black people and their communities. The contributors of this volume illuminate the political ramifications of these changes.

Black Inter-Regional Migration

At the beginning of the twentieth century, approximately 90% of Blacks lived in the South. Between World War I and the 1970s, more than 5 million Blacks moved out of the South, reducing the Black population almost by half (Frey, 2015; Pendergrass, 2013). Today, we call this six-decade exodus to cities in the Northeast, Midwest, and Western regions of the country the Great Migration. Black Americans largely followed the rail lines to larger metropolitan areas, thus making cities like New York, Philadelphia, Chicago, and Detroit popular destinations; the Pacific Coast became a new destination after World War II (Gregory, 1995). Historian James Gregory notes that scholars across disciplines "have tried to assess the myriad ways that migrants remade themselves and re-made the nation. The impacts [of the Great Migration] have been so stunning, so epochal, that to study Black migration from the South is to write about the transformations of cities, politics, popular culture, and of course citizenship in the twentieth century" (1995, p. 113).

In many ways, social scientists, including some in this volume, find themselves assessing the multitude of ways that Black migrants are remaking themselves and the nation yet again, as we are currently witnessing a "reverse" or "new" Great Migration. Demographer William Frey explains, "the reversal of the Great Migration out of the South began as a trickle in the 1970s, increased in the 1990s, and turned into a virtual evacuation from many northern areas in the first decades of the 2000s" (Frey, 2015, p. 107). The statistics are stunning. At the tail end of the Great Migration, between 1965 and 1970, states like California, Michigan, Illinois, and New Jersey were among the top ten states gaining Blacks. Between 1995 and 2000, these states were among the greatest losers of Black populations, perhaps surprisingly along with New York and Washington, DC (Frey, 2004). By 2000, states like Georgia, North Carolina, Florida, Tennessee, and South Carolina boasted some of the largest gains in their Black population. While the NYC metropolitan area has been home to the greatest number of Black folks for quite some time, the Atlanta metropolitan area recently bumped Chicago to third place; meanwhile, Miami and Houston are among the top seven metro areas with the largest Black populations (Frey, 2015). Today, just under 60% of the Black population lives in the South, and the South is now the *only* region that has a net in-migration of Black Americans (Frey, 2015).

People moved out of the South for obvious reasons—racial violence, political disenfranchisement, and Jim Crow—but they also followed employment opportunities that resulted from World Wars I and II and as agricultural opportunities in the South dwindled (Frey, 2015; Gregory, 2006). Some suggest that Black citizens have been moving (back) to the South due to the South's modernization, ranging from improved "race relations" to economic growth and also kinship ties (Frey, 1999, 2004; Stack, 1996), though other scholars have pointed out that Blacks across various socioeconomic statuses move for different reasons (Hunt, Hunt, & Falk, 2008; Pendergrass, 2013). Indeed, the South is undergoing a "brain gain," as highly educated Black Americans are leading the new migration (Frey, 2004; Hunt et al., 2008). Sociologist Sabrina Pendergrass (2013) finds that well-educated Blacks may not even have kinship ties in the South, but instead, are pulled to the region due to opportunities presented by employers and educational institutions (especially historically Black colleges and universities) and due to Black media's testimony of the good life in the South. Meanwhile, it is lower-income and lesser-educated Blacks who rely primarily on kinship ties—family and friends—when making decisions about whether and where to settle in the South.

The political implications of this movement have already been felt in national and state elections in the past decade. Barack Obama's ability to turn red states like North Carolina and Virginia blue becomes less of a paradox when we consider these vast changes. Places like Charlotte and Raleigh-Durham in North Carolina are emerging destinations for Black American migrants, and Charlotte recently elected Vi Myles, its first Black, female mayor, to boot. Virginia also elected Justin Fairfax as its lieutenant governor (three decades after Douglas Wilder's first successful statewide election). Relatedly, many have noted that as Blacks are moving out of large and also historically majority-minority cities, there seems to be a decline in the number of elected Black mayors (Greenblatt, 2017; Malloy, 2017). To be sure, the recent shift in Black Americans' residential choices—constrained or otherwise—is not the only major factor that is influencing the extent to which they have political prowess in various localities, as a number of emerging destinations for Black reverse migration participants are also "new" destinations for foreign-born Black and Latinx immigrants.

Immigration

Arguably, during the mid-1960s President Lyndon B. Johnson signed several of the nation's most important pieces of legislation. While the Civil Rights Act and Voting Rights Act are quite notable, his signature on the Immigration and Nationality Act of 1965 was also pivotal. Upon signing the bill, he made his intentions clear: "This bill says simply that from this day forth those wishing to immigrate to America shall be admitted on the basis of their skills and their close relationship to those already here" (Johnson, 1965). In the wake of the Civil Rights era, Congress and President Johnson sought to apply a higher standard of fairness, and abolish a long-standing policy that resulted in only three European countries supplying 70% of America's immigrants. Johnson's prediction that "This bill that we will sign today is not a revolutionary bill. It does not affect the lives of millions," has proven to be erroneous, as the policy has served to vastly transform the demographics of the United States. Though many attribute the influx of immigrants from Latin America (and Asia) to the Hart-Celler Act, immigrants from Africa also took advantage of the opportunities presented by the US's change in policy. Though the previous policy did not bar Caribbean immigration, issues in those countries and the loosening of race-based restrictions in the United States led to more Afro-Caribbeans to immigrate post-1965. As such, we have seen Black flight not only with native-born Blacks moving across cities or regions but also as foreign-born Blacks emigrate to the United States.

Black Immigration

Cross-Atlantic Black flight is broadening the boundaries of Black identity and Black politics. Though millions of Africans were stolen, enslaved, and brought across the Atlantic between the sixteenth and mid-nineteenth centuries, journalist Sam Roberts explains, "Between 2000 and 2010,… according to the most reliable estimates, more black Africans arrived in this country on their own than were imported directly to North America during the more than three centuries of the slave trade" (Roberts, 2014). Indeed, the number of African immigrants to the United States has doubled every decade since 1980, and today, about 2.4 million immigrants from Africa now live in the United States (Anderson, 2017). Moreover, the number of Black immigrants from the Caribbean has climbed steadily over the past several decades.

About 10% of the Black population in the United States is foreign-born. While that figure may not seem significant, there are several important caveats. This figure does not take into account the number of second-generation Black immigrants. Further, Black immigrants tend to settle in particular places, including some cities where foreign-born Black populations make up nearly a third of the Black population (e.g., Miami's Black population is 34% foreign-born, NY metro area, 28%, and Washington, DC, 15%) (Anderson, 2015).

Today, the arrival of people from African countries is not the result of a brutal transatlantic slave trade but nonetheless may involve global politics, war, and dislocation not by choice. While some of the growth of the African immigrant population derives from people benefiting from the 1990 diversity visa program, many others have come as refugees from war-riddled countries like Somalia and Ethiopia. However, on the whole, Nigeria provides the largest number of African immigrants to the US (327,000), followed closely by Ethiopia (222,000), Egypt (192,000), Ghana (155,000), Kenya (136,000) and South Africa (92,000), to name a some of the many countries that diversify Black communities in the United States (Anderson, 2017).

Meanwhile, adding to this intraracial ethnic diversity are 4 million immigrants from the Caribbean. About 90% of these immigrants hail from five countries: Cuba, the Dominican Republic, Jamaica, Haiti, and Trinidad and Tobago. The rate of growth of those from the Caribbean is not nearly as dynamic as those from Africa, but just as African immigrants have come to the US for various reasons, the same can be said for those from countries in the Caribbean (Zong & Batalova, 2016).

What may come as a surprise to many is where Black immigrants settle. Anderson (2017) explains, "African immigrants to the U.S. are more likely to settle in the South (39%) or the Northeast (25%), than in the Midwest (18%) or West (17%), while the largest numbers of African immigrants are found in Texas, New York, California, Maryland, New Jersey, Massachusetts and Virginia. Each of these states is home to at least 100,000 foreign-born Africans." Additionally, Zong and Batalova's (2016) calculations of the 2010–2014 American Community Survey data reveal, "Caribbean immigrants were heavily concentrated in Florida (40 percent), New York (28 percent), and to a lesser extent, New Jersey (8 percent)." Ultimately, 64% of Caribbeans live in two metropolitan areas: New York City and Miami (where Caribbean immigrants make up 6.5% and 20.4% of the population, respectively). The next set of metropolitan areas where Afro-Caribbeans are likely to settle are Boston, Orlando, Tampa, Philadelphia, Washington, DC, Los Angeles, and Houston, and there are an increasing number of Afro-Caribbeans moving to places like Atlanta (Tavernier, 2015; Zong & Batalova, 2016)

Black immigrants comprised only about 3% of the Black population in the 1980s but, as mentioned, now make up about 10% of the population and are expected to grow to around 16.5% by 2060. It is also important to note that Black immigrants tend to be more educated, on average, than native-born Blacks, which may partially explain the fact that their children are overrepresented in elite institutions of higher education in the US (Bleier, 2015; Massey, Charles, Lundy, & Fischer, 2008). And though they are racialized as Black in the US, they face different challenges and thus have varying policy preferences, sometimes in direct conflict with native-born Blacks' preferences (Capers & Smith, 2015; Greer, 2013; Rogers, 2004, 2006; Smith, 2014, 2017).

The movement of Black people from across the Atlantic into various states across this country serves to increase not only Black ethnic diversity but also heterogeneity in the ideological leanings, policy preferences, and political behavior of people called Black in this country. The boundaries of Blackness are shifting due to the growth of this population, but the effects are not likely to be homogeneous across localities. Again, it will be important to examine how context—rooted in the share of the population, state political culture, country of origin, and reasons for immigration—influences whether and the degree to which Black immigrants will politically incorporate, assimilate, or resist the (racial) politics of the United States altogether. The chapters in Part I of this volume provide insight into this matter.

Latinx (Im)Migrants

Though we are largely concerned about the Black geographic reconfiguration across the US, we would be remiss to not briefly discuss how Latinx migration patterns also influence Black politics. An oft-cited statistic is that Latinx citizens and denizens are now the largest ethno-racial minority group in the country, outpacing Blacks around the turn of the twenty-first century. In 1970, there were about 9.6 million Latinx residents in the US; that number grew to 50.5 million by 2010, and to be clear, most of the recent uptick is due to natural increase rather than immigration (Barreto & Segura, 2014; Frey, 2015). Aside from the growth of the population, we should like to point out that though Black and Latinx Americans have traditionally settled in very different places, this is becoming less accurate.

As Black Americans are moving about the country, Latinx people are also settling in a range of new locations (Barnett, 2011; McClain et al., 2006; McClain et al., 2011). Frey (2015) classifies 145 areas as "new destinations," or places where "less than 16 percent of the total population is Hispanic but the 2000–2010 Hispanic growth rate is at least 86%—twice the national growth rate for Hispanics." The vast majority of these locales are east of the Mississippi River, in stark contrast to the Southwest and Pacific Coast (as well as New York and south Florida) where the great majority of Latinxs have traditionally settled. Consequently, many Latinx individuals and families are now making their homes in predominately white communities in the Midwest and Northeast, or in Southern states where the population has been characterized by a historical Black–white racial binary. Among the many "new destinations" are places like Atlanta and Charlotte (whose Latinx population grew by 153% between 2000 and 2010), Knoxville, Tennessee, Wilmington, North Carolina, and Louisville, Kentucky.

Nearly half of Latinx migrants who move to these new destinations, especially those who move to the South, are foreign-born; this group is also less educated, less proficient in English, and younger than the average American (Frey, 2015). Social scientists are tasked with answering a depth of questions: To what degree will Latinx folks be welcomed and accommodated by those who already live in these "new destinations"? What challenges will members of various groups face as the population changes? Will Black Americans embrace this group as potential political allies, or see them as competition for ostensibly scarce resources?

Some of these questions have begun to be answered (see Telles et al., 2011), but even within the past decade, we continue to see fluctuating dynamics. For instance, the social construction of Latinx immigrants has undergone a major transformation over the ten years (Merolla, Ramakrishnan, & Haynes, 2013; Pérez, 2016; Schneider & Ingram, 1993). Despite being known as the "Deporter in Chief," President Obama also championed the potential implementation of the DREAM (Development, Relief and Education for Alien Minors) Act. Obama's signature presidential memorandum, Deferred Action for Childhood Arrivals (DACA), may have also served to shift how people think of young, undocumented Latinx immigrants (though DACA also covered many Asian, African, and Caribbean immigrants as well). Just as quickly, we saw yet another change in the dominant narrative of Latinx people as Trump openly described Latinx immigrants, with a special emphasis on Mexican immigrants, as people who "have lots of problems...They're bringing drugs. They're bringing crime. They're rapists" (Reilly, 2016).

Black folks have traditionally felt ambivalent about immigration (Capers & Smith, 2015; Diamond, 1998; Smith, 2014). On the one hand, Black citizens tend to have lower levels of education and income than whites and thus have been more likely to see immigrants who move to the US to do low-skilled labor as economic threats (Diamond, 1998; McClain, 1993; McClain & Karnig, 1990). On the other hand, Black people tend to want to avoid heeding the racial dog whistle politics that are quite prevalent in the Right's political rhetoric (Carter, 2007; Carter & Pérez, 2016). These interethnic dynamics are likely to differ by local context, especially as "race-space demographic profiles" across the country are shifting (Frey, 1999). For instance, there are some places in the South to which highly educated Blacks and less-educated Latinxs are heading, and this combination is not likely to lead to the intergroup conflict that we might see in a space where less-educated foreign migrants are living adjacent to low-skilled native-born populations. It is only by zooming in on various localities that we can really appreciate the myriad possibilities for Black politics in the wake of Latinx immigration, as we do in this volume.

Suburbanization

Just as the American imagination paints cities as largely Black, poor, and crime-ridden—as illustrated by Trump's words at the opening of this chapter—the stereotypical image of American suburbs can be characterized as a middle- to upper-class, white, crime-free, pristine place where the American Dream comes to fruition. As early as the 1920s, when the use of the automobile became more widespread, elite whites were able to move out of the cities and into the suburbs. Then, after the Second World War, there was a dramatic uptick in homes built in American suburbs (Frey, 2015; Vicino, 2008). As a point of reference, in 1944, about 142,000 housing units were built, but by 1946, this number rose to near a million new homes built annually, and by the end of the decade, 1.9 million, most of which were in the suburbs (Nicolaides & Weise, 2013). By 1947, the construction firm Levitt & Sons built about 12 houses per day in Levittown, Long Island, alone (and there were and still are other Levittowns) (Peltz, 1988).

White Americans, especially veterans, could buy these affordable homes costing around $6,990 to $7,990 by putting $90 down and paying the remainder in $58 installments (Nicolaides & Weise, 2013; Peltz, 1988). Becky Nicolaides and Andrew Weise (2013) explain, "In the new suburbia, older social barriers of religion, ethnicity, and class... fell away. This tolerance stopped at race" (258). These sprawling suburbs were segregated largely due to a series of government-sponsored discriminatory policies that overtly (and sometimes violently) excluded Blacks from buying and living in these pristine communities of one-family homes (Frasure-Yokley, 2015; Katznelson, 2005; Nicolaides & Weise, 2013; Rothstein, 2017). These communities served to cement the modern incarnation of middle-class whiteness (Nicolaides & Weise, 2013) and also build the foundation of the racial wealth gap that we see today (Oliver & Shapiro, 1995).

Again, shifts in policy and law, such as the Fair Housing Act, gave Blacks and other people of color greater latitude to meet their desire to move out of the city with the ability to do so. Frey asserts, "While delayed for decades, the full-scale suburbanization of blacks is finally underway" (Frey, 2015, p. 155). As such, the "chocolate cities and vanilla suburbs" trope is actually no longer very useful to describe either cities or suburbs. To begin, Latinxs, not Blacks, constitute the largest minority group residing in American cities; meanwhile, most Black, Latinx, and Asian Americans live in suburbs. People of color make up about 35% of the population in American suburbs, which is directly proportional to their composition of the American population (Frey, 2015).

Black Americans' shift to the suburbs has been slow but steady. In 1990, less than 40% of Blacks in the 100 largest metropolitan areas lived in the suburbs; that increased to just over half by 2010. Mary Pattillo explains, "In only six of the twenty largest metropolitan areas (Philadelphia, Baltimore, San Diego, New York, Detroit, and Chicago) are blacks more likely to live in the city as opposed to the suburbs" (as cited in Drake & Cayton, 1945/2015). Meanwhile, Frey notes, "the suburbs of Atlanta, Houston, Washington, D.C., and Dallas experienced the largest increases in black populations during 2000–10," along with Chicago and Detroit, where Black people are moving out of the city and into the suburbs (Frey, 2015, p. 155). The movement of Blacks into the suburbs is uneven across the country. Racial disparities and segregation are more likely to be maintained in Northern and Midwestern areas, where Blacks remain in the city and whites in the suburbs, more so than in the South (Frey, 2015).

Though the suburbs are becoming more diverse—not to be confused with exurbs, which remain very white—it does not necessarily follow that they are socially integrated, economically well-off, or politically fair. Political scientist Lorrie Frasure-Yokely notes, "[T]he contemporary rise in minority representation in U.S. suburbs has not yielded substantial declines in residential segregation. Some suburban areas are paradoxically faced with increasing minority segregation and isolation rather than racial/ethnic diversity" (2015, p. 5). In fact, research reveals that "while the vast majority of blacks and Latinos have historically lived in high-poverty suburban communities, over time, the concentration of poverty has grown acutely for black and Latino suburban populations, reproducing patterns of disadvantage commonly seen in cities" (Chen, 2017).

Ostensibly, Blacks are moving to suburbs to achieve the American Dream, but many are finding new sources of inequality. What's more, the demographic shifts in American suburbs are also bringing about new political configurations, coalitions, and potential for conflict. The interests and political preferences of those who live in the suburbs are shifting, as there is greater economic, linguistic, and cultural heterogeneity. Thus, the ways in which both citizens and their political representatives behave are also likely to evolve in the face of a greater diversity of interests and political ideologies. For our purposes, we should remind our reader that historically, Blacks have lived together in the South, then later in highly segregated and centralized portions of America's cities. With increased dispersal, we ask and seek to answer in this book: What should we expect from those who move away from historically Black communities? Will the ties that bind stretch across the interstate?

Neighborhood Change

Lastly, we consider, perhaps, the smallest scale of demographic change: racialized neighborhood change. Words like "schools," "neighbors," and "friends" might come to mind when we think of neighborhoods, just as easily as words like "enclaves," "segregation," and "fences." The word "ghetto" might also come to mind. Americans have a way of avoiding certain words that explicitly reference patterns of structural racism, often exchanging them for euphemisms. In this case, phrases such as "across the tracks," "bad schools," and "rough areas" come to mind, but we ought to be clear that a ghetto "accurately describes a neighborhood where government has not only concentrated a minority but established barriers to its exit" (Rothstein, 2017, p. xvi). Indeed, between the Emancipation Proclamation and the 1970s, Black segregation in American ghettos "continued unabated" (Frey, 2015, p. 169). We point this out to make clear that while many Americans have come to believe that neighborhoods are segregated because people naturally aim to live with their own kind—in this case, alongside their racial group—the segregation in neighborhoods that we have seen over time has occurred because the American government and dominant members of society have made it so through redlining, blockbusting, racial covenants, and prevention of access to government-backed, low interest loans, to name a few mechanisms (Coates, 2014; Katznelson, 2005; Rothstein, 2017).

But, as we have discussed, changes in the extent to which Americans live in racially segregated neighborhoods can have an effect on the shape of American democracy. Since the 1970s, Black–white segregation levels have declined. The dissimilarity index is one way of measuring racial segregation; this index ranges from 0, indicating full integration, to 100, indicating full segregation; scores above 60 are understood among social scientists to be high, while those below 30 are deemed low. In 1970, the American Black–white dissimilarity measure was 70, meaning that 70% of Black folks would need to move to another neighborhood in order for communities to be more evenly representative of the population; by 2010, this number creeped to just below 50 (Frey, 2015).[4]

Needless to say, national averages don't necessarily provide the nuance required to understand segregation and its influence on politics at the state and local levels. In fact, and perhaps counterintuitively, some of the most segregated areas are in the Midwest and Northeast, and places where integration is increasing at a faster clip are in Southern metropolitan areas. Not to put too fine a point on it, even at this "reduced" level of segregation, Black and Latinx people still remain targets and victims of disparate housing policies. For instance, Massey, Rugh, Steil, and Albright (2016) revealed that one of the most predictive determinants of neighborhoods having homes financed by subprime mortgages and experiencing foreclosure was residential segregation and racial isolation measures, whereby Black and Latinx homeowners bore the brunt of the fiscal meltdown we now call the Great Recession (Rugh, Albright, & Massey, 2015).

Overall, neighborhoods are changing as well-educated, young Blacks are moving across the country to settle in new neighborhoods. That is to say, these folks are helping to drive (statistical) integration, but gentrification is another mechanism of neighborhood change. In the former instance, Blacks are diversifying historically white communities, but gentrification is largely understood as a white- and middle-class-led diversification process of poor, often Black, neighborhoods. Each process has their own special set of political ramifications, as explained by a number of scholars (Martin, 2007; Newman, Velez, & Pearson-Merkowitz, 2016), including some of our contributors.

Book Overview

The chapters in this volume challenge what we know about Black politics in the twenty-first century given the vast changes in the geography of Black Metropolises. To be more precise, the authors illuminate the ways in which the aforementioned demographic dynamics challenge traditional conceptualizations and theories of Black politics. They examine the extent to which tried-and-true theories of Black politics still help us to explain what we see empirically and outline what we should predict for the future, and they do so by analyzing Black politics at the state and local level. Second, they describe and analyze the changing and expanding points of focus with which Black politics must contend in the face of these processes. Altogether, they consider the implications for demographic change on Black politics in practice and as an area of scholarship. This book is composed of four parts, each of which homes in on the effects of immigration, suburbanization, and gentrification. These processes are not mutually exclusive, and as the readers will find, the chapters speak to each other.

The two chapters in Part I, "All in the Family?", explore the myriad of possibilities for Black politics in the face of increasing ethnic diversity. First, Sharon Wright Austin takes us to the home of the largest number of African Americans: New York City. Though New York remains a stronghold for Blacks, it too is changing. African Americans have attempted to increase their political representation in New York for decades, but since the 1980s, a distinct Afro-Caribbean constituency has emerged. In response, African American political figures have had to find ways to develop coalitions with this new group, but these relationships have been marked more often by conflict than coalition. Additionally, the Dominican population has also increased dramatically and presented both prospects for coalitions and challenges for African American political development in New York. This chapter traces the political ascendancy of African Americans, Afro-Caribbeans, and Dominicans; challenges our conceptions of "descriptive" representation; and helps us to gain a better understanding of how Black New Yorkers view politics, not across racial lines, but instead within them.

While New York is a major thoroughfare for Blacks across many ethnic groups, the effects of ethnic diversity on Black politics is likely to be localized. Historically, there have been times and places where Black immigrants attempt to assimilate into the larger Black community, while at other times, they actively distance themselves from native-born Blacks (Candelario, 2007; Dunn, 1997; Smith, 2014). Relatedly, there are only a few places in this country where people can and do differentiate between Black immigrants and African Americans. Despite the range in the salience of Black ethnic diversity, there is a limited analysis of Afro-Caribbean identity in settings where the Afro-Caribbean community is not as visible (i.e., large and elevated) in the public consciousness. Cory Charles Gooding rectifies this problem in the second chapter of this book. Gooding asks and seeks to answer this question: How does ethnic visibility impact identity and politics in the US? Using Afro-Caribbeans as a case study, this chapter examines the impact of public recognition of immigrant populations on the identity and sociopolitical attitudes of the group across two starkly different sites: New York, NY, and Los Angeles, CA.

Part II of this book, "Black (In)Visibility in Majority-Minority Cities," is also concerned with immigration, but it shifts our focus to examine the ways in which Blacks have fared in "new destination," majority-minority cities. These chapters focus on the circumstances under which interethnic conflict and co-alition arise in these places and determine whether new demographic trends challenge or support existing theories of intergroup contact.

Chapters 3 and 4 comprise Part II, which provides insights into the evolving dynamics of majority-minority cities. In Chapter 3, Niambi Carter examines the growing trend of so-called sanctuary cities in traditionally, or majority, Black localities and asks, "What are the political and racial implications of establishing these spaces as sanctuaries for undocumented persons?" Utilizing survey data from Prince George's County, the long-term residence of many Blacks in the DC Metropolitan area, Carter seeks to illuminate whether and the extent to which Blacks have become stakeholders in this ongoing debate around immigration. In Chapter 4, Andrea Benjamin revisits Browning, Marshall, and Tabb's (1984) notion of political incorporation in her examination of Black politics in another "new destination": Durham, North Carolina. Using original data from a 2015 mayoral election, Benjamin presents a quandary for Blacks in this majority-minority city: they have achieved full incorporation, according to the original conceptualization, but still face major political challenges. What lessons can be learned for Black politics in the New South as well as for Latinx communities who have made cities like Durham home?

Next, we turn from those who have immigrated to the US in order to focus on those who have migrated within the US. Part III, "Keeping Up with the Joneses," examines the effects of suburbanization on Black politics. Ernest McGowen, in Chapter 5, offers a retrospective analysis. He analyzes data collected when Blacks just began to move to predominately white suburban neighborhoods in order to get a sense of the extent to which these early movers were political anomalies, or harbingers of the rightward shift we see today in the sentiments of the Black political elite and middle class (Cohen, 2010; Tate, 2010). Taking a closer look at Black pioneers to newly opened areas in the geography of opportunity, McGowen provides insight about the extent to which Black suburbanites distanced and differentiated themselves politically from those who remained in concentrated Black neighborhoods during the 1980s and early 1990s. In Chapter 6, Reuel Rogers explores the effects of suburbanization on African American political attitudes decades later, in the twenty-first century. Considering that migration to the suburbs represents a major restructuring in the spatial architecture of the networks that shape linked fate bonds among Blacks, Rogers analyzes whether and the extent to which living in a suburban setting—whose populations are now more racially and ethnically diverse than ever—affects the political viewpoints of Black Americans, particularly their policy preferences and perceptions of linked racial fate.

In Part IV of this volume, "There Goes the Neighborhood," two scholars examine the politics of racialized neighborhood change. Jessica Lynn Stewart provides much-needed nuance in the larger conversation on neighborhood change. Just as we have seen throughout this introductory chapter, there are major regional differences concerning where Black folks live. Stewart, in Chapter 7, provides both an explanation for why regional differences are so stark and further delineates what these differences mean for Blacks' well-being and level of vulnerability in the face of gentrification. Sarah Mayorga-Gallo, in Chapter 8, provides a detailed depiction of how these regional differences play out at the street level in her analysis of interpersonal interactions in two neighborhoods. As Blacks seek to "move on up," they sometimes find themselves in neighborhoods that whites have left behind; in other instances, they find that their neighborhood is changing due to white-led diversification. Though neighborhoods marked by racial and ethnic diversity characterize America's utopian ideals of racial harmony, Mayorga-Gallo's work sheds light on the promises and perils that Black Americans face in multiracial neighborhoods.

Closing Remarks

We are motivated to examine immigration, gentrification, and suburbanization because with reconfigurations in the key elements of a particular space, we ought to expect some transition in that local political landscape. These mechanisms of demographic change have political consequences for the shape of Black politics, but we know full well that the challenges that are presented by these demographic shifts are by no means the only ones that Black Americans face. By the close of the first self-identified African American president's second term in office, the challenges that many Blacks face across this country became evident to a wider array of Americans, and the era of the 45th president does not seem to suggest any major positive outcomes for people of color, generally speaking. We suspect that Trump will not earn 95% of Blacks' support by the close of his presidency, despite his "promise."

There's a phrase that is all too prescient: history doesn't repeat, but it often rhymes. Whether Blacks from the Diaspora immigrate to the United States or Black Americans move from Detroit to Durham, they are likely to face problems rooted in structural racism (Bonilla-Silva, 1997). What this means is that as Black folks move to and about the country, they are likely to find new problems or old ones with new faces. For example, as low-income Black folks move into the suburbs, they face new challenges related to transportation, employment, social services, and the like (Anacker, 2015; Frasure-Yokley, 2015; Peltz, 1988). Or, on the matter of similarities, the Department of Justice found that police treat Black citizens more harshly than white Americans in cities like both Chicago and Baltimore, as well as small, majority-minority suburbs like Ferguson.

Demographic changes like gentrification or neighborhood diversification can exacerbate problems faced by Black communities as well. As white newcomers seek to imprint their fingerprint on a location, they are more likely to see the police as allies who can control Black, longtime residents (Mayorga-Gallo, 2014; Smith & Mayorga-Gallo, 2017). Needless to say, there is plenty of evidence that Black communities are likely to be surveilled more, and that everyday interactions with police—such as traffic stops—do not bode as well for people of color as they do for whites (Baumgartner, Epp, Shoub, & Love, 2017). Meanwhile, research shows that as neighborhoods become more diverse, residents are less likely to support raising and spending more on schools, roads, and public goods (Hopkins, 2009) and more like "hunker down" (Putnam, 2007). Trends in integration at the neighborhood level and in suburbs may serve to aggravate the extent to which Black people and other people of color are at the short end of this stick. Blacks have historically been marginalized from quality neighborhoods and the schools that come with them; it becomes incumbent upon social scientists to keep in mind the downsides that come with ostensibly good outcomes, such as racial integration.

Despite the political rhetoric of the 45th president, we should also note that Black folks have called attention to and resisted against ever-evolving racial inequality, well-marked by the rise of the Black Lives Matter Movement as well as the Contemporary Movement for Black Lives. This leaderful movement centers on a Black feminist ideology and takes seriously the idea that Black liberation requires the issues of Blacks who have faced secondary marginalization (Cohen, 1999)—such as formerly incarcerated Blacks, lesbian, gay, and transgender Blacks, undocumented Black immigrants—or those who have experienced the brunt of respectability politics—such as young Blacks and Black women—to also be centered on "the" Black political agenda (Cohen, 2010; Obasogie & Newman, 2016; Taylor, 2016). Among the many lessons this movement has taught us, as social scientists and citizens, is that we ought to be thinking more about politics at the local level. Due to the United States' system of federalism, there is a great deal of heterogeneity across states and even across localities within a state. As such, we should become more cognizant of the ways in which our street-level bureaucrats, city councils, mayors, elected judges, and district attorneys shape the life chances of Americans at the local level.

Historically, the study of Black politics focused on the political dynamics of the local level to provide insight on the social, economic, and political well-being of Blacks (Browning et al., 1984; Drake & Cayton, 1945/2015; Du Bois & Eaton, 1899/2003; Sonenshein, 1993), but over time, scholars have shifted much of their attention towards national-level trends in political attitudes and behaviors as well as Congressional outcomes. Though this latter body of literature has provided a great deal of clarity on the complexities of Black politics, we believe the most cutting-edge work that helps us better understand the nuances of twenty-first century Black politics analyzes what is going on at the local level. This work leverages local diversity to uncover important patterns as well as anomalies in America's democratic experiment. The study of Black politics is only necessary insofar as it provides insight to bring about better outcomes for all Americans. Our contributors provide an excellent set of examples of how we can accomplish that through scholarship.

Notes

1 My thanks goes to Rose Buckelew, Chrissy Greer and Sarah Mayorga-Gallo for their close reading and feedback. Errors, egregious or otherwise, are my own.
2 The Supreme Court of the United States held, "Private agreements to exclude persons of designated race or color from the use or occupancy of real estate for residential purposes do not violate the Fourteenth Amendment; but it is violation of the equal protection clause of the Fourteenth Amendment for state courts to enforce them" in *Shelley v. Kraemer* (1948).
3 Ira Katznelson's seminal text, *When Affirmative Action was White*, highlights the fact that though the GI Bill was race-neutral in its language, the policy was implemented at the state level, thus allowing norms of white supremacy to prevent the overwhelming majority of Black GIs from fully enjoying the benefits of the policy.
4 Average levels for Asian and Latinx Americans have not seen a similar decline, and over the same time period, there has been an uptick in segregation for these two groups in the US's largest metropolitan areas.

References

Anacker, K.B. (2015). Introduction. In K.B. Anacker (Ed.), *The new American suburb: Poverty, race and the economic crisis* (pp. 1–11). Farnham, Surrey: Ashgate Ltd.

Anderson, M. (2015). *A rising share of the U.S. black population is foreign born.* Washington, D.C.: Pew Research Center.

Anderson, M. (2017). African immigrant population in U.S. steadily climbs. Retrieved from http://www.pewresearch.org/fact-tank/2017/02/14/african-immigrant-population-in-u-s-steadily-climbs/

Austin, S.D.W., Middleton, R.T., & Yon, R. (2012). The effect of racial group consciousness on the political participation of African Americans and black ethnics in Miami-Dade County, Florida. *Political Research Quarterly, 65*(3), 629–641.

Barnett, E. (2011). *"Somos Costeños": Afro-Mexican transnational migration and community formation in Mexico and Winston-Salem, NC.* Connecticut College: New London, CT.

Barreto, M., & Segura, G. (2014). *Latino America: How America's most dynamic population is poised to transform the politics of the nation.* New York, NY: Public Affairs.

Baumgartner, F.R., Epp, D.A., Shoub, K., & Love, B. (2017). Targeting young men of color for search and arrest during traffic stops: evidence from North Carolina, 2002–2013. *Politics, Groups, and Identities, 5*(1), 107–131.

Bleier, E. (2015). Growing numbers of immigrants from Africa and the Caribbean are reshaping the US and now account for almost ten per cent of overall black population in America *Daily Mail.* Retrieved from http://www.dailymail.co.uk/news/article-3034000/African-Caribbean-immigrants-reshaping-black-population-America.html

Bonilla-Silva, E. (1997). Rethinking racism: Toward a structural interpretation. *American Sociological Review, 62*(3), 465–480.

Boyd, R.L. (2012). The 'Black Metropolis' revisited: A comparative analysis of northern and southern cities in the United States in the early 20th century. *Urban Studies, 49*(4), 845–860.

Browning, R.P., Marshall, D.R., & Tabb, D.H. (1984). *Protest is not enough: The struggle of blacks and Hispanics for equality in urban politics.* Berkeley, CA: University of California Press.

Candelario, G.E.B. (2007). *Black behind the ears: Dominican racial identity from museums to beauty shops.* Durham: Duke University Press.

Capers, K.J., & Smith, C.W. (2015). Straddling identities: Identity cross-pressures on black immigrants' policy preferences. *Politics, Groups, and Identities, 4*(3), 393–424.

Carter, N.M. (2007). *The black/white paradigm revisited: African Americans, immigration, race, and nation in Durham, North Carolina.* (Ph.D.), Duke Univeristy, Durham.

Carter, N.M., & Pérez, E.O. (2016). Race and nation: How racial hierarchy shapes national attachments. *Political Psychology, 37*(4), 497–513.

Chen, M. (2017). Why are America's suburbs becoming poorer. *The Nation.* Retrieved from https://www.thenation.com/article/why-are-americas-suburbs-becoming-poorer/

Coates, T.-N. (2014). The case for reparations. *The Atlantic, 313*(5), 54–71.

Cohen, C.J. (1999). *The boundaries of blackness: AIDS and the breakdown of black politics.* Chicago, IL: University of Chicago Press.

Cohen, C.J. (2010). *Democracy remixed: Black youth and the future of American politics.* Oxford, England: Oxford University Press.

Dawson, M.C. (1994). A black counterpublic? Economic earthquakes, racial agenda(s), and black politics. *Public Culture, 7*(1), 195–223.

Dawson, M.C. (2001). *Black visions: The root of contemporary African-American political ideologies.* Chicago, IL: University of Chicago Press.

Diamond, J. (1998). African-American attitudes towards united states immigration policy. *International Migration Review, 32*(2), 451–470.

Drake, S. C., & Cayton, H. R. (2015). *Black metropolis: A study of negro life in a northern city, with a foreword by Mary Pattillo.* Chicago, IL: University of Chicago Press. (Original work published 1945)

Du Bois, W. E. B., & Eaton, I. (2003). *The Philadelphia negro: A social study.* Whitefish: Kessinger. (Original work published 1899)

Dunn, M. (1997). *Black Miami in the twentieth century.* Gainesville, FL: Univeristy Press of Florida.

Frasure-Yokley, L. (2015). *Racial and ethnic politics in American suburbs.* New York, NY: Cambridge University Press.

Frazier, F. (1957). *The black bourgeoisie: The rise of the new middle class in the United States.* New York, NY: The Free Press.

Frey, W. H. (1999). New black migration patterns in the United States: Are they affected by recent immigration. In F. D. Bean & S. Bell-Rose (Eds.), *Immigration and opportunity: Race, ethnicity, and employment in the United States.* New York, NY: Russell Sage.

Frey, W. H. (2004). *The new great migration: Black Americans' return to the South, 1965–2000.* Washington, DC: Center on Urban and Metropolitan Policy, the Brookings Institution.

Frey, W. H. (2015). *Diversity explosion: How new racial demographics are remaking America.* Washington, DC: Brookings Institution Press.

Greenblatt, A. (2017). Where have all the black mayors gone? Retrieved from http://www.governing.com/topics/politics/gov-cities-vanishing-black-mayors.html

Greer, C. (2013). *Black ethnics: Race, immigration, and the pursuit of the American dream.* New York, NY: Oxford University Press.

Gregory, J. N. (1995). The southern diaspora and the urban dispossessed: Demonstrating the census public use microdata samples. *The Journal of American History, 82*(1), 111–134.

Gregory, J. N. (2006). *The southern diaspora: How the great migrations of black and white southerners transformed America.* Chapel Hill, NC: Univerisity of North Carolina Press.

Harris-Lacewell, M. (2004). *Barbershops, bibles, and BET: Everyday talk and black political thought.* Princeton, NY: Princeton University Press.

Haynie, K.L. (2001). *African American legislators in the American States.* New York, NY: Columbia University Press.

Hayward, C.R., & Swanstrom, T. (2011). Introduction. In C.R. Hayward & T. Swanstrom (Eds.), *Justice and the American metropolis* (pp. 1–29). Minneapolis, MN: University of Minnesota Press.

Hopkins, D. J. (2009). The diversity discount: When increasing ethnic and racial diversity prevents tax increases. *The Journal of Politics, 71*(1), 160–177.

Hunt, L. L., Hunt, M. O., & Falk, W. W. (2008). Who is headed south? US migration trends in black and white, 1970–2000. *Social Forces, 87*(1), 95–119.

Johnson, L. B. (1965). Remarks at the signing of the immigration bill. In. Liberty Island, New York.

Katznelson, I. (2005). *When affirmative action was white: An untold history of racial inequality in twentieth-century America.* New York, NY: W.W. Norton.

Malloy, D. (2017). Are America's big-city black mayors a thing of the past? *OZY.* Retrieved from http://www.ozy.com/politics-and-power/are-americas-big-city-black-mayors-a-thing-of-the-past/79455

Martin, L. (2007). Fighting for control: political displacement in Atlanta's gentrifying neighborhoods. *Urban Affairs Review, 42*(5), 603–628.

Massey, D. S., Charles, C. Z., Lundy, G., & Fischer, M. J. (2008). *The source of the river: The social origins of freshmen at America's selective colleges and universities.* Princeton, NJ: Princeton University Press.

Massey, D. S., Rugh, J. S., Steil, J. P., & Albright, L. (2016). Riding the stagecoach to hell: A qualitative analysis of racial discrimination in mortgage lending. *City & Community, 15*(2), 118–136.

Mayorga-Gallo, S. (2014). *Behind the white picket fence: Power and privilege in a multiethnic neighborhood.* Chapel Hill, NC: The University of North Carolina Press.

McClain, P. D. (1993). The changing dynamics of urban politics: Black and hispanic municipal employment--is there competition? *The Journal of Politics, 55*(2), 399–414.

McClain, P. D., Carter, N. M., DeFrancesco Soto, V. M., & Lyle, M. L. (2006). Racial distancing in a Southern city: Latino immigrants' views of black Americans. *Journal of Politics, 68*(3), 571–584.

McClain, P. D., & Karnig, A. K. (1990). Black and hispanic socioeconomic and political competition. *American Political Science Review, 84*(2), 535–545.

McClain, P. D., Lackey, G. E., Perez, E. O., Carter, N. M., Carew, J. D. J., Smith, C. W.,...Nunnally, S. C. (2011). Intergroup relations in three southern cities. In E. Telles, M. Q. Sawyer, & G. Rivera-Salgado (Eds.), *Just neighbors? Research on African American and Latinos relations in the United States.* New York, NY: Russell Sage Foundation.

Merolla, J., Ramakrishnan, S. K., & Haynes, C. (2013). "Illegal,""Undocumented," or "Unauthorized": Equivalency frames, issue frames, and public opinion on immigration. *Perspectives on Politics, 11*(3), 789–807.

Newman, B. J., Velez, Y., & Pearson-Merkowitz, S. (2016). Diversity of a different kind: Gentrification and its impact on social capital and political participation in black communities. *Journal of Race, Ethnicity and Politics, 1*(2), 316–347.

Nicolaides, B., & Weise, A. (Eds.). (2013). *The suburb reader.* New York, NY: Routledge.

Obasogie, O. K., & Newman, Z. (2016). Black lives matter and respectability politics in local news accounts of officer-involved civilian deaths: An early empirical assessment. *Wisconsin Law Review, 2016,* 541.

Oliver, M., & Shapiro, T. (1995). *Black wealth/White wealth: A new perspective on racial inequality.* New York, NY: Routledge.

Pattillo, M. (2017). The future of black metropolis. Duke University, Department of Sociology: Race Workshop Lecture Series.

Peltz, J. F. (1988). It started with Levittown in 1947: Nation's 1st planned community transformed suburbia. *LA Times.* Retrieved from http://articles.latimes.com/1988-06-21/business/fi-4744_1_levittown-house

Pendergrass, S. (2013). Routing black migration to the urban US South: social class and sources of social capital in the destination selection process. *Journal of Ethnic and Migration Studies, 39*(9), 1441–1459.

Pérez, E. O. (2016). *Unspoken: Implicit attitudes and political thinking.* New York, NY: Cambridge University Press.

Putnam, R. D. (2007). E pluribus unum: Diversity and community in the twenty-first century the 2006 Johan Skytte Prize Lecture. *Scandinavian Political Studies, 30*(2), 137–174.

Reilly, K. (2016). Here are all the times Donald Trump insulted Mexico. *Time.* Retrieved from http://time.com/4473972/donald-trump-mexico-meeting-insult/

Roberts, S. (2014, September 2). Influx of African immigrants shifting national and New York demographics. *New York Times.* https://www.nytimes.com/2014/09/02/nyregion/influx-of-african-immigrants-shifting-national-and-new-york-demographics.html.

Rogers, R. R. (2004). Race-based coalitions among minority groups Afro-Caribbean immigrants and African-Americans in New York City. *Urban Affairs Review, 39*(3), 283–317.

Rogers, R. R. (2006). *Afro-Caribbean immigrants and the politics of incorporation: Ethnicity, exception, or exit.* New York, NY: Cambridge University Press.

Rothstein, R. (2017). *The color of law: A forgotten history of how our government segregated America.* New York, NY: Liveright Publishing Corporation.

Rugh, J.S., Albright, L., & Massey, D.S. (2015). Race, space, and cumulative disadvantage: A case study of the subprime lending collapse. *Social Problems, 62*(2), 186–218.

Schneider, A., & Ingram, H. (1993). Social construction of target populations: Implications for politics and policy. *American Political Science Review, 87*(2), 334–347.

Smith, C. W. (2014). *Black mosaic: The politics of black pan-ethnicity.* New York, NY: New York University Press.

Smith, C. W. (2017). Black immigrants in the U.S. face big challenges. Will African Americans rally to their side? *The Washington Post.* Retrieved from https://www.washingtonpost.com/news/monkey-cage/wp/2017/09/18/black-immigrants-in-the-u-s-face-big-challenges-will-african-americans-rally-to-their-side/?utm_term=.bc34b946a703

Smith, C. W., & Mayorga-Gallo, S. (2017). The new principle-policy gap: how diversity ideology subverts diversity initiatives. *Sociological Perspectives, 60*(5), 889–911.

Sonenshein, R. J. (1993). *Politics in Black and White.* Princeton, NY: Princeton University Press.

Spence, L.K., McClerking, H.K., & Brown, R. (2009). Revisiting black incorporation and local political participation. *Urban Affairs Review, 45*(2), 274–285.

Stack, C. (1996). *Call to home: African Americans reclaim the rural South*. New York, NY: Basic Books.

Tate, K. (1994). *From protest to politics: The new black voters in American elections*. Cambridge, MA: Harvard University Press.

Tate, K. (2010). *What's going on? Political incorporation and the transformation of black public opinion*. Washington, D.C.: Georgetown University Press.

Tavernier, L. A. (2015). *On the midnight train to Georgia: Afro-Caribbeans and the new great migration to Atlanta*. (Doctor of Philosophy), New York, NY: City University of New York.

Taylor, K.-Y. (2016). *From #BlackLivesMatter to Black Liberation*. Chicago, IL: Haymarket Books.

Telles, E., Sawyer, M., & Rivera-Salgado, G. (2011). *Just neighbors?: Research on African American and latino relations in the United States*. New York, NY: Russell Sage Foundation.

U.S. Supreme Court (1948). Shelley v. Kraemer, 334 U.S.1.

Vicino, T. (2008). *Transforming race and class in suburbia: Decline in metropolitan Baltimore*. New York, NY: Palgrave Macmillan.

Wilkerson, I. (2010). *The warmth of other suns: The epic story of America's great migration*. New York, NY: Random House.

Zong, J., & Batalova, J. (2016). Caribbean immigrants in the United States. *Migration Policy Institute*. Retrieved from https://www.migrationpolicy.org/article/caribbean-immigrants-united-states

PART I

All in the Family?

The Political Dynamics of
Black Ethnic Immigration and
Diversification

1

AFRICAN AMERICAN, BLACK ETHNIC, AND DOMINICAN POLITICAL RELATIONS IN CONTEMPORARY NEW YORK CITY

Sharon D. Wright Austin

This chapter examines the political relationships among native-born African Americans, Dominicans, Haitians, and West Indians in New York City.[1] African Americans have attempted to increase their political representation in New York since the city's earliest founding. Over the past three decades, a Black ethnic constituency has also emerged.[2] The growth of new racial and ethnic immigrant populations presents both prospects and challenges for African American political development in New York.

Given the historical ups and downs of the relationship between various groups of Black immigrants and African Americans, what should we expect for "Black" politics in the twenty-first century? The "minority group model" assumes that people of color will develop electoral coalitions and vote for minority candidates who further their interests (Carmichael & Hamilton, 1967; Eisinger, 1976, pp. 17–18; Rich, 1996; Sonenshein, 1993). It is expected that these collaborations will, in turn, result in an increase in overall minority political incorporation.

This chapter argues that African American political figures have had to find ways to develop coalitions with Dominicans, Haitians, and West Indians; yet, these relationships have been more conflictual than collaborative. What's more, through an examination of an original survey conducted in 2013 with over 700 foreign- and native-born Blacks, this chapter highlights both the prospects for future cross-ethnic coalitions as well as the perceived obstacles that hinder intraracial coalitions from coming to fruition.

Black Political Efforts in New York City

The charter for the city of New York stipulates that a strong mayor–weak city council system will govern the city. As the city's most influential elected official, the mayor serves for four years in one term with a two-term limit. The unicameral New York City Council consists of 51 members who each represent their districts for four-year terms and are also limited to a maximum of two possible consecutive terms. The city also consists of five boroughs that encompass five counties: Manhattan (New York County), Queens (Queens County), Brooklyn (Kings County), the Bronx (Bronx County), and Staten Island (Richmond County). Each borough has a president who advises the mayor about the needs and issues of their individual borough. Created by a 1901 charter, the borough president is its main representative, but the person has little citywide or countywide political power. A charter reform effort in 1989 awarded more power to the city mayor and council but reduced the borough president's influence. Since then, the borough president has mainly had an advisory role over development, zoning, and planning affairs (Austin, 2018).

African American Political Evolution

Throughout the city's history, African Americans have had limited political success in the city's five boroughs. During the earliest years of Black officeholding, African Americans and West Indians were the city's largest Black minority groups. All candidates of African descent were classified as "Black" rather than African and Caribbean candidates. However, during the 1980s, a shift occurred when West Indian candidates and constituencies began to distinguish themselves from African Americans. West Indians acknowledged that they possessed interests that often differed from those of African Americans.

Like in many northern cities, machine politics dominated New York City politics for several decades. Many years before Chicago's infamous Richard J. Daley machine, the Tammany Hall was founded in the 1780s and remained dominant until the 1960s. It controlled patronage and Democratic Party elections in Manhattan while also controlling New York City and state political affairs. White immigrants, mostly Irish, expanded their political influence by working in the machine. However, African Americans and Black ethnics were often the targets of racial prejudice within the machine (Thompson, 2006).

Whereas Richard J. Daley was the face of the Chicago machine, William M. Tweed (or Boss Tweed as he was known) dominated the Tammany machine. Beginning with the mayoral victory of Fernando Wood in 1854, the New York City machine rewarded its Irish Catholic supporters with jobs, naturalization assistance, and neighborhood enhancements, but not other racial/ethnic groups (Rich, 2007). In addition, the Tammany machine cared little about cultivating Black politicians into their fold.

The earliest African American elected officials had several things in common. They worked in predominantly Black middle-class political clubs that received some financial support from white progressives. This support allowed them to win office in predominantly Black areas (primarily in Harlem), but not citywide (Rich, 2007). In addition, they were disadvantaged by the separation of Black neighborhoods in the five boroughs and the absence of "cross-borough coalitions" (Rich, 2007; Thompson, 2006).

Despite their lack of electoral victories in the current local political scene, some of the first Black elected officials were of West Indian descent. These candidates ran as Black rather than Caribbean candidates, represented issues of pressing concern to Black voters, and often deliberately downplayed their Caribbean ancestry (Foner, 1998). Many did so because West Indians were at the bottom of the city's racial totem pole. They endured bigotry from all races of people in New York including native-born African Americans, Puerto Ricans, and other "non-whites of Caribbean ancestry" (Bryce-LaPorte, 1979).

Despite the widespread bigotry, beginning in the mid-1930s, West Indians were represented in local political offices. In 1935, Herbert Bruce, a native of Barbados, won the election as a Tammany district leader (Kasinitz, 1992). This victory made him the first Black man to reach a position of prominence during the Tammany era, though some in the African American community viewed the political victory of a West Indian with suspicion. Bruce, as a result, had to reassure the African American community that he was committed to Black interests generally rather than to Caribbean interests (Kasinitz, 1992).

Bertram Baker, a naturalized citizen from the Caribbean island of Nevis, became the first Black member of the New York State Assembly from Brooklyn in 1948. In 1966, Baker became the first Black assemblyman to hold a leadership position as majority whip (Waggoner, 1985). Thus, West Indians revealed both their political interests and savvy in winning elections in local and state politics. By the beginning of the 1950s, most of the highest-ranking Democratic district representatives (four out of five), as well as the only Black district leader in Brooklyn (Baker), were of West Indian descent.

In 1953, Hulan Jack, a naturalized citizen from St. Lucia, was elected as the first Black borough president of Manhattan. Jack was one of the few Black politicians with an active career during Tammany Hall when he represented Harlem from 1941 to 1953 (Biondi, 2003). Although the borough position carried little influence at the time, it was a symbolic political victory for African Americans locally (Rich, 2007).

In 1964, J. Raymond Jones became the first African American chairman of the New York City County Democratic Party during the last years of the Tammany Hall political machine. Although Tammany Hall had lost its appeal to voters, Jones' position was still significant. He was described as "the quintessential go-along-to-get-along politician" (Rich, 2007, p. 27).

For many years, Harlem was the epicenter of Black political power in New York City. The most powerful African American politicians in the city were, first, Adam Clayton Powell, Jr., a civil rights activist and the pastor of Harlem's Abyssinian Baptist Church and US Representative (D.-NY) from 1944 to 1970;

second, Charles B. Rangel succeeded Powell in the House of Representatives in 1970 and represented his congressional district until 2016. Despite their national influence, their citywide political influence was limited.

For much of the city's history, Black New Yorkers could only win elections in Brooklyn or Harlem. Shirley Chisholm became Brooklyn's most prominent African American political figure after winning election to Congress in 1968. She represented the 12th congressional district for seven terms and was later the first Black candidate to seriously compete for a major party nomination for the presidency in 1972.

Besides Powell and later Rangel, Harlem's "Gang of Four"[3] consisted of politically influential African American and Black ethnic men in Harlem. David Dinkins was deputy mayor, Manhattan borough president, and later mayor of New York City. Basil Paterson served in the state senate, as deputy mayor, and New York secretary of state. Paterson was born in Harlem but was of Jamaican and Carriacouan descent. He and Shirley Chisholm, whose parents were born in the British Guiana and Barbados respectively, were two of New York City's first elected West Indian legislators. As the only Black ethnic member of the Gang of Four and the first Black secretary of state from 1979 to 1982, Paterson represented Black interests with no distinction between African American and Black ethnic interests. In 1966, Charles Rangel began his political career as a state representative before winning election to Congress in 1970. Finally, Percy Sutton was a state representative in 1965 and 1966 and the Manhattan borough president in 1966 (Salazar, 2014).

The experience of 1976 mayoral candidate Percy Sutton demonstrates the challenges for Black candidates in citywide elections. Besides being a member of the Gang of Four, Sutton was a former National Association for the Advancement of Colored People (NAACP) president, civil rights activist, and high-profile attorney for clients such as Malcolm X. He needed to assemble a multiracial coalition of Blacks, whites, and Puerto Ricans in order to be elected, but votes from these groups split among white liberal candidates Mario Cuomo, Ed Koch, and Bella Abzug and Puerto Rican candidate Herman Badillo (Rich, 2007). Some individuals in Black, white, and Latinx communities believed that 1976 was not an opportune time for a Black or Latinx candidate to run for mayor because of a fiscal crisis that left the city on the verge of bankruptcy. In the Democratic primary, Sutton received 14% of the vote and Badillo 11%. Mario Cuomo and Ed Koch competed in the year's runoff election that Koch eventually won (Rich, 2007). Sutton was also disadvantaged by a low turnout among Black voters. He received less than 50% of the Black vote and practically no white votes (Thompson, 2006). For a brief time during his mayoral campaign, Sutton used right-wing rhetoric that alienated the Black electorate, and some Black citizens interpreted his anti-crime rhetoric as insulting and condescending toward people of color. For example, he accused "criminals" of driving away tourists, but failed to address the underlying causes of crime during a time of high unemployment rates and a citywide fiscal crisis (Sandbrook, 2011). The research of Charles Green and Basil Wilson (1989) indicates other possible reasons for the diminished enthusiasm among Blacks for Sutton's campaign: "Sutton chose to run for mayor when the white backlash movement was at its zenith and initially chose not to base his campaign in the Black community." Percy Sutton also received less radio, newspaper, and television coverage than Cuomo and Koch because of his perception as a less serious contender (Rich, 2007). He financed his campaign with $400,000 of his own money but received few other campaign funds. He also had few supporters outside of the Manhattan borough. A Black mayor would not wage a successful mayoral campaign until the 1989 David Dinkins victory.

Dinkins, a former New York State Assemblyman and Manhattan borough president, won the city's mayoral election because of a successful mayoral campaign and a number of events that worked in his favor. First, Dinkins motivated voters to support him out of a sense of racial solidarity and the belief that his administration would benefit all groups. In addition, Dinkins benefited from his image as a "healer" who promoted the idea of diversity as a "beautiful mosaic." After several racially charged incidents occurred in New York City during the 1980s, he portrayed himself as the candidate who could alleviate the city's racial divide. African Americans and Black ethnics supported him because the victims of racial attacks were of both African American and Caribbean descent. Thus, African Americans and Black ethnics did not perceive his campaign in "us against them" terms.

The Dinkins campaign also secured the backing of a multiracial coalition of voters because of his name recognition. Additionally, the 1984 and 1988 Jesse Jackson presidential bids had motivated African Americans and Black ethnics to register to vote nationwide and develop multiracial coalitions (Foner, 1998; Rich, 2007). African Americans, voters of Caribbean descent, white progressives, and to a lesser extent Latinos, united to support both the Jackson and Dinkins campaigns.

In the 1989 Democratic primary, David Dinkins eventually defeated Ed Koch by a margin of 51% to 42%. He received approximately 29% of the white vote, 94% of the Black vote, and 26% of the Jewish vote (Rich, 2007). African Americans and Black ethnics were the most cohesive bloc of voters to support him in the election (Rogers, 2004; Zephir, 1996). From the early 1990s to the 2013 election of Bill DeBlasio, Republican fiscal conservatives won mayoral elections, even though New York City was a heavily Democratic city during the 1980s and remained a boastful 6-to-1 Democratic Party registrants for the next two decades. As a result, Dinkins was assured of victory in the general election after winning the primary (Rich, 2007).

In the general election, Dinkins defeated Rudolph Giuliani, an Italian American former US Attorney General, in the general election by only 47,000 votes (Thompson, 2006). On election night, Dinkins received 28% of the white vote, 70% of the Latinx vote, and 90% of the African American/Black ethnic vote (Carsey, 2001). Thus in 1989, African American, Black ethnics, and other voters in New York City finally elected an African American mayor despite being disadvantaged by machine rule, intraracial conflicts, and the competitive political nature of the city's borough residents.

Dinkins served for only one term as mayor, however. In 1993, Giuliani defeated him by a narrow margin of approximately 2%. Giuliani benefited from the support he received from white ethnic wards in Brooklyn, Queens, and Staten Island and from perceptions that the city's crime rate was out of control. In addition, the turnout rate among the members of Dinkins' coalition was a disappointment.

During Dinkins' mayoral term, African American and Black ethnic citizens failed to substantially increase their political standing. Few Black officeholders won elections. Although Mayor Dinkins appointed minorities and women to key positions in his administration, the overall economic standing of poor and working-class people of color did not improve significantly. Because of the city's severe recession during his term and the opposition he encountered from local politicians, Dinkins could only do so much for them (Mollenkopf, 2003; Rich, 2007).

The members of the Dinkins electoral coalition hoped that the presence of an African American mayor would lead them on the path to full political incorporation (a concept that Andrea Benjamin elaborates upon in this volume). This entails the election and reelection of a minority mayor for several terms, victories for other minority candidates, and "governmental responsiveness"—a dominant role in a governing coalition that is committed to their interests (Browning et al., 2003). Unfortunately, this did not occur because of Dinkins' one term in office and inability to assist minority candidates and citizens to their satisfaction.

The Black political elite has been ethnically diverse in New York City for many decades. Despite the existence of ideological and strategic fissures among these Black political "firsts," African Americans and Black ethnics have historically worked together to expand their political position in the city, perhaps motivated by the assumption that all people of African descent benefit from African American and Black ethnic officeholding.

West Indian Political Participation in New York

New York City's Caribbean immigrants have come mainly from Jamaica, Guyana, Trinidad/Tobago, Barbados, Haiti, and Martinique (Crowder, 1999). Shortly after the turn of the twentieth century, West Indian immigrants comprised about 1% of the Black population in the US, with most residing in New York City. By 1930, over half of the 72,000 Afro-Caribbeans in the United States lived in New York City (Foner, 2001). During the 1940s and 1950s,

West Indian immigration declined dramatically, in part, because of immigration restrictions, a 1924 federal immigration law, and the 1952 McCarran-Walter Act (Foner, 1979).

The numbers of West Indian migrants rebounded after passage of the 1965 Hart-Celler Immigration Reform Act. By 1980, over 50,000 West Indians of diverse origin were entering the United States annually, with over half of them settling in New York City (Crowder, 1999). By 1990, nearly half of all West Indians in the United States lived in New York State and another 7% in New Jersey, with the population in each state heavily concentrated in the major cities of New York City and Newark. Also, by the 1990s, approximately one-third of the city's Black population was foreign-born (Foner, 2001). By the late 1990s, West Indians had become the largest immigrant group in New York City and are the second-largest group (behind Dominicans) there today (City of New York, 2016). New York City's West Indian population increased from 274,366 in 1980 to over 1 million in 2010 (Crowder & Tebow, 2001; Zong & Batalova, 2016). Although New York City has the most sizable West Indian population in the nation, few West Indians have run for and won elections since the 1980s.

New York's African American and West Indian communities have several similar political experiences. Both groups were active members of the Republican Party before the mid-1960s. During this time, their Republican identifications placed them at a political disadvantage in a city dominated by Democrats (Kasinitz, 1992). During the 80-year heyday of the Tammany Hall machine from 1854 to 1934, both African Americans and Black ethnics were excluded from leadership positions (Kasinitz, 1992). The failure of the Democratic machine to solicit Black ethnic support and their support of "radical" political organizations placed them at a disadvantage (Rogers, 2000). Concerning the latter, the United Negro Improvement Association (UNIA) was the most well-known of these "radical," nationalist groups. Jamaican immigrant Marcus Garvey founded the group in 1914 with the goal of empowering economically and politically disfranchised people of African descent. Despite the criticisms of some African Americans that the UNIA and the Garvey movement were too "West Indian controlled," many African Americans held leadership positions in its national chapter and over 1,000 local chapters. The UNIA ended in 1927 after Garvey's deportation to Jamaica.

As mentioned, the first West Indian candidates to win office ran in predominantly Black districts and refused to emphasize their Caribbean heritage. It would have been an unlikelihood that candidates like Hulan Jack and Basil Paterson and the other earliest West Indian candidates would win by appealing separately to West Indians because of the absence of a visible West Indian constituency (Rogers, 2000). Therefore, these candidates addressed issues of concern to Black New Yorkers without confronting the unique interests of Caribbean-born Black citizens (Kasinitz, 1992).

The 1977 Caribbeans for [Percy] Sutton organization, was the first effort of West Indians to support candidates and promote issues as a Caribbean rather than an African American group. The formation of this group revealed the presence of a separate Black Caribbean electorate that could be mobilized separately from African Americans (Kasinitz, 1992). The Caribbean factions continued to grow and mobilize separately from African Americans during the 1980s. In 1980, Colin Moore, former state senator Waldaba Steward, and Trinidadian-born Congressman Mervyn Dymally (D-CA) founded the Caribbean Action Lobby (CAL). The CAL mobilized Black ethnics to advocate for Caribbean interests at both the local and national levels of government (Kasinitz, 1992).

After 1980 redistricting, predominantly Black districts in New York City included a greater number of West Indians. As a result, African Americans became more concerned about the growing and distinct Caribbean constituency that politicians had now begun to mobilize (Kasinitz, 1992). West Indian candidates appealed to their supporters after the growth of West Indian neighborhoods in central Brooklyn, the northeast Bronx, and southeastern Queens (Foner, 1998). By the decade's end, West Indian print and broadcast publications had also expanded, as did other predominantly West Indian institutions that emphasized the need to address Black issues while at the same time address Black Caribbean issues.

"Caribbeans for" groups continued to organize in support of candidates, but their endorsements sometimes contradicted African American endorsements. For example, the Caribbeans for Koch group endorsed Mayor Ed Koch's 1985 reelection effort even though most of the African American civil rights and political organizations opposed it. This group only consisted of approximately 150 members, but their endorsement angered many African Americans. The members of the group believed that their endorsement would persuade Koch to promote Caribbean interests as mayor (Rogers, 2004). However, Koch had tense relationships with the African American community. When several racially motivated incidents occurred in New York City during the 1980s, Koch took unyielding stances that many believe exacerbated racial tensions. African Americans believed that Black ethnics should have been equally offended by Koch's actions and rhetoric (Rogers, 2004).

African Americans also objected to Caribbeans for Koch because it was formed during a time when they were trying to replace Koch with a Black mayor. The Coalition for a Just New York group solicited an African American candidate to run against Koch so that they could finance his campaign and mobilize a multiracial coalition of voters. The group's mission failed after Koch defeated African American assemblyman Herman "Danny" Ferrell in the Democratic primary by a landslide. Koch later defeated white Democrat Carol Bellamy and white Republican Diane McGrath in the 1985 general election by an impressive number of votes (Rogers, 2004).

After the 1980s, West Indians continued to address issues of significance to them. As their population grew, both white and African American politicians had to acknowledge and respect the West Indian voting bloc. White politicians, realizing the benefits they could receive from this group, appointed "Caribbean liaisons" and "Caribbean community advisors" to reach out to Caribbean voters (Kasinitz, 1992).

Initially, African American candidates resisted West Indian political efforts because of fears that their victories would diminish African American political power. After refusing to acknowledge the presence of a West Indian constituency and support Caribbean candidates for years, African Americans also had to discover ways to form coalitions with these candidates and communities (Rogers, 2004). However, due to a number of challenges presented to African Americans and Black ethnics due to their shared racial identity, racial issues continued to unite them into a cohesive voting bloc, thereby making moot the efforts of some West Indian contenders to appeal to unique Caribbean interests in local politics (Foner, 1998; Kasinitz, 1992).

West Indians continued their political activities in New York City. West Indian candidates won office at this time by emphasizing both their Black and West Indian heritage. For example, David Paterson, the son of Basil Paterson and the 55th governor of New York, utilized this tactic when seeking election to the state senate in 1985 (Pierre-Pierre, 1993). During the early 1990s, a reform of the city charter expanded the council from 35 to 51 seats (Guarnizo, 2001). Due to population shifts, the legislature created a new predominantly African American and Dominican district in the Washington Heights area (Guarnizo, 2001). Also, two predominantly West Indian districts were created in Brooklyn during this expansion (Foner, 2001).

While West Indians were able to gain more latitude to campaign on issues specific to their co-ethics due to changes in district boundaries, they were still subsumed by matters that influenced them due to their race. Consequently, some West Indian candidates were motivated to run for office because of racial hate crimes that involved West Indian victims. These incidents included the 1984 shooting of four Black teenagers by white engineer Bernard Goetz in a subway station in what Goetz claimed was an attempted mugging. In 1986, Trinidadian-born Michael Griffith died after being chased onto an expressway by a group of bat-wielding young white men. Years later in 1991, seven-year-old Gavin Cato, a Guyanese boy, was killed after a Hasidic Jewish man accidentally struck him and his cousin in the Crown Heights section of Brooklyn. Four days of ugly racial clashes occurred after his death, and a Jewish student was murdered in retaliation (Pierre-Pierre, 1993).

These crimes resulted in an emotional and political solidarity between African Americans and Black ethnics, but evidence of competition was simultaneously evident. For instance, in 1991, Una S.T. Clarke, a Jamaican woman, became the first Caribbean-born member of the New York City Council.

Although she had worked to elect several African American candidates, many failed to endorse her campaign while others endorsed her opponents. After the election, African American candidate Carl Andrews filed a legal challenge to Clarke's victory (Rogers, 2004).

By the year 2000, African American and Black ethnic candidates were openly competing against each other because African Americans no longer comprised the majority in districts they once predominated. In 2001, Una Clarke challenged Major Owens, a nine-term incumbent, for his congressional seat. By this time, the district had a 55% Black population, two-thirds of which was West Indian (Rogers, 2004). Owens eventually defeated Clarke in a very contentious race in which he faced his first serious challenge since 1982 (Rogers, 2004).

Clarke and Owens had worked together as political allies for years before she announced her candidacy. When she sought a seat on the council in 1991, Owens was one of the few African American elected officials to support her candidacy partly out of a belief that backing her would assure his future reelections in a district with a growing Caribbean population. As a result of their collaborative relationship, Owens was personally offended when Clarke decided to run against him. He had considered himself her mentor while she served on the council (a relationship that Clarke denied) (Rogers, 2004). Her campaign appealed to both African American and Black ethnic voters, but she described Owens as being "anti-immigrant" and failing to effectively serve both African American and West Indian communities (Rogers, 2004). The predominantly African American Coalition for Community Empowerment urged her to exit the race to avoid splitting the Black vote (Brown, 2012). She refused but lost the election.

Owens also defeated Clarke's daughter Yvette in 2004 (Gamble, 2010). He referred to the congressional candidacies of Una and Yvette Clarke as a "long-term double-cross and stab in the back" (Bernstein, 2013). After Owens declined a reelection bid in 2006, Yvette Clarke defeated his son Chris by a wide margin. She currently represents this district, which was created decades earlier to facilitate the election of an African American (Kasinitz, Mollenkopf, Waters, & Holdaway, 2008).

The race between Major Owens and the Clarkes is an indication of the African American-West Indian political tensions in New York City. In *Afro-Caribbean Immigrants and the Politics of Incorporation: Ethnicity, Exception, or Exit* (2006), Reuel R. Rogers points out the political conflicts among African Americans and Blacks of Caribbean descent. The groups have united to support causes of concern to them as Black citizens but also have major differences. West Indians perceive African American politicians and voters as trying to limit their political successes out of a fear that such victories will derail the prospects for African American political gains (Rogers, 2006). On the other hand, West Indians also believed that African American leaders erroneously presumed that they were competing with them (Rogers, 2004).

The Political Participation of Dominicans in New York City

The earliest wave of Dominican immigrants moved to the US after the end of Rafael Trujillo's regime in 1961 and the deterioration of its economy (Itzigsohn & Dore-Cabral, 2000). As the economy continued to decline, many poor and working-class Dominicans moved to the US in search of jobs and other opportunities. Increasing numbers emigrated after the 1965 US military intervention in the Dominican Republic and the ratification of Hart-Celler. After the Dominican economy declined in the 1980s, another wave of Dominicans from various class backgrounds fled the island in search of economic opportunities (Itzigsohn & Dore-Cabral, 2000; Liberato & Feagin, 2007). Most settled in New York City, while others moved to New Jersey, Florida, Massachusetts, Rhode Island, and Connecticut (Hernandez & Torres-Saillant, 1996). Currently, New York City has the second-largest Dominican voting population in the world (Pantoja, 2005). Only Santo Domingo, Dominican Republic has a higher concentration of Dominican voters.

After the growth of their populations, Dominicans became interested in American political issues while maintaining interests in their home country's political affairs. Scholarly research has found that Dominicans are not as interested in voting as they are in other forms of political participation, such as involvements in neighborhood associations and running for office. Their lower interest in voting has been attributed to their preoccupation with the politics of the Dominican Republic and their desire to return there (Levitt, 2001). Many Dominicans consider themselves as "sojourners" who live in the US because of their desire to take advantage of economic opportunities but believe that the Dominican Republic is their true home (Pantoja, 2005). There were institutional mechanisms in their home country that prevented Dominicans from fully participating in politics in the US. For instance, prior to 1994, Dominicans had to relinquish their home country citizenship after becoming American citizens (Levitt, 2001), but this law has since changed; in 1997, the legislature passed a law (that took effect in 2004) that allows Dominicans to retain their home country citizenship (and thus their voting rights) after they emigrate to any country.

In the New York political arena, Dominicans are disadvantaged in several ways. Both the Republican and Democratic parties have historically failed to actively solicit their support because of their low naturalization and voter turnout rates (Levitt, 2001). Additionally, many Dominicans in the US live below the poverty line. Research shows that socioeconomic status is an important driver of political participation, thus further contributing to the political neglect of Dominicans.

About one-third of New York City's Dominican population identifies as Afro-Dominican, but unlike West Indians, most have not formed electoral coalitions with African Americans. In part because of their growing population over the past decade or so, Dominicans have begun establishing a political power base in Washington Heights, which traditionally has been dominated by African Americans (Ramirez, 2011); however, by 2010, the district that is composed of Washington Heights, Inwood, Harlem, parts of the Upper West and East sides, and part of Northwest Queens was 46% Latino, 26% African American, and 21%white (Ramirez, 2011). For more than 65 years, this district had been represented by Charles Rangel and the late Adam Clayton Powell, Jr. (Colvin, 2012). As a result of the change in the population, Adriano Espaillat became the first Dominican American member of Congress in January 2017. He is the first person who is not African American to represent the 13th congressional district since 1944.

The electoral victory of Espaillat was not an easy one. In 2012, Espaillat, a former state senator, challenged Rangel for this seat. Representative Rangel had been the target of recent corruption and ethics probes but had never faced a serious challenger since winning the seat. Adriano Espaillat emphasized his Dominican heritage and the need for a Dominican representative in a predominately Dominican district. Because of Rangel's popularity with his African American base and a respectable amount of support from Puerto Rican voters in the district, he defeated Espaillat by a small margin. In 2014, Rangel again defeated Espaillat by less than 2,000 votes to win a twenty-third term in Congress but shortly thereafter announced that he would not seek reelection in 2016 (Karni, 2014). Espaillat defeated seven candidates in the Democratic primary with 37% of the vote. His contenders included Adam Clayton Powell IV, the son of the late congressman, and New York Assemblyman Keith Wright, whom Rangel endorsed (Ngo, 2016). The winner of the New York Democratic primary almost assuredly wins the general election because of the dominance of the party in local politics.

The Espaillat congressional victory was perceived as a loss of "Black" political power. The congressional district he now represents was configured with a majority Black population decades earlier with the intention of electing a Black member of Congress. Because it now has a predominantly Dominican population, many African American and Black ethnic citizens believe that they have lost the ability to elect a Black representative in what was once a predominantly Black district. Dominicans also have been elected as state assembly members, city council members, and state senators. In addition, Carmen De La Rose represents District 12 in the New York State Assembly and Ydanis Rodriguez represents District 10 on the New York City Council. Both of these districts include Washington Heights.

Haitian American Politics in New York City

New York has a sizable population of Haitians. The earliest Haitian immigrants began arriving in the city between 1915 and 1934 (Laguerre, 1984). Another influx arrived between 1957 and 1971 during the oppressive administrations of Francois Duvalier (Papa Doc) and his son, Jean-Claude (Baby Doc). This exodus occurred because of political instabilities but also because of the dire economic situation. The earlier Haitian immigrants were more affluent than the Haitian "boat people" who arrived around 1972 when Baby Doc succeeded his father as president for life (Laguerre, 1984).

The earliest leaders avoided local political involvements because they planned to return to Haiti. They focused on overthrowing Papa Doc and improving conditions there. Because of their preoccupation with Haitian affairs, these leaders discouraged the hometown associations' members from engaging in local American political affairs. They believed that the distractions posed by US political issues diverted their members' attention and resources away from more important issues in Haiti (Pierre-Louis, 2006). As such, Haitian New Yorkers have an extensive history of participating in hometown associations dating back to the late 1950s and early 1960s.

The first wave of Haitian immigrants established two types of associations— one primarily political and another combining political and community service efforts (Wah and Pierre-Louis, 2004, p. 151). The political aspect of these groups has almost solely focused on political matters in their homeland. These groups primarily provide opportunities for Haitian transmigrants to assimilate into American life while also maintaining ties to Haiti. In addition to sending funds and other aid to Haiti, these groups allow Haitian immigrants and citizens to network and support each other and, at the same time, celebrate their Haitian identity (Pierre-Louis, 2006). Few of the hometown associations work in congruence with other, non-Haitian community and political organizations (or with churches) even when their interests coincide (Pierre-Louis, 2006).

Perhaps, it follows that Haitians are one of the most politically underrepresented Black groups in New York City. Currently, they are as interested in politics as African Americans and West Indians, but Haitian voters desiring to elect one of their own to office have been disappointed because of fragmented votes. For example, ten Haitian candidates competed for a city council seat vacated by Jamaican American Yvette Clarke after her election to the US House of Representatives. Although Haitian community activists desired a consensus candidate to avoid split votes, none of the candidates withdrew (Greer, 2013). These types of dilemmas (i.e., the splitting of votes among several candidates) have been commonplace among Haitian New Yorkers and have prevented them from uniting to expand their political influence for many decades (Buchanan, 1979).

The most pressing dilemma for Haitian American New Yorkers is their inability to make their voices heard in the local electoral arena (Pierre-Louis, 2006). Currently, Dr. Mathieu Eugene is the only Haitian elected official in the local political arena. In 2007, he became the first Haitian American to win an elective office after his election to the city council. In 2016, Clyde Vanel became the second Haitian

American to win an elective office after his victory in a New York State Assembly race. African Americans, West Indians, Dominicans, and Haitians have had mixed successes in electing representatives from their racial or ethnic group.

Data and Methods

Given the historical complexity of Black identity and politics in the face of growing ethnic diversity, what are our expectations for the shifting boundaries of contemporary Black politics in New York City? I examine the racial identities, political attitudes, and activities of Black respondents across an array of ethnic groups from my 2013 survey to provide some insight.

During the week of June 23 in 2013, I distributed the *African American, Afro Caribbean, and Afro Latino Solidarity and Political Participation Survey* to individuals at New York City churches, libraries, schools, and small businesses in the predominantly African American, Black ethnic, and Dominican sections of Harlem and Washington Heights section of Manhattan as well as the Eastern, Northern, and Flatbush sections of Brooklyn. This research is part of a larger book project that examines African American and Afro-Caribbean political power in urban cities.

For this chapter, I also interviewed native-born African Americans, Black ethnics, and Dominicans because of my desire to determine the racial identification of individuals US society classifies as Black. Additionally, I want to determine the extent to which they engage in political activities and whether their participation rates are similar. A total of 219 African Americans, 110 Dominicans, 162 Haitians, and 253 West Indians provided written answers to several survey questions that assess their racial identities, political activities, and beliefs about coalitions.

Results

Identification

"What do our respondents state is their primary racial identification?" Whereas most of the African American and Black ethnic respondents identify as Black, most of the Dominican respondents identify as Hispanic/Latino. The survey includes two racial identification questions. The first is, "What is your racial identification?" Possible answers include Black, White, Latinx, Asian, and Other. Between 98% and 100% of native-born African Americans, Haitians, and West Indians refer to their racial identity as Black. However, most first- (71%) and second-generation (62%) Dominicans (including the Afro-Dominicans in the sample) identify as Latinx (see Table 1.1).

The responses can largely be characterized by homogeneity, whereby most respondents affirm a Black identity, with the unique exception of Dominicans.

TABLE 1.1 Racial Group Identification Across Ethnic Groups and Generations

	African Americans (n = 219)	Dominican		Haitian		West Indian	
		First Generation (n = 112)	Second Generation (n = 118)	First Generation (n = 81)	Second Generation (n = 81)	First Generation (n = 225)	Second Generation (n = 228)
Black	100%	25%	33%	98%	99%	98%	100%
White	0%	0%	0%	0%	0%	0%	0%
Latinx	0%	71%	62%	0%	0%	0%	0%
Other	0%	4%	5%	2%	1%	2%	0%

Source: Data from the African American, Afro-Caribbean, and Afro-Latino Solidarity and Political Participation Survey, 2013.

Intuitively, a shared sense of racial identity may portend a shared political outlook, but a deeper analysis of respondents' attitudes toward collaboration reveals the fact that Black New Yorkers are well aware of the difficulties of inter- and intraracial political coalitions.

Potential for and Perceptions of Collaboration

The growth of Dominican, Haitian, and West Indian populations in New York City and their settlements in what were once predominantly African American neighborhoods raise important questions about minority coalition-building. In order to assess their views on collaborations, I asked the participants, "Should the members of your group work together or separately with people of African descent to gain political power?" and "Should the members of your group work together or separately with individuals born in the Caribbean and Latin America to gain political power?" Possible answers are yes or no.

As shown in Table 1.2, most African Americans (99%) view coalitions with Dominicans, Haitians, and West Indians favorably (see Table 1.2). African American interview respondents elaborated on their overwhelmingly positive opinions about coalitions. One African American respondent noted, "We should be willing to work with anyone who will work with us to expand our local, state, and national political status." Another pointed out,

> Black people have never had prejudiced views toward other people, but they have prejudiced views toward us. In the past, Black candidates represented everyone, but white and Hispanic candidates put their people first. People of color won't get anywhere if we allow others to divide and conquer us.

Another respondent asserted, "The only time African Americans have ever won is when they had coalitions. Dinkins showed us what is possible through coalitions".

In addition, most first- and second-generation Haitians (93% and 95% respectively) and West Indians (90% and 93% respectively) support multiracial

TABLE 1.2 Support for Political Coalitions

African Americans (n = 219)	Dominican		Haitian		West Indian	
	First Generation (n = 112)	Second Generation (n = 118)	First Generation (n = 81)	Second Generation (n = 81)	First Generation (n = 225)	Second Generation (n = 228)
99%	67%	89%	93%	95%	90%	93%

Source: Data from the African American, Afro-Caribbean, and Afro-Latino Solidarity and Political Participation Study, 2013.

Note. African Americans were asked, "Should the members of your group work together with individuals born in the Caribbean and Latin America to gain political power?" Other groups were asked, "Should the members of your group work together with people of African descent to gain political power?" Affirmative responses are reported.

coalitions. One Haitian respondent said, "Haitians won't win without help from Black, white, and Hispanic people because so many of us are undocumented and can't vote. So, we need as many allies as we can find." Meanwhile, another said, "Haitians are from a country where there is a lot of turmoil. In America, we are surprised at the political freedoms we have. It will be foolish for us to refuse to work with other people. We won't get too far if we don't."

I distinguish the responses of first- and second-generation participants because their support for coalitions with individuals from different racial and ethnic groups differs at times. First-generation Black ethnics often harbor more negative stereotypical images of African Americans than second-generation Black ethnics (Bryce-LaPorte, 1972; Vickerman, 1994). What's more, second- and third-generation Black ethnic citizens are more likely to have racial solidarity with native-born African Americans (Rogers, 2001). Second-generation Black ethnics are also more supportive of political coalitions with African Americans than the members of the first generation (Austin, 2018). In addition, second-generation Black ethnics whose families have resided in the US for longer periods of time are more likely to have a common racial group identification with other Blacks (Benson, 2006, p. 237). The most common explanation for this is that Black and Latinx immigrants are exposed to more racial discrimination the longer they remain in American cities and, as a result, develop a racial identification with other racial and ethnic groups because of these experiences (Jones-Correa, 1998; Vickerman, 1999; Waters, 1999). Another explanation is that Black and Latinx immigrants abandon the stereotypes they have of African Americans after interacting with them over a period of years.

Visible differences are evident between first- and second-generation Dominicans, however. While 89% of second-generation Dominicans support collaborations, only 67% of first-generation Dominicans do. Most of the first- and second-generation Dominicans support coalitions, but the gap among the first- and second-generation respondents is wider than the generational gap of other ethnic groups. Many of the second-generation Dominicans favor coalitions because according to them, "It's common sense," as one respondent notes. Another second-generation Dominican explained, "We can't make it politically in this country if we try to work only with our own kind." One respondent added, "We need to set an example for the younger Dominicans by working with other people to show that we aren't prejudiced." As a final example of this sentiment, "We respect this country because it's our country and everyone in it. So, we should work with everyone in it."

First-generation Dominicans who oppose coalitions made comments such as, "African Americans are selfish and only look out for their own kind." One first-generation Dominican respondent expressed their apprehension this way: "We will be pushed into the background if we work with other races of people. They don't respect what we need in our communities." Similarly, another asserted, "Blacks are ungrateful for the opportunities they have. They can go to school for free, apply for financial aid to college, live and work wherever they want to, but all they do is whine about police brutality." Yet another first-generation Dominican respondent elaborated, "Black people don't know how good they've got it. Immigrants come here and want to work and take advantage of opportunities in the land of opportunity, but Blacks have a different mindset. We can't work with Blacks because of this."

Ironically, most of our respondents desire collaborative relationships with other people of color but also acknowledge that their groups compete for political influence. As shown in Table 1.3, these percentages range from 51% for second-generation Haitians to 75% for first-generation West Indians (see Table 1.3). According to written responses, this competition stems from the small number of offices available to minority candidates—most of whom win elective offices representing predominantly minority districts. According to one first-generation West Indian respondent,

> It's hard for anyone to win a political office in New York City. Minorities are supposed to be able to win any of them, but we know the truth. Black and Hispanic candidates can only win in a few Black and Hispanic districts. That's sad, but it's true. This means that the competition is fierce. Everyone wants to elect someone from their group, but there are only a few places where we can win so what are we to do?

Another African American interviewee expresses resentment toward Black ethnic candidates and states,

> For years, Black people struggled and fought for civil rights. Now we have to compete with people who came here and took advantage of the opportunities that resulted from our struggles. Some of the Caribbean people have views toward us that are just as negative as white people's.

TABLE 1.3 Perceptions of Intraracial Political Competition

African Americans (n = 219)	Dominican		Haitian		West Indian	
	First Generation (n = 112)	Second Generation (n = 118)	First Generation (n = 81)	Second Generation (n = 81)	First Generation (n = 225)	Second Generation (n = 228)
60%	74%	69%	55%	51%	75%	72%

Source: Data from the African American, Afro-Caribbean, and Afro-Latino Solidarity and Political Participation Study, 2013.

Note. African Americans were asked, "Do African Americans compete with Caribbean and Latin American citizens for political influence?" Other groups were asked, "Do African Americans compete with the members of your group for political influence?" Affirmative responses are reported.

These responses about collaboration and competition provide evidence of the kinds of challenges faced by minority candidates in a multiracial and multiethnic city. Is it a contradiction that they support coalition political efforts but also compete for political influence? What should we make of these observations on the part of my respondents? It seems that a contradiction exists between "what people want" versus "what people think is possible." The surveys indicate that they want to work with other groups for their political gains. They believe this is possible, but not without competing for the few political offices in minority districts that minority elected officials represent. Despite the victories of former President Barack Obama and statewide officials such as former Massachusetts Governor Deval Patrick, US Senator Corey Booker (D.-NJ), and US Senator Kamala Harris (D.-CA), many minority voters still believe that they can only win a few select offices and must compete.

Political Participation

My survey also includes questions about both traditional political activities (such as voting, donating funds, interacting with elected officials, and volunteering for political efforts) and those of a nontraditional nature (i.e., the signing of petitions and attendance of political rallies). According to the responses, African Americans, Dominicans, Haitians, and West Indians have a high level of interest in voting. I asked the respondents, "How often do you vote in local, state, and national elections?" As shown in Table 1.4, 77% of African Americans report always voting, or sometimes missing one. In addition, second-generation Dominicans, Haitians, and West Indians vote at higher rates than first-generation respondents (see Table 1.4). According to the survey, 61% of first-generation Dominicans, 60% of second-generation Dominicans, 55% of first-generation Haitians, 68% of second-generation Haitians, 50% of first-generation West Indians, and 63% of second-generation West Indians always or sometimes vote.

TABLE 1.4 Political Participation and Interests Across Ethnic Groups

	African Americans (n = 219)	Dominican First Generation (n = 112)	Dominican Second Generation (n = 118)	Haitian First Generation (n = 81)	Haitian Second Generation (n = 81)	West Indian First Generation (n = 225)	West Indian Second Generation (n = 228)
How often do you vote in local, state, and national elections? (% Always, or sometimes missing one)	77%	61%	60%	55%	68%	50%	63%
How often do you donate funds to candidates or on behalf of political functions? (% Frequently, four or five times a year)	17%	3%	1%	21%	29%	13%	8%
How often do you discuss American political issues? (% Quite Frequently, four or five times a month)	75%	82%	59%	72%	74%	62%	76%
Are you more interested in the politics of your home country or the US? (% US)	—	60%	82%	64%	84%	68%	87%

Source: African American, Afro–Caribbean, and Afro–Latino Solidarity and Political Participation Study, 2013.

These turnout rates closely align with national Black and Latinx turnout rates. Nearly 60% of African American and Black ethnic voters went to the polls in 1964, but this percentage would not be reached again until the 2008 presidential election when Black voters had an approximately 72% turnout. From the 1970s to the early 2000s, Black turnout averaged from the high 40-percentile to the mid-50-percentile range (US Census Bureau, 2017). Latinx turnout rates were usually about ten percentage points lower than Black turnout rates.

The voting participation is much higher than the other political activities of those interviewed. When asked, "How often do you donate funds to candidates or on behalf of political functions?" few respondents report having a habit of donating; instead, over 79% of our respondents occasionally or seldom donate funds for political causes. The failure, or possibly the unwillingness, of African American, Black ethnic, and Dominican citizens to donate funds may stem from several possible reasons. First, candidates may not be reaching out to these voters sufficiently for campaign funds. Another explanation may be the financial status of these voters. Many may not be able to afford to donate to these campaigns. Third, they may not understand the importance of donating to political candidates.

I also asked the respondents about the extent to which they discuss political issues because of my desire to determine their interest in American politics. Since some of the respondents (or their parents) have lived in other countries, they may be more interested in the politics of those countries rather than in American politics. Substantial percentages of them discuss politics on a regular basis. I asked, "How often do you discuss American political issues?" The responses were "quite frequently" (four or five times a month), "frequently" (two or three times a month), "occasionally" (once or twice every six months), and "seldom" (once or twice a year). First-generation Dominicans discuss political issues at a higher rate than the other respondents, but overall, respondents seem knowledgeable about political issues and participate in discussing politics frequently. While 82% of first-generation Dominicans discuss American political affairs, they are followed closely by second-generation West Indians (76%), African Americans (75%), second-generation Haitians (75%), first-generation Haitians (72%), first-generation West Indians (62%), and lastly, second-generation Dominicans (59%).

Dominicans, Haitians, and West Indians who were born outside of the US are also more interested in American politics than the politics of their home countries. As shown in Table 1.4, second-generation respondents across ethnic groups were more interested in American politics than the members of the first generation. When asked, "Are you more interested in the politics of your home country or the US?" the first-generation respondents who answered "American politics" were in the 60-percentile range while those giving the same answer among our second-generation respondents were in the 80-percentile range.

Conclusion

In conclusion, I find little evidence of a disdain for political coalitions among the respondents. To the contrary, native-born African American and Black ethnic citizens have a high level of solidarity and realize the importance of coalitions to win elections. African Americans, Dominicans, Haitians, and West Indians have many political similarities that could lead to coalition development. They vote at high rates and frequently discuss American political issues. In addition, most of the Dominicans, Haitians, and West Indians interviewed for this study are more interested in American political affairs than those in their home countries. This is especially the case for the second-generation respondents. However, small percentages of those interviewed donate funds to political causes.

I also found evidence of barriers to their coalition development. According to the written survey responses, these groups compete for political influence in a city with a long history of marginalizing the economic and political interests of people of color. Moreover, African Americans have voted for Haitian, West Indian, and Dominican candidates, but some are disappointed. This disappointment stems from the belief that after years of struggling to elect African American politicians and experiencing limited success in these attempts, they now have more difficulty electing their own. African Americans reside in districts that were once predominantly African American, but now consist mostly of Blacks from the Caribbean. On the other hand, some Dominican, Haitian, and West Indian candidates communicated their perceptions that African Americans are jealous of their political victories.

Overall, what are their prospects for political power? It will remain difficult to elect minorities in New York City because of racial polarization, competition among boroughs, and the city's machine structure. New York's minority communities need a candidate who can develop multiracial coalitions among the city's diverse electorate. Because New York City is a melting pot of cultures, white and minority politicians have to be mindful of differences among the various groups and address issues of common concern to them.

Notes

1 This study distinguishes Haitians and Dominicans from West Indians even though Haiti and the Dominican Republic are geographically located on the island of Hispaniola in the Greater Antilles region of the West Indies. The West Indian respondents in the chapter trace their ancestries to Jamaica, Guyana, Trinidad/Tobago, and Barbados and to the Dutch- and French-speaking countries of Martinique, Aruba, and Curacao.

2 I use the term "Black ethnics" to refer to people of African descent who also have a Caribbean lineage. In this research, Haitians and West Indians are categorized as Black ethnics. I refer to these individuals as both Black ethnic and Black in this study. I refer to individuals with a native-born African American heritage as African American.

3 The "Gang of Four" was comprised of Charles Rangel, David Dinkins, Basil Paterson, and Percy Sutton.

References

Austin, S. D. (2018) *The Caribbeanization of black politics: Race, group consciousness, and political participation in America.* Albany, NY: State University of New York Press.

Benson, J. E. (2006). Exploring the racial identities of black immigrants in the United States. *Sociological Forum, 21*(2), 219–247.

Bernstein, A. (2013, October 22). Major R. Owens, Former Congressman, Dies at 77. *New York Times.* Retrieved from https://www.washingtonpost.com/politics/major-r-owens-former-congressman-dies-at-77/2013/10/22/692d7c00-3b31-11e3-b6a9-da62c264f40e_story.html

Biondi, M. (2003). *To stand and fight: The struggle for civil rights in postwar New York City.* Cambridge, MA: Harvard University Press.

Brown, E. (2012). An ethnography of local politics in a Brooklyn Caribbean community. *The world in Brooklyn: Gentrification, immigration, and ethnic politics in a global city.* New York, NY: Rowman and Littlefield.

Browning, R. P., Marshall, D. R., & Tabb, D. H., eds. (2003). *Racial politics in American cities. Second Edition.* New York, NY: Longman.

Bryce-LaPorte, R. S. (1972). Black immigrants: The experience of invisibility and inequality. *Journal of Black Studies, 3*(1), 29–56.

Bryce-LaPorte, R. S. (1979). New York City and the New Caribbean immigration: A contextual statement. *International Migration Review, 23,* 214–234.

Buchanan, S. H. (1979). Language and identity: Haitians in New York City. *International Migration Review, 13*(2), 298–313.

Carmichael, S., & Hamilton, C. V. (1967). Black power: The politics of liberation in America. New York, NY: Vintage Books.

Carsey, T. M. (2001). *Racial context and racial voting in New York City mayoral elections revisited.* Paper Presented at the Annual Meeting of the Southern Political Science Association. November 7–10, 2001. Atlanta, GA. Retrieved from http://www.unc.edu/~carsey/research/workingpapers/Carsey-Southern2001.pdf

Colvin, J. (20152012, February 15). Support growing for New York to get first Dominican congressional district. *DNAinfo.* Retrieved from http://www.dnainfo.com/new-york/20120215/washington-heights-inwood/support-growing-for-new-york-get-first-dominican-congressional-district

Crowder, K. (1999). Residential segregation of West Indians in the New York/New Jersey metropolitan area: The roles of race and ethnicity. *International Migration Review, 33,* 79–113.

Crowder, K., & Tebow, L. M. (2001). West Indians and the residential landscape of New York. In *Islands in the city: West Indian migration to New York* (pp. 81–114). Berkeley, CA: University of California Press.

Eisinger, P. K. (1976). *Patterns of interracial politics: Conflict and cooperation in the city.* New York, NY: Academic Press.

Foner, N. (1979). West Indians in New York City and London: A comparative analysis. *International Migration Review, 13*(2), 284–297.

Foner, N. (1998). West Indian identity in the diaspora: Comparative and historical perspectives. *Latin American Perspectives, 25*(3), 173–188.

Foner, N. (2001). Introduction: West Indian migration to New York: An overview. In *Islands in the City: West Indian migration to New York* (pp. 1–22). Berkeley, CA: University of California Press.

Gamble, K. (2010). Young, gifted, black, and female: Why aren't there more Yvette Clarkes in congress? In *whose black politics? Cases in post-racial black leadership* (pp. 293–308). New York, NY: Longman.

Greer, C. M. (2013). *Black ethnics: Race, immigration, and the pursuit of the American dream.* Oxford, England: Oxford University Press.

Green, C., & Wilson, B. (1989). *The struggle for black empowerment in New York City.* Westport, CT: Praeger.

Guarnizo, L. E. (2001). On the political participation of transnational migrants: Old practices and new trends. In *E pluribus unum? Contemporary and historical perspectives on immigrant political incorporation* (pp. 213–265). New York, NY: Russell Sage Foundation.

Hernandez, R., & Torres-Saillant, S. (1996). Dominicans in New York: Men, women and prospects. In *Latinos in New York: Communities in transition* (pp. 30–56). Notre Dame, IN: University of Notre Dame Press.

Itzigsohn, J. & Dore-Cabral, C. (2000). Competing Identities? Race Ethnicity, and Panethnicity among Dominicans in the United States. *Sociological Forum, 15.* 225–247.

Jones-Correa, M. (1998). Between two nations: The political predicament of Latinos in New York City. Ithaca, NY: Cornell University Press.

Kasinitz, P., Mollenkopf, J. H., Waters, M. C., & Holdaway, J. (2008). *Inheriting the city: The children of immigrants come of age.* New York, NY: Russell Sage Foundation.

Laguerre, M. S. (1984). *American Odyssey: Haitians in New York City.* Ithaca, NY: Cornell University Press.

Levitt, P. (2001). *The transnational villagers.* Berkeley, CA: University of California Press.

Liberato, A. S., & Feagin, J. R. (2007). Becoming American and maintaining an ethnic identity: The case of Dominican Americans. In *The other African Americans: Contemporary African and Caribbean immigrants in the United States* (pp. 177–215). New York, NY: Rowman and Littlefield.

Ngo, E. (2016, June 29). Adriano Espaillat, Keith Wright lead democratic party to succeed Charles Rangel. *New York Daily News.* Retrieved from http://www.newsday.com/news/new-york/voters-go-to-the-polls-in-13th-congressional-district-1.11980888

Pantoja, A. D. (2005). Transnational ties and immigrant political incorporation: The case of Dominicans in Washington heights, New York. *International Migration Review, 43*(4), 123–144.

Philip, K. (1992). Caribbean New York: Black immigrants and the politics of Race. Ithaca, NY: Cornell University Press.

Pierre-Louis, F., Jr. (2006). *Haitians in New York City: Transnationalism and hometown associations.* Gainesville, FL: University of Florida Press.

Pierre-Pierre, G. (1993, September 6). West Indians adding clout at ballot box. *New York Times.* Accessed June 9, 2015. http://www.nytimes.com/1993/09/06/nyregion/west-indians-adding-clout-at-ballot-box.html.

Purdum, T. S. (1993, November 3). The 1993 Elections: Mayor; Giuliani Ousts Dinkins by a Thin Margin; Whitman is an upset winner over Florio. *New York Times.* Retrieved June 9, 2015.

Ramirez, D. (2011, August 29). Dominicans in New York: A strong and growing political presence." *Huffington Post Latino Voices.* Accessed June 24, 2015. http://www.huffingtonpost.com/2011/08/29/dominicans-prevalence-in-new-york-stronger-than-you-think_n_940232.html.

Rich, W.C. (1996). *The politics of minority coalitions: Race, ethnicity, and shared uncertain ties.* Westport, CT: Praeger Publishers.

Rich, W. C. (2007). *David Dinkins and New York City politics: Race, images, and the media.* Albany, NY: State University of New York Press.

Rogers, R. (2001). Black like who?' Afro-Caribbean immigrants, African Americans, and the politics of group identity. In *Islands in the city: West Indian migration to New York* (pp. 163–192). Berkeley, CA: University of California Press.

Rogers, R. (2004). Race-based coalitions among minority groups: Afro-Caribbean immigrants and African-Americans in New York City. *Urban Affairs Review, 39*(3), 283–317.

Rogers, R. R. (2000). Afro-Caribbean immigrants, African Americans, and the politics of group identity. In *Black and multiracial politics in America* (pp. 15–59). New York, NY: New York University Press.

Rogers, R. R. (2006). *Afro-Caribbean immigrants and the politics of incorporation: Ethnicity, exception, or exit.* New York, NY: Cambridge University Press.

Salazar, C. (n.d.). Basil Patterson and the Gang of Four: Power and politics in Harlem. *AmNewYork.* Retrieved from http://www.amny.com/news/basil-paterson-and-the-gang-of-four-power-and-politics-in-harlem-1.7737420

Sandbrook, D. (2011). Mad as hell: The crisis of the 1970s and the rise of the populist right. New York, NY: Alfred A. Knopf.

Sonenshein, R. (1993). *Politics in black and white: Race and power in Los Angeles.* Princeton, NJ: Princeton University Press.

Thompson, P., III (2006). *Double trouble: Black mayors, Black communities, and the call for a deep democracy.* New York, NY: Oxford University Press.

Vickerman, Milton. (1994). The responses of West Indians to African-Americans: Distancing and identification.*Research in Race and Ethnic Relations* 7:83-128.

Vickerman, M. (1999). *Crosscurrents: West Indian immigrants and race.* New York, NY: Oxford University Press.

Waggoner, W. H. (1985, March 10). Bertram Baker, 87, Is Dead; Ex-Brooklyn AssemblymanBertram Baker, 87, Is Dead; Ex-Brooklyn Assemblyman. *New York Times.* Retrieved from http://www.nytimes.com/1985/03/10/nyregion/bertram-baker-87-is-dead-ex-brooklyn-assemblyman.html

Wah, T., & Pierre-Louis, F. (2004). Evolution of Haitian immigrant organizations and community development in New York City. *Journal of Haitian Studies, 10*(1), 146–161.

Waters, M. C. (1999). *Black identities: West Indian immigrant dreams and American realities.* Cambridge, MA: Harvard University Press and Russell Sage Foundation.

Zephir, F. (1996). *Haitian immigrants in Black America: A sociological and sociolinguistic portrait.* Westport, CT: Bergin and Garvey.

Zong, J., & Jeanne B. (2016, September 14). Caribbean Immigrants in the United States. Retrieved from http://www.migrationpolicy.org/article/caribbean-immigrants-united-states

2

BLACK IMMIGRATION AND ETHNIC RESPECTABILITY

A Tale of Two Cities, New York and Los Angeles

Cory Charles Gooding

All too frequently, Black politics and immigration politics are conceptualized as separate areas of interest in the United States. Such conceptualizations tend to rest on assumptions about immigration as originating exclusively from Latin America and Asia and ideas about a monolithic Black[1] community. A growing community of scholars (Greer, 2013; Rogers, 2006; Smith, 2014), including the contributors to this volume, resist these assumptions and provide nuance to the Black politics scholarship through rigorous studies of Black immigrant attitudes and political behavior. Such studies provide necessary complexity to the study of Black politics and the politics of immigration. This volume answers the call for the more expansive research that is needed to excavate the contextual factors that inspire, inform, and constrain Black politics in immigrant communities.

In particular, studies of Black immigration frequently focus on locales that maintain a large Black immigrant population. New York City, for example, represents the most popular site of study for understanding the social, economic, and political incorporation of Afro-Caribbeans (see Austin, this volume; Foner, 2001; Greer, 2013; Kasinitz, 1992; Model, 2008; Rogers, 2006; Waters, 1999). New York serves as the center of Afro-Caribbean immigration and is home to 38% of the Afro-Caribbean immigrant population in the United States (Thomas, 2012). The large size of the Black immigrant population, the local context, and the geography of New York City[2] make this an important site of study for understanding Afro-Caribbean political incorporation and its relationship to Black politics more broadly.

While New York remains a critical site of study, non-gateway settings can provide greater clarity around the contextual factors that influence political incorporation. For example, Los Angeles County has a population of 10 million people spread across 4,061 square miles (US Census Bureau, 2017). Yet, the Caribbean population comprises only 1% of the Black population, which equates to approximately 12,600 Caribbeans in Los Angeles County (Nichols, 2005). The vast geographic and demographic differences between New York and Los Angeles create radically different social, cultural, and political landscapes for Afro-Caribbeans to navigate.

In each of these settings, Afro-Caribbeans face different obstacles in balancing their identity with ensuring their social and political interests are addressed. Mary Waters (1999, p. 44), in her influential work on Black immigrants in New York, highlights the importance of local context in understanding social identity:

> Social identities are unlike material objects. Whereas material objects have a concrete existence whether or not people recognize their existence, social identities do not... It is only in the act of naming an identity, defining an identity or stereotyping an identity that identity emerges as a concrete reality. Not only does that identity have no social relevance when it is not named; it simply does not exist when it has not been conceived and elevated to public consciousness.

The dependence of identity on the public consciousness accentuates the need to understand Black immigrant identity and politics in settings where the immigrant community is not as elevated in the public consciousness, as the recognition of racial and ethnic identity proves to be a powerful motivator of political behavior and policy in US politics at the local and national levels. New York–based studies find culture to be a prominent factor in helping Afro-Caribbeans raise their community profile, distinguish themselves from African Americans, and make political claims. Yet, how does a lack of public consciousness about the Afro-Caribbean community impact their identity, political attitudes, and political engagement? A near-exclusive focus on places like New York City, where Caribbean immigrants experience an elevated status in the public consciousness, leaves this question unanswered.

This chapter examines how social context impacts Afro-Caribbean identity. It focuses on the sociopolitical factors that inform Afro-Caribbean negotiations of racial politics and the strategies Afro-Caribbeans use to improve their social and political standing in local communities. I argue that Afro-Caribbeans balance their country of origin and their ethnic and racial identities simultaneously. Whether in New York or Los Angeles, Afro-Caribbeans recognize the role of race and racism in American society historically and in the contemporary moment. In navigating racial structures locally, the visibility of the ethnic group in the public sphere proves to be a significant factor in determining how they engage their community and the government.

To be specific, my study complicates and expands upon the discourse on respectability politics, which is typically understood as an exclusively African American strategy for navigating racial discrimination. My findings reveal that

Afro-Caribbeans deploy what I call *ethnic respectability*: the effort to use cultural difference to distance the self and group from racial stigma, improve sociopolitical standing, and insulate the group from structural racism. The prevalence of ethnic respectability as a strategy varies between New York and Los Angeles largely due to the elevation of the group in the public consciousness.

To understand the social factors that influence Afro-Caribbean identity and politics, I rely on in-depth interviews conducted with 71 Afro-Caribbean immigrants in New York and Los Angeles. In a semi-structured interview format, participants were asked to describe their background and identity, the racial/ethnic makeup of their personal networks and residential neighborhoods, and the nature of their interactions with non-Caribbeans. Reoccurring themes of group consciousness, group reputation management, and efforts to gain recognition from political officials form the basis of conclusions made in this chapter. My goal is to illustrate and describe the impact of social context on the identity and politics of Afro-Caribbean immigrants in various urban settings today. This chapter continues the effort of resisting conceptions of Black political attitudes as monolithic by unpacking the multiple identities that Black immigrants embody. The analysis centers Afro-Caribbean management of multiple identities in different social and political spaces, and it introduces an analysis of a previously unstudied population, Afro-Caribbeans, in a city where they do not constitute a large portion of the Black population, Los Angeles.

I proceed by first exploring the relationship between identity and social location as understood in the social sciences. I then highlight the contextual factors that influence Afro-Caribbean identity through an analysis of interview responses in New York and Los Angeles. I move to describing how contextual factors constrain, open, and transform opportunities for political engagement. Lastly, I address the implications of the study and practice of Black immigrant politics.

Background and Context: Identity, Visibility, and Social Location

The dominant definition of social identity focuses on the individual's self-image as informed by their ascribed membership to a broader group (Tajfel, 1979; Tajfel & Turner, 1979). In other words, an individual's identity is influenced by how others classify them. Such identities are not merely abstract classifications. In the case of race and ethnicity, identities are developed with the recognition that phenotype is instructive of an individual's behavior. Omi and Winant (2015, p. 126) describe the perceived relationship between appearance and behavior as such:

> Our ability to interpret racial meanings depends on preconceived notions of a racialized social structure. Comments such as "Funny, you don't look black" betray an underlying image of what black should look like.

We expect people to act out their apparent racial identities. Phenotype and performativity should match up. Indeed, we become disoriented and anxious when they do not.

Embedded in this conception of race in the social structure is the recognition that racial systems depend on the individual and their ability to represent a broader community. If there are no preexisting ideas about how members of a specific group behave then there is no need to reconcile the behavior of the individual.

In the case of Black people in the United States, racial meanings attached to a particular range of phenotypes are heavily associated with negative conceptions of aggression, low intelligence, hypersexuality, low economic status, and a range of other stereotypes. Such stereotypes are compared with other groups and employed to rationalize decreased social standing. As such, the social standing of Black people in the United States is informed by their perceived inferiority to other groups.

Relatedly, Claire Kim (1999) describes the social location of Asian Americans as positioned in relation to African Americans and white Americans in terms of their placement on two axes. First, Asian Americans are perceived to be culturally superior to African Americans though inferior to whites by dominant members of society. Kim's theory of racial triangulation also emphasizes the notion that Asian Americans are considered to be perpetual foreigners, on the second insider/outsider axis. This theory of racial triangulation is not only useful for understanding Asian American standing in America's "field of racial positions" but other immigrant groups as well, including Black immigrants.

Recognizing that "groups become racialized in comparison to one another and that they are differently racialized" (Kim, 1999, p. 107), individuals develop diverse ideological beliefs and strategies for improving the social standing, individually and as members of the broader group. For some, ideological beliefs about their group's social standing inspire a commitment to collective action as the best means for improving that standing. Such beliefs and preferences compose group consciousness (McClain, Johnson Carew, Walton, & Watts, 2009). It is important to note that group consciousness does not determine the nature of group attitudes. Two members of the same group can share a sense of group consciousness, without necessarily agreeing about the most effective or expedient strategy for improving the standing of the group (Dawson, 2001).

Bringing more nuance to the relationship between identity and politics, the immigrant incorporation scholarship emphasizes the diversity that exists on the basis of country of origin (Jones-Correa, 1998; Rogers, 2006). Country-of-origin differences can yield different ideological beliefs toward race; for example, Jamaicans and Trinidadians, while both Caribbean, come from nations with unique histories of race relations. The same can be said for Dominicans and Puerto Ricans, Mexicans and Colombians, Japanese and Koreans, and Ghanaians and Nigerians. Beltrán (2010) highlights the internal tensions that can arise among Latinx political movements as a result of this diversity.

The intersectionality literature is also useful in accounting for intragroup diversity, as it reminds us that every individual functions at the intersection of multiple identities, including but not limited to race, class, and gender. Existing at such intersections means that some individuals face overlapping systems of oppression such as racism, classism, sexism, and nativism (Collins, 2008; Crenshaw, 1991). This recognition inspires Greer's analysis of Black ethnic identity. Greer states, "Indeed, black immigrants face both the black-white binary and the binary of native-born versus foreign born that exists within the black community living in the United States. Therefore, black ethnics maintain a 'Du Boisian tripart Negro experience'" (Greer, 2013, p. 27). Drawing on and expanding Du Bois' (1903) concept of double consciousness, Greer emphasizes the multifaceted nature of identity and the existence of multiple versions of a Black experience. Given the multifaceted nature of identity and the multiple systems of oppression operating in the United States, Black immigrants must develop strategies for dealing with such systems, and these strategies may differ from African Americans who do not experience exclusion due to immigration status.

The Politics of Ethnic Respectability

Historically, some Black Americans have sought to challenge and avoid the consequences of negative stereotypes by conscientiously distancing themselves from the stigmatized behaviors that are assigned to blackness. A growing literature traces this strategy in African American history and politics, describing it as a politics of respectability. Higginbotham (1993, p. 187) describes respectability politics as emphasizing "reform of individual behavior and attitudes both as a goal in itself and as a strategy for reform of the entire structural system of American race relations." The belief embedded in the use of respectability politics is that one can alter the negative racial meanings that are assigned to Black people by consciously comporting one's self in opposition to those stereotypes and in line with white norms of behavior. Respectability can be used to advance the interests of a single individual. For example, by comporting one's self in a manner that counters negative stereotypes, one may be able to avoid racist or discriminatory interactions and develop acceptance among whites. Respectability politics is also a strategy used to advance the interests of a well-defined group of similarly situated individuals, as the logic of respectability suggests that an individual may be assigned to a broader group described as "good" or "well-behaved" according to white American standards.

Randall Kennedy (2015) describes respectability politics as historically and contemporarily useful in challenging white supremacy in the United States. While disparaging the racial structures that create the need for such extreme self-consciousness, Kennedy argues that being sensitive to one's public image has been successful in the fight for greater liberty and equality for people of color, citing the Civil Rights Movement and President Barack Obama as exemplars of respectability politics at work.

Critiques of respectability politics abound (e.g., Obasogie & Newman, 2016; Reynolds, 2015), arguing that respectability politics advance the false narrative that if you work hard and play by the rules you can succeed, regardless of your race, ethnicity, or social class. Critics note that an emphasis on individual behavior does not challenge racist systems but rather reinforces them by suggesting that individual behavior exclusively explains negative outcomes.[3] Many of these critiques focus on African Americans' use of the strategy and start with the assumed goal of unraveling racist systems. However, they do not frequently consider how other groups may use, reject, or transform respectability politics to their own ends.

While not traditionally engaged in the framework of respectability politics, the scholarship on Afro-Caribbeans describes a similar approach to the racial social structure. In her analysis, Waters (1999) finds that ethnic distancing best characterizes the Afro-Caribbean relationship with African Americans. Waters emphasizes the different impressions that the dominant society has of the two groups and the extent to which Caribbean immigrants work to distance themselves from the racial stigma that is frequently attached to African Americans by the dominant society. Such stigma and stereotypes can result in decreased job opportunities and increased racial discrimination for the African American community. As such, Afro-Caribbeans seek to maintain a positive reputation, particularly in the workforce, by actively distinguishing themselves from African Americans.

Similarly, in her theory of elevated minority status, Greer (2013) emphasizes the extent to which whites promote Afro-Caribbeans, as well as African immigrants, to an elevated group status over native-born Black populations in New York. This promotion incentivizes Afro-Caribbeans to remain outside of the Black–white binary and capitalize on the improved status that foreignness can provide, as seen in Kim's (1999) theorization of racial triangulation and the Asian American experience.

While Greer (2013) and Waters (1999) examine Afro-Caribbeans' efforts to navigate America's racial hierarchy, both studies are based in New York where Black ethnic identity has a salient, well-understood social meaning, and both presume that Afro-Caribbeans are working toward a white standard to improve their social standing. Given that there is limited analysis of Afro-Caribbean identity in settings where the co-ethnic community is not as elevated in the public consciousness, and given the significance of public recognition in the existence of social identities and locations, this chapter examines the social factors that influence Afro-Caribbean group attachment in New York City and Los Angeles County. With an eye toward identity, visibility, and the sociopolitical strategies of members of the group, the chapter seeks to understand how Afro-Caribbean populations understand their identity. What are the sociopolitical factors that inform their negotiation of racial politics, and what types of strategies do they deploy to navigate a sociopolitical landscape where those ascribed as Black are placed at the bottom of the racial hierarchy?

I argue that Afro-Caribbeans maintain attachments to multiple groups simultaneously, including the country of origin, ethnic, and racial groups. These attachments are maintained with a keen awareness of how each group is perceived in the public sphere. As such, their attachments manifest themselves differently based on the visibility and reputation of the various groups. While a single attachment may prove more salient for an individual, an emphasized attachment does not negate the existence of the other prevailing attachments. Therefore, to analyze group attachment without accounting for the role that space and place play in the development of multiple identities inherently neglects the social aspect of social identity.

I find that Afro-Caribbeans use cultural practices to garner group recognition and signal ethnic respectability. While the dominant use of respectability politics relies on conformity to Victorian or dominant white cultural norms to gain recognition, ethnic respectability consciously seeks to signal cultural difference from the Black–white binary to avoid the consequences of negative stereotypes typically associated with blackness and African Americans, in particular. Ethnic respectability utilizes foreignness in the field of racial positions to improve social standing. This strategy is worth noting because it rests on the belief that acceptance is rooted in dominant values; it does not demand cultural performativity that is consistent with white cultural norms. The theory of ethnic respectability offers a more nuanced and accurate description of the relationship between social identity, context, and sociopolitical strategy.

Data and Methods

The conclusions developed in this chapter are based on 71 in-depth interviews that I conducted in New York City and Los Angeles County over approximately a year and a half. The interviews lasted from approximately 17 minutes to an hour and 42 minutes. Initial contact with study participants in New York developed through personal networks. Meanwhile, Caribbean restaurants, concerts, and cultural festivals provided opportunities for initial contact with study participants in Los Angeles, where the Caribbean population is harder to find. The initial participants in both sites then recommended other potential contributors, a technique known as snowball sampling.

Jamaica and Trinidad are among the largest segments of the Caribbean population in both study sites and immigrants from these countries maintain significant visibility in their communities.[4] As such, I focused on interviewing Jamaicans and Trinidadians in order to observe attitudinal differences based on country of origin.[5] Participants included first- through second-generation immigrants[6] with an eye toward observing attitudinal changes that develop with more time in the United States. Of the participants, 37 were from New York, while 34 interviews were conducted in Los Angeles. New York participants resided in Brooklyn, Manhattan, Queens, and the Bronx. Los Angeles–based participants resided in South Los Angles, Mid City, Westwood, Bellflower, Long Beach, Inglewood, and the San Fernando Valley. Study sample characteristics are included in Table 2.1 (see Table 2.1).

TABLE 2.1 Interview Sample Demographic Characteristics

City of Residence	
New York	52%
Los Angeles	48%
Nation of Origin	
Jamaica	52%
Trinidad	48%
Gender	
Female	61%
Male	39%
Immigration Arrival	
First Generation	40%
1.5 Generation	16%
Second Generation	44%
Age Distribution	
18–24	16%
25–34	39%
35–44	18%
45–54	9%
55–64	18%
Marital Status	
Single	58%
Married/Living w Partner	34%
Separated	1%
Divorced	7%
Residential Status	
Own	28%
Rent	48%
Neither (e.g. live with parent)	24%
Political Affiliation	
Democrat	65%
Independent	18%
Republican	4%
Don't know	10%
Other	3%
Political Leaning	
Liberal	40%
Conservative	11%
Moderate	27%
Don't know	21%

Source: Data from the Afro-Caribbean Social Survey, 2011–2013.

Note. Sample size = 71; reported percentages are rounded.

The interview protocol focused on six key themes: background, identity attachments and interethnic relations, political interests, political engagement, the Barack Obama Presidency, and cultural symbols.[7] In order to solicit honest responses, I shared my Barbadian heritage (second generation) with study participants, and I changed participant names to protect their identity. The interviews were digitally recorded and transcribed. Content analysis of major themes of discussion was coded by hand. Themes from the New York sites were then compared with Los Angeles sites. Where possible, key themes were quantified and analyzed.

Country of Origin, Ethnicity, and Race in Context

Consistent with previous studies on Afro-Caribbean identity, my interview findings suggest that Afro-Caribbeans in both sites maintain attachments to their distinct country of origin, their ethnic group, as well as a racial group understood as the Black diaspora.[8] Each attachment informs Afro-Caribbean interaction with others within those groups' boundaries and outside them. Moreover, each attachment bears perceived social responsibilities that are neither static nor complimentary. Rather, they are dynamic and at times in sharp contrast with each other. Despite this complexity, Afro-Caribbeans navigate multiple attachments in order to maximize the potential for positive social and economic outcomes.

Between Home and the Diaspora

Two forces serve to shape study participants' negotiation of identity politics, deep connections to the country of origin, and recognition of historical and contemporary systems of racial oppression. As an immigrant population, Afro-Caribbeans in both cities maintain a strong primary attachment to the country of origin, particularly among the first generation. Regardless of their citizenship status, the country of origin remains the primary emotional attachment for many study participants. The country-of-origin attachment is exhibited by Lana, a first-generation Trinidadian in Los Angeles, who describes her attachment to Trinidad as follows: "I am a Trinidadian wherever I go... It's an opportunity to be here [in the United States], but I represent Trinidad wherever." Similar sentiments are expressed by participants in both sites with deep emotional, familial, and, in many cases, financial connections to the country of origin. The attachment to the country of origin described by study participants suggests that despite naturalization oaths, Afro-Caribbeans maintain a strong allegiance to the country of origin that echoes the findings in the transnational literature (see Rogers, 2006).

Amidst this country-of-origin attachment, Afro-Caribbeans also maintain an attachment to the pan-African diaspora that is rooted in historical and present day anti-Black racism and discrimination. This finding resonates with Smith's (2014) study of Black immigrants. When asked about what relationship, if any, he feels to the African continent and diaspora, Charles, a first-generation Jamaican in Los Angeles, emphasizes the African continent as the roots of his heritage. Meanwhile, 1.5 generation Los Angeles–based Trinidadian, Frank lifts up the transatlantic slave trade as a history shared by Black people across the Americas. Likewise, Luke, a second-generation Jamaican in New York, discusses the prevalence of anti-Black racism stating, "It may not be something that we want to talk about, but there is still so much racism out in the world." Across the study sites, the consciousness of a broader African diaspora was informed by the realities of historical and contemporary racial oppression.

Beyond the consciousness drawn out by questions focused on the African diaspora, study participants also described experiences of race-based discrimination that range from microaggressions, such as being followed by store clerks while shopping, to violent and systemic interactions with law-enforcement and institutional structures that resulted in significant trauma. When asked about experiences with racism or discrimination, first-generation Jamaican Charles recalls one such experience as driving with his family on a Los Angeles freeway and being rear-ended by a semitruck, flipping the car with his family over the median. While his family escaped without serious injury, the white driver was cited by law enforcement for relevant traffic violations. The accident resulted in a civil case against the truck driver, which was held shortly after the O.J. Simpson verdict. The jury consisted of nine whites and three people of color, with all nine white jurors finding the white truck driver not responsible for any damages and the three minority jurors finding for the plaintiff. While the facts of the case are not laid bare here, the fact that Charles understood the verdict as the product of racism speaks to his racial group attachment and its development in conversation with a racially unjust society.

Similarly, Charlene, a second-generation Trinidadian in Los Angeles, describes the worst experience of her life as calling 911 for help when she was attacked by a white neighbor and subsequently being arrested by the police officers that arrived on the scene. Consistent with previous works, Afro-Caribbeans express a racial group attachment that responds to anti-Black racism in the United States and globally based on historical injustices as well as on their personal experience with race-based discrimination (Hackshaw, 2008).

Ultimately, participants highlight the importance of ethnicity in balancing the country of origin and diasporic attachments. The following section examines the presence of such attachments in two settings where Afro-Caribbeans occupy contrasting locations in the public consciousness. In New York, Caribbean culture and identity are readily recognized as distinct from native-born Blacks and other Black immigrant groups. Meanwhile, in Los Angeles, the relative absence of a large Caribbean community renders Afro-Caribbean identity as largely invisible to the public consciousness. The work of Stepick, Eugene,

Teed, and Labissiere (2001) highlights the importance of public perception in creating social and political opportunities for immigrant populations. As such, how Afro-Caribbeans understand themselves, their group's social location, and their political opportunities must be framed by the public perception of these groups in the local and national context.

Caribbean Visibility and Public Consciousness in New York

Caribbeans represent a large ethnic group in New York City, comprising over a quarter of the Black population. The large, concentrated population is highly visible not only to Caribbean immigrants but also the wider community. Rogers (2001, p. 163) paints a particularly vivid picture in his groundbreaking study on Afro-Caribbean incorporation:

> Walking around Brooklyn's Flatbush Avenue, one immediately notices that the Caribbean has come to New York. All along the avenue, signals of a vibrant Caribbean immigrant presence shout at even the most casual observer. Storefronts advertise Caribbean symbolism—the bright colors of a flag, a palm tree, a stack of island newspapers in the window. Small, garrulous groups of men and women congregate in front of Caribbean bakeries and restaurants to discuss the news from "back home." Their animated conversations are thick with the distinctive inflexions of Caribbean dialects. Jitney vans and dollar vans perilously jockey for positions as they compete for fares along the busy thoroughfare and above the din, the sounds of calypso and reggae music ring out. This is black New York.

The density of the Caribbean population in New York increases the occasions when an Afro-Caribbean may come into contact with cultural forms of expression that can reify psychological connections to the ethnic group or country of origin while simultaneously signaling the meaningful presence of the ethnic community to the broader city.

This description speaks to the impact of Afro-Caribbean immigration on New York. For Afro-Caribbeans, the widespread presence of Caribbean people, culture, businesses, and organizations in New York mitigates the sharp distinction between life in the Caribbean and life in the United States. Andre, a second-generation Trinidadian, provides a portrayal of life in New York that is largely representative of New York participant responses, describing it as "comfortable because the community is vast with other Caribbeans who understand my culture, language, needs and wants. It's almost like living in Trinidad."

The presence of Caribbean culture is evident in the day-to-day elements of life in New York as well as in an annual celebration of Caribbean culture that includes a large Carnival-inspired parade in Brooklyn every September on Labor Day, the West Indian Day Parade. Held in Harlem from 1947 until 1964,[9] the parade moved to the Crown Heights section of Brooklyn in 1969 where it attracts over 1 million participants each year, placing it among the city's largest cultural events. Urban radio stations serving the tristate area (New York, New Jersey, and Connecticut) play reggae, soca, and calypso music from the Caribbean throughout the weekend as local newspapers and television networks cover the parade. Kasinitz (1992) describes the Carnival as a generator of ethnic identity, as it highlights the presence of a vibrant Caribbean community in Brooklyn and across the region, therefore strengthening pan-ethnic ties and raising the visibility of the Caribbean population.

Carolyn, a second-generation Trinidadian explains how the parade and the high visibility of Caribbean culture facilitate interpersonal interactions:

> I think it is easier because you will find a lot of people who will identify with you or your culture, especially because we have a parade. So even if you don't understand Trinidad or the culture, it's like, "Oh, it's West Indians. They have that parade," so it ties back to that. ... Everyone wants to be around people like themselves. In New York, it's that much easier [than living in other cities with fewer West Indians].

Carolyn's description of life in New York highlights the parade's capacity to facilitate public recognition of Afro-Caribbeans as a distinct cultural group. She also alludes to a preference for living in close proximity to other members of the group. Existing studies find Caribbean residential patterns in New York tend to be dense and concentrated in central Brooklyn, northern Bronx, and eastern Queens (Crowder & Tedrow, 2001). Similarly, New York participants for this study resided primarily in central Brooklyn. Carolyn describes the benefits of living in the Crown Heights neighborhood of central Brooklyn as the Caribbean community has grown:

> Growing up in this neighborhood [Crown Heights]... I've met with first generation people who came over in their adolescence who felt like [being from the Caribbean] was something that they had to hide or shy away from because they didn't want to be ridiculed...everybody trying to fit in when they were growing up. I never thought that way. It was always a source of pride. I remember in high school with the whole coconut music and I was like I am perfectly fine with my coconut music. I love your country and everything, but that's just not where I am from. I think the fact that there is so many of us here it's like okay and a strong community.

Carolyn describes the experience of living within the ethnic enclave as insulating her from the ridicule experienced by earlier immigrants and the strength of the community as enforcing a sense of ethnic pride. She stresses her ability to emphasize her culture as a marker of her ethnic difference. Carolyn's response is significant because, in New York, she is able to maintain such a strong attachment to the country of origin that, as a second-generation Trinidadian, she still describes the United States as "your" country when discussing a hypothetical American response to her attachment to her culture.

Similarly, Lionel, a second-generation Trinidadian, describes what it means to be Trinidadian in New York and specifically in his neighborhood of East Flatbush: "It's almost like the norm, you hardly hear somebody say 'I'm American' around here." The benefits of such co-ethnic interactions extend to participant social networks as well. Tim, a first-generation Trinidadian, discussed New York as providing opportunities for him to pass on his culture to his daughter. Tim highlights the importance of his daughter playing steel pan with people from across the Caribbean as a member of the Caribbean-American Sports & Cultural Youth Movement, Inc. (CASYM) Steel Orchestra.

While New York respondents describe their neighborhoods as largely Afro-Caribbean, the length of time in the United States serves to impact social networks. First-generation respondents largely describe their networks as predominately immigrant, consisting mostly of other Afro-Caribbean and Latino immigrants. The immigrant experience is unique and provides important opportunities for bonding based on past experiences, the process of incorporation, and the effort to hold on to home culture.

Meanwhile, second-generation respondents describe their networks as pan-ethnically Black (i.e., African immigrant, African American, and Afro-Caribbean). The second generation establishes relationships on the basis of a common Black experience in the United States; additionally, socialization in American schools facilitates network-building across ethnic communities. Taken together, such choices make sense, as people choose networks based on common ground, that is, immigration status versus Black racial identity.

The building of such networks is informed by a popular understanding of what it means to be from the Caribbean. In Los Angeles, this popular understanding does not exist. As a result, the experience of Afro-Caribbeans is vastly different in terms of interpersonal relations, cultural experience, and ultimately political engagement.

Ethnic Invisibility: Black in Los Angeles

Los Angeles County serves as a stark contrast to the New York City context, and the setting differs particularly with respect to the size of the Afro-Caribbean population. Despite a Caribbean population of less than 13,000 (State of Black Los Angeles, 2005), Los Angeles is a county where demographic trends shift dramatically as a result of immigration. Increasing immigrant populations from Mexico, Central America, and the Caribbean now occupy neighborhoods traditionally viewed as African American. Medina (2012) describes the changing face of Los Angeles as such:

Today, immigrants from Mexico and Central America live on blocks that generations ago were the only places African-Americans could live. In the former center of black culture in Los Angeles, Spanish is often the only language heard on the streets. Now, signs for "You buy, we fry" fish markets catering to Southern palates have been replaced by Mexican mariscos and Salvadoran pupuserias. In the historic jazz corridor, where music legends once stayed when they were barred from wealthy white neighborhoods in the city, botanicas sell folk and herbal remedies from Latin America.

The changing face of Los Angeles is the result of multiple forces. Since the 1990s, Black flight to the suburbs in search of homeownership has been one such force changing the face of Los Angeles (Hunt & Ramon, 2010; Medina, 2012). More recently, Los Angeles, like many other US cities, is also changing as a result of aggressive investment and redevelopment in urban centers. New expansions of public transportation, downtown renovations, and business development place many Los Angeles neighborhoods and communities in the midst of major demographic transformations. The increasing diversity raises questions about how Black immigrants understand themselves in relation to a growing Latinx community, a fluctuating African American population that still maintains important seats of power in the community, and the existing white population who maintain economic and political power across the county.

The size of the immigrant community in Los Angeles places immigration at the center of the public consciousness, impacting every facet of local politics and culture. With 35.3% of the county's population being foreign-born, the social, residential, and cultural landscapes of the county are shifting as a result of the changing demographics. As greater attention is paid to Latino immigration in Los Angeles, the Afro-Caribbean presence has largely been unnoticed by political officials. Still, Afro-Caribbeans are increasingly making their presence felt in the county.

Study participants reside across Los Angeles County in primarily African American and Latinx neighborhoods with a few living in the surrounding area. There is a notable absence of Caribbean enclaves, as one might find in New York, and this absence made finding Los Angeles participants more difficult. Despite the lack of a geographic community, 59% of first-generation Afro-Caribbean respondents in Los Angeles described their personal networks as composed primarily of Caribbean immigrants. While additional research would be necessary to determine whether an ethnic enclave serves to strengthen such ties, this finding suggests that an ethnic enclave is not a requirement for the development of an ethnic community. In addition to co-ethnic ties, first-generation participants also identify their networks as comprised of other first-generation immigrants from Latin America, Africa, and the Pacific Islands.

Often, the basis of such networks is described in terms of perceived cultural commonalities such as food and music.

While first-generation respondents are able to maintain connections to other members of the Caribbean community and facilitate cultural events, Afro-Caribbeans remain relatively invisible in the public consciousness. The local press does not extensively cover such events, and ideas about who is Caribbean and what it means to be Caribbean are not well-known.

Jones, a 1.5 generation immigrant, shares the perspective of an individual who accepts this invisibility as a social reality in Los Angeles. In answering the question, "What does it mean to be Jamaican in Los Angeles?" Jones responds:

> I'm just a regular Black dude in L.A. In New York or Miami, you feel like you can be with your own more. A lot of the Jamaicans here, you don't know they're Jamaican unless they tell you. Even myself, people wouldn't know I was Jamaican unless I tell them because I'm so westernized now. I've been here for 19 years. I picked up a lot of the African American culture. Depending on when you came to L.A. or California or whatever you can kind of lose your culture.

While Jones describes his perspective as a 1.5 generation Jamaican who migrated as a young child, the description of his own social identity highlights a trend that was echoed among second-generation respondents. This is explained by the reduced outward projection of Afro-Caribbean identity described by Jones. Similarly, Tyler, a second-generation Jamaican responds to the same question stating, "I feel like it's not something that comes up often. Nobody can tell I'm Jamaican. I'm just a Black girl. I don't feel like it really distinguishes me from anyone."

Second-generation participants largely describe their country of origin and ethnic attachments as a private affair, shared among family and close friends. For instance, Joyce explains, "When it comes to Jamaica, I kind of vibe off of my family. I don't think about it too much. Aside from my family everyone that I hang out with is just American." Similarly, in her description of what it means to be Trinidadian in Los Angeles, Rebecca, a second-generation Trinidadian in LA, describes a specific type of responsibility that comes with ethnic invisibility: "In school, I have to educate others, including my professors." The responsibility of educating others falls upon those who choose to emphasize country-of-origin or ethnic attachments.

For those respondents who moved to Los Angeles from other regions with a larger Caribbean population, Afro-Caribbean invisibility is a source of frustration. Tanisha, a second-generation Jamaican who had previously resided in the northeast region of the US as well as Toronto, Canada, which has a large Afro-Caribbean population and a significant presence in the public consciousness, expresses this frustration: "I have to fight to keep my culture. It's a very hard thing." The role that cultural reinforcement and public consciousness play in-group attachment echoes the findings of Zhou and Bankston (1999, p. 224), who argue that "families do not and cannot sustain and pass on cultural values in isolation. Rather, they exist and function in wider webs of social relations in the community." As such, the relative absence of a physical Afro-Caribbean community and the private nature of ethnic attachment among the 1.5 and second generations highlight the centrality of cultural reinforcement to social identity. The visibility of the community is an important factor for the group in its entirety, as well as for individual conceptions of the self as the length of time in the United States increases.

On the surface, the invisibility of Afro-Caribbeans in Los Angeles does not significantly alter group attachments among the first generation. As seen in New York, this attachment is rooted in cultural pride and an upright representation of the country of origin and ethnic groups. However, where New York and Los Angeles differ is in terms of the relationship with African Americans. In Los Angeles, first-generation participants reported their networks as having fewer African Americans than first-generation New Yorkers. First-generation Afro-Caribbeans in Los Angeles emphasized their frustration about being lumped in with African Americans on surveys and in popular conceptions of blackness. Afro-Caribbeans in Los Angeles also draw larger distinctions between Afro-Caribbeans and African Americans in terms of their outlook on life and values.

This trend dissipates significantly among 1.5 and second-generation Angelenos. Afro-Caribbean identity becomes a personal matter, shared among family and close friends but not a major part of interpersonal relations. Those socialized in the US readily connect and identify with their African American counterparts. Whereas respondents in both cities readily connect with the term Black, first-generation Angelenos maintained a heightened need for a national identifier as well. This difference in identity is likely the result of different patterns of interpersonal interactions and visibility in the public consciousness.

Improving Social Standing Through Ethnic Respectability

The politics of respectability is deeply committed to managing group visibility. Obasogie and Newman (2016, p. 541) argue, "Respectability politics is ultimately a performance and project of moving from the position of 'other,' to being incorporated into the normal, dominant and hegemonic." This conception of respectability politics places a group or individual (African Americans) in the position of performer attempting to gain the acceptance of the audience (white Americans) by mirroring the audience's behavior. Ostensibly, it is this performance that will unlock the door to opportunities available to those deemed normal. This framework is useful but doesn't fully capture the strategies of all Black groups. Like the traditional politics of respectability, ethnic respectability is also concerned with the audience and how they perceive the actor. However, unlike the politics of respectability, ethnic respectability is not concerned with mirroring white behavior. Rather, ethnic respectability accentuates the actor's position as an "other" through cultural signaling. This conscious othering is used to distance racial stigma and emphasize shared hegemonic values with the dominant group. This requires raising the profile of the group and policing representations of the group in the public sphere. In the case of Afro-Caribbeans, this produces different considerations in New York in comparison to Los Angeles.

In New York, where the Caribbean community has a high profile, attachment to the country of origin proves to be an important factor in understanding Afro-Caribbean emphasis on visibility and representations of the group. Johnson, a first-generation Jamaican in New York, suggests that the relationship between the country of origin and the host country bears tangible consequences.

> People back home are counting on you to send something back and you have to make something of yourself here. You have to be an ambassador. So, you are selling Jamaica in the US and provide some reality to those still living in Jamaica.

Johnson emphasizes his role as ambassador with a particular responsibility to succeed, inform friends and family back home about life in the United States, and represent the country of origin well. Johnson's interpretation of his role speaks to a larger trend among Afro-Caribbeans in New York to be mindful of the group's reputation.

Respondents describe a sense of responsibility to advance positive depictions of Caribbean culture that distinguishes the group from others and challenges negative interpretations of the national origin group specifically and the Caribbean community more generally. Andre, a second-generation Trinidadian in New York, highlights the positive attributes and distinctions of Caribbean culture as such:

> West Indian culture differs [from African Americans] in terms of work ethic. It could stem from a history as laborers. The Jamaican stereotype applies to the whole Caribbean. Non-West Indians don't have that. We still are pushed by our parents. American parents don't have the same push. They make fun of me. "He must be West Indian because he works so much." It's a different kind of hustle. If you can't hustle, Americans get welfare and social services. West Indians don't do that.

Andre describes the group in terms of a common culture of hard work consistent with dominant values, and this culture is contrasted with negative depictions of

"African American culture." Making such claims is crucial to developing what Greer (2013) calls an elevated group status. However, beyond such interethnic distinctions, Rachel, a first-generation Jamaican in New York, also highlights the management of negative stereotypes that are sometimes validated by other Afro-Caribbeans:

> Because of the reputation of the few who make a bad name for us,... people... think negatively. There's the standing, "So you got some of that good stuff to smoke, right." That's the standing thing, but I take that lightly. But there are people who really have no clue what life in the Caribbean is like so it's a great opportunity for me to teach people about that when I can. There's this whole notion that you are from Jamaica or the Caribbean you come over here and take our jobs from Blacks who are native to America. But there are those who from the minute they hear Jamaican, they say Jamaicans are really bright; they are this. So being a Jamaican in NY is interesting because NY is such a melting pot. You are comfortable in certain ways, and you feel like you bring something to the texture and culture of NYC, but in a lot of ways you feel like you're on the side just competing because of some of the perceptions and misperceptions that people have.

While much of the literature on Black immigration in New York highlights the ethnic distancing between Afro-Caribbeans and African Americans (Waters, 1999), this study finds that the story is more complicated than the literature suggests. Respondents demonstrate not only a distancing between themselves and "bad" African American stereotypes but also between themselves and "bad" Afro-Caribbean reputations. In their study of Haitians in Miami, Stepick et al. (2001) highlight the powerful effect that a negative perception in the public consciousness can have on access to social, political, and economic opportunities, particularly among the second generation. Participant responses reveal an effort to maintain ethnic respectability in the public consciousness that will improve social and economic outcomes for themselves and their families back in the Caribbean.

While New York–based participants are aware of this reality and work to police the reputation of the group, Los Angeles–based respondents must overcome a lack of recognition in order to attain an elevated status. Like in New York, Los Angeles participants describe a desire to represent their country of origin and Afro-Caribbeans well. Monique, a second-generation Jamaican, is cognizant of how her actions may translate to broader group inferences. She responds to the question of what it means to be a Jamaican in Los Angeles by explaining that as a Jamaican, she has to "be mindful of how you portray yourself." Attempting to police the public perceptions of the national origin and ethnic groups causes Monique to be sensitive to the external perceptions of the group. Similarly, Pam is encouraged to draw distinctions between Afro-Caribbeans and African Americans, as seen in New York:

> [W]e have a different mentality and we conduct ourselves differently and we can see that we're worlds apart from an [African] American. Even though we have the same skin tone, our thinking is different... We don't come here expecting this country to give us something, we come here with the expectation that there is so much to achieve and in order for us to achieve it, we have to work our asses off to get it... We don't go and sit on the welfare system to collect a check.

Smith (2014) finds in her particularly nuanced study of Black immigrants that the term "Black" is a satisfactory shared identifier, yet Afro-Caribbeans in both sites identify the distinctions in outlook between African Americans and Afro-Caribbeans. Despite the similarities in managing group reputation between New York and Los Angeles, the lower profile of Afro-Caribbeans in Los Angeles results in a concerted effort to highlight Caribbean culture. First-generation Trinidadian Jonathan argues that what it means to be a Trinidadian in Los Angeles is

> Unique from[the] perspective[that] they don't have much of us here, so that's one aspect. Secondly, with my accent, I draw people close to me. People will stop me and say, "I hear an accent, where is that from?" and I tell them, "Trinidad," so it gives me the opportunity to explain to them and show them Trinidad, because most people don't know about Trinidad. On the east coast, yes, but here... when you tell them you're from Trinidad, [they ask] "What part of Africa is that?"

Such circumstances result in the need to raise the profile of the community as an individual and as a collective effort. Louis, a first-generation Jamaican in Los Angeles, describes what it means to be a Jamaican in Los Angeles as

> Pride. Confidence. Hard work... Promoting the whole culture and what we do in Jamaica is what I'm about, so I'm unique and different because some people like to sit back and enjoy but it's my job and it's my life, so being a Jamaican in SoCal is promoting Jamaica for me.

While participants in both sites balance the layered attitudes toward Afro-Caribbeans in the public consciousness, a higher profile allows New Yorkers to mark themselves as distinct and manage their social location in relation to other present groups. Angelenos, on the other hand, emphasize a need to uplift, educate, and represent what it means to be a part of the group in a positive light.

In order to distinguish the group and manage its reputation, participants rely on cultural explanations for group success in the United States. They emphasize education, hard work, and the absence of social safety net programs such as unemployment and welfare in the Caribbean as evidence of the inherent self-reliance of the group.[10] This emphasis on hard work does not stand alone to improve group reputation, rather cultural practices and events serve to signal ethnic difference and to raise the profile of the group.

Developing Recognition through Cultural Signaling

For some political scientists, the concept of culture is closely related to essentialist claims about group traits and characteristics (Almond, 1956; Almond & Verba, 1963; Huntington, 1996). Scholars such as Samuel Huntington (1993, 1996) espouse interpretations of culture that are used to explain a variety of political hypotheses including why democratization is more or less successful in certain countries and why certain groups do not adhere to various models of political behavior. Lisa Wedeen (2002, p. 715) points out some of the fundamental problems with these interpretations of culture and what it means to political science as a discipline:

> The understanding of culture as a specific group's primordial values or traits is untenable empirically. It ignores the historical conditions and relevant power relationships that give rise to political phenomena such as "democratization," ethnic conflicts, and contemporary radical Islamicist movements. The group traits version of culture, moreover, rides roughshod over the diversity of views and the experiences of contention within the group or groups under study.

Wedeen highlights the problem with addressing culture as an inherent value or trait, a conceptualization that is unable to address the internal diversity of a given group. This problem with engaging culture as a group value or trait prompts other scholars, particularly in sociology, to engage culture in terms of group norms and practices. Zhou and Bankston (1999, p. 11) define immigrant culture in particular as

> an entire way of life, including languages, ideas, beliefs, values, behavioral patterns, and all that immigrants bring with them as they arrive in their new country. The original culture may be seen as hindering the adaptation of the ethnic group (the assimilationist perspective) or as promoting this adaptation (the multiculturalist perspective).

Such an interpretation of culture shifts the focus from inherent traits to an emphasis on the in-group means of communication and interaction. While Zhou and Bankston (1999) highlight the tension that exists between maintaining and shedding the immigrant culture in the host country, the use of culture to navigate relationships is politically significant insomuch as cultural practices produce political effects.

Guidry and Sawyer (2003) identify culture as an area of concern for political science, particularly in the case of marginalized groups. Guidry and Sawyer (2003, p. 273) explain, "Attempts by marginalized groups to gain a foothold in the public sphere can contribute to the development of democracy, even when these actors aren't consciously organizing for the purpose of advancing democracy." The impact that an individual or group can exert on the nature and substance of political discourse and policy is significant despite a desire to remain removed from it. Such moments where cultural practices meet political activity highlight the possibility for seemingly nonpolitical actions to produce political change.

Evidence of the influence exerted by Afro-Caribbean cultural claims-making is most evident during the annual West Indian Day Parade in New York. Between 2009 and 2013 alone, the political significance of Caribbean culture in local politics resulted in high-ranking political officials serving as grand marshals, including Secretary of State Colin Powell (2009), New York Governor Andrew Cuomo (2011), New York Mayor Michael Bloomberg (2011), and City Council Speaker and Mayoral candidate Christine Quinn (2012). Kasinitz (1992) traces this trend to the early 1980s. In the desire to make the political nature of the parade more explicit, Sultan, (42, second-generation Trinidadian in NY) states as much by saying,

> [The best way for Afro- Caribbeans to achieve their political goals is to] use some of the existing organizations to drive political goals like WIADCA (West Indian American Day Carnival Association). We organize for those things culturally but maybe we can advance political goals as well.

To be sure, the Black immigrant population in New York warrants political attention due to the size alone. Afro-Caribbeans have electoral prowess, influence, and the institutional setup in New York elections incentivizes politicians to pay special attention to this group (Rogers, 2004). Yet, the presence of a large Caribbean community in New York also provides Afro-Caribbeans with alternative forms of political participation not afforded to Afro-Caribbeans in settings with a smaller population and public presence, such as Los Angeles.

While politics are engaged in intimate cultural settings among members of the group in LA, larger displays of Caribbean culture such as the Los Angeles Caribbean Carnival and the Hollywood Carnival are largely devoid of political messaging and mobilization efforts. Since 1995, a small festival has taken place in the middle-class neighborhood of West Chester emphasizing Caribbean culture and community. Started by a University of California, Los Angeles (UCLA) graduate student from Jamaica, the event has grown and developed into an annual event. Still, as the event grows, similar events are developing in other parts of the county. During this study's fieldwork, the first annual Hollywood Caribbean parade took place in June of 2012. Similarly, a small annual carnival paralleling Trinidad and Tobago's Carnival in February also sprung up in downtown Los Angeles. Such events speak to a growing community that is largely unknown to the larger Los Angeles community but encourages academic and political attention. The growth of Caribbean cultural events is dependent on a well-connected community of Afro-Caribbeans who stimulate memories of home and maintain spaces where cultural traditions and norms are sustained. Such traditions are preserved in the relative absence of clearly defined Caribbean enclaves in Los Angeles.

Despite the absence of such enclaves, the seemingly apolitical work of carnival-organizing in Los Angeles yields political results. Through a collaboration between Hollywood Carnival organizers and City Councilman Marqueece Harris-Dawson, the Los Angeles City Council declared June 21, 2017, the inaugural celebration of an annual Caribbean Heritage Recognition Day. Caribbean flags were draped around City Hall, stilt walkers, dancers, and steel drum music filled the council chamber as members of the city council looked on and some highlighted the contributions of the Caribbean community in Los Angeles. This celebration served to raise the profile of the Caribbean population. The use of cultural practices to highlight ethnic differences became an explicitly political project in Los Angeles. Such recognition and symbolic representation by Harris-Dawson prompts more substantive questions from those seeking and maintaining elected office such as "What are the interests of this population?" and "How do I connect with them and represent them effectively?" Carnival events represent potential sites of engagement, claims-making, and mobilization. While the size of the population in New York means that cultural events exist in conversation with more substantive and sustained political projects, time will tell whether and how cultural practices will be used to make political claims on behalf of the Black immigrant population in Los Angeles.

Conclusion

Black immigration challenges conceptions of a monolithic Black community at every turn. Diverse countries of origin, cultural practices, and migration circumstances translate into distinct patterns of engagement with co-ethnics, African Americans, other racial groups, and the government. The Afro-Caribbean population provides a useful window into understanding identity, intergroup relations, and political engagement in this growing segment of the Black political landscape.

Scholars seeking to understand identity and intergroup relations among Afro-Caribbeans in the US find considerable variation. Sometimes members of the group are seen as distancing themselves from African Americans, and at other times they are seen as advantageously identifying with their African American counterparts. Amidst this variation, there is little discussion about when, where, and how Afro-Caribbeans reconcile this variation for themselves. This gap in the literature underscores the complexity of racial and ethnic group attachments, their dynamic nature, and the potential political impact of such attachments.

This chapter seeks to address this gap by examining the social factors that influence Afro-Caribbean group identity in New York City and Los Angeles County. It argues that Afro-Caribbeans maintain three distinct group attachments: country of origin, ethnic, and racial. Each attachment bears with it social responsibilities that Afro-Caribbeans seek to navigate through ethnic respectability. Study participants maintain an acute awareness of group image in the public consciousness in order to maximize personal success and to improve opportunities for other members of the group. As such, cultural practices and values serve as a tool for managing group image in the local public consciousness.

Participants attempt to manage essentialist claims used by the dominant society to explain socioeconomic mobility or lack thereof. The inability to attain socioeconomic success is coded as the result of cultural deficiencies that warrant the less-than-full acceptance as a member of the polity. The persistence of such group-based assessments causes Afro-Caribbeans to tread lightly in their deployment of their various group attachments.

The chapter finds that the size of the Afro-Caribbean communities in New York and Los Angeles has implications for the visibility of the community, the interpersonal interactions of group members, and the deployment of identity-based attachments. While social context bears little impact on the social identity of the first generation, second-generation Afro-Caribbeans understand their attachments very differently in New York and Los Angeles, as exemplified by their perceived group allies, commonalities, and shared values.

Culture serves as a language of meaning, constructing a lens through which to understand potential allies, as well as identity and group attachment in the host country. Home country attachment reinforces a concept of self that is primarily immigrant, particularly among first-generation respondents in Los Angeles where there is only a small scattered community of co-ethnics and relative invisibility in the Los Angeles public sphere. Meanwhile, a large community of co-ethnics and higher visibility in the city's public sphere produces a two-way assimilation process that facilitates social and political attachments with African Americans in New York.

My results confirm Rogers' findings that Afro-Caribbeans who are firmly enmeshed in African American networks are more inclined to tap into race-based group attachments. Meanwhile, a large Afro-Caribbean community in New York serves to strengthen the country of origin and ethnic group attachments from the first generation through to the second generation. The chapter challenges Waters' findings by suggesting that a theory of ethnic distancing ignores Afro-Caribbean membership and identification as Black. It suggests a more nuanced approach to Afro-Caribbean identity, as the local community can be a powerful force that facilitates incorporation into a new country while also maintaining strong bonds to the country of origin.

Ethnic respectability provides a roadmap for understanding Afro-Caribbean incorporation in places like New York. This strategy provides Afro-Caribbeans in New York with the capacity to evade some of the stigma associated with blackness in the US and improve access to opportunities by using culture to retain their foreignness. This strategy provides hints for what might be expected in other cities where small immigrant populations struggle to gain recognition from the political establishment. In Los Angeles, for example, the growing profile of the Caribbean community is likely to gain greater attention of elected officials, including an increased presence of elected officials at cultural events such as the Carnival. While ethnic respectability may not immediately produce explicitly political claims in cultural venues, as the population and profile grows, political organization on the basis of ethnicity may push the Black political establishment to engage immigration, not only as a Latin American phenomenon, but also as an issue that is personal to a more diverse Black community.

Notes

1 The term Black refers to people who trace their lineage to the African continent and identify as members of the African diaspora. African American is used to reference members of the Black community who trace their lineage through slavery in the United States, while Afro-Caribbean is used for members of the Black community who more recently immigrated from one of the nations situated in or bordering the Caribbean Sea.

2 New York City maintains a population of over 8.5 million people concentrated in an area of 469 square miles.

3 The Black Lives Matter movement that developed in response to police violence inflicted on Black people in the United States rejects respectability politics as a viable strategy for systemic reform. Movement leaders are critical of narratives that seek to paint victims of state violence as more or less deserving of the violence inflicted on them based on what they were wearing or whether they were comporting themselves according to dominant middle-class white values. Rather, the movement calls for basic human rights and the recognition of human dignity for all Black people.

4 Members of these communities have also made a significant mark on the political landscape in both cities. For example, Congresswoman Yvette Clarke of New York's then eleventh and now ninth district (2007–present) is a second-generation Jamaican, and Congressman Mervyn Dymally of California's thirty-first district (1981–1993) was first-generation Trinidadian.

5 Country-of-origin differences are not addressed in this chapter.

6 First-generation respondents represent those who were born and raised in the country of origin. The sociology literature highlights the importance of recognizing the country of socialization; as such, I distinguish participants who were born in the country of origin but migrated to the United States before the age of 13 as "1.5 generation." Meanwhile, those born in the US to at least one parent from Jamaica or Trinidad are coded as second generation.

7 The interview protocol was adapted from protocols utilized by Rogers (2006) and Jackson, Hutchings, Brown, and Wong (2009).

8 Studies of transnationalism describe a strong attachment to the country of origin that manifests in various ways, including the maintenance of dual citizenship, participation in transnational organizations, continued electoral participation in the country of origin, and a desire to return home to the country of origin at some point (usually retirement) (Basch, Schiller, & Blanc, 1994; Escobar, 2004; Jones-Correa, 1998; Lee, Ramakrishnan & Ramírez, 200; Rogers, 2006).

9 The Harlem parade ended when the parade permit was revoked in 1964. The parade did not resurface until 1969 in Brooklyn (Brooklyn Public Library, 2005; Kasinitz, 1992).

10 In her innovative and influential study of Black ethnicity in New York, Greer (2013) finds that Afro-Caribbean union members maintain attitudes towards welfare that are consistent with those of African American union members. Responses to this study set the stage for an extension of Greer's work to examine such attitudes among Afro-Caribbeans in Los Angeles and with nonunion members, who may not be as politically engaged.

References

Almond, G. A. (1956). Comparative political systems. *Journal of Politics, 18*(3), 391–409.

Almond, G. A., & Verba, S. (1963). *The civic culture: Political attitudes and democracy in five nations*. Princeton, NJ: Princeton University Press.

Basch, L., Schiller, N. G., & Blanc, C. S. (1994). *Nations unbound: Transnational projects, postcolonial predicaments, and deterritorialized nation-states*. Langhorne, PA: Gordon and Breach.

Beltrán, C. (2010). *The trouble with unity: Latino politics and the creation of identity*. Oxford, England: Oxford University Press.

Brooklyn Public Library. (2005). Our Brooklyn: West Indian Carnival. Retrieved from https://www.bklynlibrary.org/ourbrooklyn/carnival/index.html

Collins, P. (2008). *Black feminist thought: Knowledge, consciousness, and the politics of empowerment*. New York, NY: Routledge.

Crenshaw, K. (1991). Mapping the margins: Intersectionality, identity politics, and violence against women of color. *Stanford Law Review, 43*(6), 1241–1299.

Crowder, K. D., & Tedrow, L.M. (2001). West Indians and the residential landscape of New York. In N. Foner (Ed.), *Islands in the city: West Indian migration to New York* (pp. 81–114). Berkeley, CA: University of California Press.

Dawson, M. C. (2001). *Black visions: The roots of contemporary African-American political ideologies*. Chicago, IL: University of Chicago Press.

Escobar, C. (2004). Dual citizenship and political participation: Migrants in the interplay of United States and Colombian politics. *Latino Studies, 2*(1), 45–69.

Foner, N. (2001). *Islands in the city: West Indian migration to New York*. Berkeley, CA: University of California Press.

Greer, C. M. (2013). *Black ethnics: Race, immigration, and the pursuit of the American dream*. New York, NY: Oxford University Press.

Guidry, J. A., & Sawyer, M. Q. (2003). Contentious pluralism: The public sphere and democracy. *Perspective on Politics*, *1*(2), 273–289.

Hackshaw, A. C. (2008). *Ethnic diversity and Pan-Black racial solidarity: Locating the bonds of political unity among Black Americans and Black Caribbean immigrants in the U.S.* (Doctoral Dissertation). Retrieved from Deep Blue, University of Michigan. (2008-08-25T20:57:03Z).

Higginbotham, E. B. (1993). *Righteous discontent: The women's movement in the Black Baptist Church, 1880–1920*. Cambridge, MA: Harvard University Press.

Hunt, D., & Ramon, A.-C. (2010). *Black Los Angeles: American dreams and racial realities*. New York, NY: New York University Press.

Huntington, S. P. (1993). The clash of civilizations? *Foreign Affairs*, *72*(3), 22–49.

Huntington, S. P. (1996). *The clash of civilizations and the remaking of world order*. New York, NY: Simon and Schuster.

Jackson, J. S., Hutchings, V. L., Brown, R., Wong, C., & Inter University Consortium for Political and Social Research. (2009). *National politics study, 2004*. Ann Arbor, MI: Inter-university Consortium for Political and Social Research [distributor].

Jones-Correa, M. (1998). *Between two nations: The political predicament of Latinos in New York City*. Ithaca, NY: Cornell University Press.

Kasinitz, P. (1992). *Caribbean New York: Black immigrants and the politics of race*. Ithaca, NY: Cornell University Press.

Kennedy, R. (2015, October). Lifting as we climb: A progressive defense of respectability politics. *Harper's Magazine*. Retrieved from https://harpers.org/archive/2015/10/lifting-as-we-climb/

Kim, C. (1999). The racial triangulation of Asian Americans. *Politics & Society*, *27*(1), 105–138.

Lee, T., Ramakrishnan, S. K., & Ramírez, R. (2007). *Transforming politics, transforming America: The political and civic incorporation of immigrants in the United States*. Charlottesville, VA: University of Virginia Press.

McClain, P. D., Johnson Carew, J. D., Walton, E., & Watts, C. S. (2009). Group membership, group identity, and group consciousness: Measures of racial identity in American politics? *Annual Review of Political Science*, *12*(1), 471–485.

Medina, J. (2012, April 24). In South Los Angeles, a changed complexion since the riots. *The New York Times*. Retrieved from http://www.nytimes.com/2012/04/25/us/in-south-los-angeles-a-changed-complexion-since-the-riots.html

Model, S. (2008). *West Indian immigrants: A Black success story?* New York, NY: Russell Sage Foundation.

Nichols, M. (2005). *The state of Black Los Angeles*. Los Angeles, CA: Los Angeles Urban League and United Way of Greater Los Angeles. This is an online report. The URL is as follows: http://cretscmhd.psych.ucla.edu/healthfair/PDF%20articles%20for%20fact%20sheet%20linking/BlackHealth_UnitedWay.pdf

Obasogie, O. K., & Newman, Z. (2016). Black Lives Matter and respectability politics in local news accounts of officer-involved civilian deaths: An early empirical assessment. *Wisconsin Law Review*, *2016*(3), 541–571.

Omi, M., & Winant, H. (2015). *Racial formation in the United States* (3rd ed.). New York, NY: Routledge.

Reynolds, B. (2015, August 24) I was a civil rights activist in the 1960s. But it's hard for me to get behind Black Lives Matter. *The Washington Post*. Retrieved from https://www.washingtonpost.com/posteverything/wp/2015/08/24/i-was-a-civilrights-activist-in-the-1960s-but-its-hard-for-me-to-get-behind-black-livesmatter/?postshare=5221440433170944&utm_term=.aca38fbecf30

Rogers, R. R. (2001). Black like who? Afro-Caribbean immigrants, African Americans, and the politics of group identity. In N. Foner (Ed.), *Islands in the city: West Indian migration to New York* (pp. 163–192). Berkeley, CA: University of California Press.

Rogers, R. R. (2004). Race-based coalitions among minority groups: Afro-Caribbean immigrants and African-Americans in New York City. *Urban Affairs Review, 39*(3), 283–317.

Rogers, R. R. (2006). *Afro-Caribbean immigrants and the politics of incorporation ethnicity, exception, or exit.* Cambridge; New York: Cambridge University Press.

Smith, C. W. (2014). *Black mosaic: The politics of pan-ethnic diversity.* New York, NY: New York University Press.

Stepick, A., Stepick C. D., Eugene, E., Teed, D., & Labissiere, Y. (2001). Shifting identities and intergenerational conflict: Growing up Haitian in Miami. In R. Rumbaut, & A. Portes (Eds.), *Ethnicities: Children of immigrants in America* (pp. 229–266). Los Angeles, CA: University of California Press.

Tajfel, H. (1979). Individuals and groups in social psychology. *British Journal of Clinical Psychology, 18*(2), 183–190.

Tajfel, H., & Turner, J. C. (1979). An integrative theory of inter-group conflict. In W. G. Austin, & S. Worchel (Eds.), *The social psychology of inter-group relations* (pp. 33–47). Monterey, CA: Brooks/Cole.

Thomas, K. J. A. (2012). A demographic profile of Black Caribbean immigrants in the United States. Migration Policy Institute National Center on Immigrant Integration Policy.

U.S. Census Bureau (2017). Annual estimates of the resident population: April 1, 2010 to July 1, 2017. Retrieved from https://factfinder.census.gov/faces/tableservices/jsf/pages/productview.xhtml?src=CF.

Waters, M. C. (1999). *Black identities West Indian immigrant dreams and American realities.* Cambridge, MA: Harvard University Press.

Wedeen, L. (2002). Conceptualizing culture: Possibilities for political science. *American Political Science Review, 96*(4), 713–728.

Zhou, M., & Bankston, C., III. (1999). *Growing up American: How Vietnamese children adapt to life in the United States.* New York, NY: Russell Sage Foundation.

PART II

Black (In)Visibility

New Insights on Majority–Minority Cities

3

A SANCTUARY FOR WHOM?

Race, Immigration, and the Black Public Sphere

Niambi M. Carter

In many ways, the politics of Washington, DC have always been about race. The movement of DC from simply a federal district to more political independence has always been accompanied by conversations about race. In fact, from the neighborhoods to the distribution of employment in the city, race is an organizing principle in the District. As the District grew to be a majority Black city, it has also been a haven for immigrants (Jamison, 2016; Simon, 2014). In the contemporary moment where sanctuary cities are gaining more political attention, it is important to note that this Black city under a Black mayor has been an official sanctuary city for more than 30 years. While this progressive political style has been a characteristic of the city, it is also true that native-born Black[1] engagement with the city has been simultaneously characterized by visibility and invisibility.

For many Blacks on the East Coast, DC has traditionally been a beacon for those hoping to achieve upward social mobility. This is still true. Yet, economic forces have made the gaps between the "haves" and "have-nots" more pronounced (Reel, 2003). Those with fewer resources, however, have not found themselves in a position to take advantage of the city's bounty; their tenure in the city has been characterized by marginalization, exclusion, and failures in service. The once "chocolate city" is now characterized as a "latte city," indicating there is still a strong Black presence, but this has been accompanied by an influx of affluent whites and services that the city's poorest citizens cannot access (Dvorak, 2015; Hyra, 2015). What is more, the District has witnessed an influx of immigrant residents (Simon, 2014). DC has a large Salvadoran population that rivals larger cities like Los Angeles; it is a preferred destination of African refugees and immigrants; and most immigrants, regardless of country of origin, arrived after 1980 (Wilson, 2008). While this immigration has calmed amid the city's rising cost of living and the Great Recession, it is nonetheless a preferred immigrant gateway. Given the seemingly hasty exodus of Blacks from the city which has accompanied the aforementioned changes, how do the city's Black residents think about immigration? More importantly, is the decreasing presence of Blacks in the city at odds with its sanctuary status, a status that was established and reaffirmed by the city's Black leadership?

This chapter presents arguments on two fronts. The first provides a better understanding of Black public opinion on immigration. This is significant because in the literature on minority relations, competition is one of the primary lenses employed to understand these relations (Bonacich, 1972; Jones-Correa, 2001; McClain et al., 2006). Using DC as a case, I argue that native-born Blacks, in general, are not opposed to immigration, including undocumented immigration. The second line of analysis provides a better understanding of how Blacks see themselves as stakeholders in the city. Black Washingtonians are far more concerned with their everyday lives where crime is still a reality in the poorer wards of the city; rents are increasing and the average salary to live comfortably in the city tops $100,000; and public education continues to fail too many of its most needy residents. This ostensible contradiction is significant to identify, as DC reintroduces itself to the local area as a preferred destination for young professionals and families on par with the near suburbs and a hub of economic development.

Establishing DC as a welcoming place for our most vulnerable citizens is a necessity in the hostile political climate; this sanctuary status, however, seems at odds with the realities many native-born Blacks encounter simply trying to *remain* citizens of the city. To be clear, this is not written to suggest an either/or scenario of native-born Blacks versus immigrants. Moreover, it is not to suggest that all Black residents of the District are poor. Blacks represent a diverse community of people in the District. Yet, it is also true that the Black median income in the city is $41,000; I think it fair to say the Black middle-class' hold on the city is tenuous. Rather, it is a call for the District to send similarly explicit messages of care to native-born Black residents.

What is a Sanctuary City?

The increasing prominence of "sanctuary cities," localities that are not in compliance with federal immigration enforcement, is the direct result of evolving US immigration policy. The first manifestation of the "sanctuary" movement occurred during the 1980s when religious institutions and localities began offering assistance to Central American refugees who were refused admittance by the federal government (Villazor, 2008). These groups' "use of the word sanctuary conveyed a sense of moral and ethical obligation" and is the primary justification for defying federal immigration enforcement (Villazor, 2008, p. 135). Though sanctuary cities are not legal designations, they are statements about what that locality views as its primary responsibility. By designating itself as a "sanctuary," a jurisdiction effectively establishes that it will not cooperate with federal immigration authorities. This means local law enforcement is barred from inquiring about an individual's immigration status, and local jails will not detain people because of their status or share this information with federal authorities.

While sanctuary cities have been in existence for more than 30 years, they have gained a new prominence in today's political environment. Currently, Attorney General Sessions is trying to use his authority to legally define sanctuary jurisdictions as "a term for local governments that refuse to fully comply with federal immigration laws" (Bernal, 2017). By defining this term legally and broadly, Sessions is attempting to force these localities and, in some cases, states, to comply with federal immigration laws or face sanctions in the form of withholding federal funding from the Departments of Justice or Homeland Security. This is related to President Trump's executive order attempting to crack down on sanctuary cities. The executive order states,

> Sanctuary jurisdictions across the United States willfully violate Federal law in an attempt to shield aliens from removal from the United States. These jurisdictions have caused immeasurable harm to the American people and to the very fabric of our Republic.

While Trump's executive order was halted, it has not stopped Attorney General Sessions from attempting to force compliance from these jurisdictions (Bernal, 2017). The matter is still being adjudicated, as it is unclear that a locality's choice to designate itself a sanctuary is in violation of federal law (Casselman, Casteel, & Koeze, 2017).

As the federal government increasingly focused on border enforcement as a way to insure US domestic safety over the last three decades, the need for more humane immigration practices has once again brought sanctuary cities to the fore. A consequence of focusing on border enforcement is that individuals fleeing civil conflicts are also construed as threats, especially those from countries with governments viewed as being hostile to American interests; these immigrants were treated as proxies for their governments by ideologically conservative politicians, policies, and political pundits (Huntington, 1993; Kinder & Kam, 2010; Lee, 2002; Rodriguez, 2007). Thus, non-European immigrants who lack proficiency in English and deign to access city and state services are treated with a certain kind of suspicion. Not only are they seen as being disinterested in being incorporated into the body politic and a danger to the country's identity, they are viewed as illegitimate usurpers of American bounty who take jobs and services American taxpayers provide (Massey & Pren, 2012; Viladrich, 2012). While the Reagan years provided a model of what amnesty for undocumented immigrants could look like, the framing of this group as "illegal" gained renewed prominence in the 1980s and remains the dominant frame for discussing undocumented persons (Flores, 2003; Jeong, Miller, Schofield, & Sened, 2011; Mehan, 1997). This sense that people without papers are dangerous has only become solidified since the enactment of the Immigration Reform and Control Act (IRCA).

After 9/11, the preoccupation with American safety made undocumented immigration a matter of national security. President Bush ushered in a generational preoccupation with border enforcement that continued under the Obama administration. One of the most beloved modern presidents President Obama deported more undocumented people than any of his predecessors and introduced the Secure Communities program. Secure Communities was a program started in 2008 where local authorities would share information on inmates with federal authorities to ascertain one's citizenship status. Those in police custody found to be in the country without authorization were then detained until federal authorities came and took custody of these individuals. By framing undocumented immigration as a matter of national security, federal authorities effectively enjoined local and state police to their federal mission of immigration enforcement. Federalism issues aside, Secure Communities raised a number of issues for localities at its initial rollout.

One of the first issues was the uneven application of the program's key provisions. Initially, local authorities could create memoranda of understanding with the federal government outlining the parameters of their relationship and involvement with the program. For example, under Chief Ramsey, the Metropolitan Police Department (MPD) agreed not to inquire about an individual's status for the purposes of immigration enforcement. Rather, Chief Ramsey advised MPD to focus on enforcing the law and leave all immigration matters to federal authorities; if it was determined an individual was in the country without authorization, the MPD would inform the federal government but that would be treated separately from the original offense (Aguilar, 2005). While these memoranda were favored by local police forces, it created some confusion, as there was no single policy of enforcement. Therefore, each state and their localities could potentially have a different relationship with the federal government depending on the termination clauses negotiated by their states.[2] This practice was ended in 2010, as the Department of Homeland Security favored uniform application of the policy. In fact, the Obama administration argued state compliance with Secure Communities was not required for the federal government to enforce immigration law. Any police organization that shared fingerprint data with the federal government was supplying enough information for the federal government to detain and deport any person who came into contact with the legal system (Hing, 2011). The result of this top-down manner of enforcement left fewer considerations for state and local law enforcement agencies. While these changes may have addressed issues of implementation, Secure Communities still received a lot of pushback from localities because of the Fourth Amendment issues raised by some of its key provisions (Chen, 2016).

As Secure Communities was initially conceived, there was no real distinction between the worst criminal offenders and those who were relatively harmless. If a detainer was issued for an individual, the locality could hold them for a maximum of 48 hours without probable cause. Because localities would be the authority in charge of the detention, they were potentially liable for any lawsuits resulting from such violations. In effect, federal law required local authorities to keep people confined for longer periods than legally allowed given the initial offense that led to their jailing. Additionally, the folks being detained had yet to be convicted of any crime but were remanded. While many localities resisted these practices on ethical grounds and sound policing strategy, money was also a part of their decisions to resist complying with the Secure Communities program.

Beyond lawsuits, having to house individuals for extended periods of time put a financial burden on already stressed local jail facilities. While there were some funds available to reimburse localities for essentially functioning as federal detention facilities, these funds did not make up for the increased responsibilities and training of police forces, the increased personnel needed to guard facilities, and the potential financial liabilities arising from the constitutional violations of these detentions (Cheh, 2012).

All of these practical matters, however, ignore the real difficulties federal enforcement made for community policing. Community policing is an approach to law enforcement where police foster trust with the local community to increase reporting of crimes. Community policing advocates argued that not only would the reporting of crimes decrease under a more punitive immigration enforcement regime but also convincing individuals to come forward as witnesses would be increasingly difficult if they were concerned they would be treated as criminals. As such, Marion Barry declared by executive order that the city would not comply with any federal immigration enforcement, thereby making the District the head of a wave in 1984.

In order to understand the District's symbolic and real importance in this debate, it is necessary to understand how the city became demographically and politically Black-identified and what this means for the city's identity. The next section offers a brief look at the uniqueness of the District and its native-born Black residents.

Demographics and Political Power

The District is unique for a few reasons. The first of the "chocolate cities" in America, DC was majority Black by 1960.[3] The District is not a state, it is a federal district. Until 1973, it was run by an unelected Board of Commissioners generally hostile to Black Washingtonians (Fauntroy, 2003; Price, 1998; Yon, 2010). Until 1973, the only representation the District had in Congress was the relatively low-prestige Committee on the District of Columbia, which was headed by the likes of Rep. Ron Dellums (D-CA) and other Blacks who were elected to Congress after the passage of the Voting Rights Act (1965). Advocacy for increased autonomy for Washington became the norm as Black Democrats assumed leadership of the committee. As a consequence of their agitation, the District of Columbia Home Rule Act of 1973 was passed.

According to the provisions of the Home Rule Act, city residents are allowed to elect their own mayor, city council, and nonvoting congressional leadership. The city, however, is subject to federal authority in ways that do not apply to the states. The city's legislation is subject to federal oversight; their members of Congress, like Puerto Rico, cannot vote. More than what the city can do, it is what it cannot do that creates a tension between DC and the federal government (Fauntroy, 2003). For example, the federal government is the largest employer in the city, and region, occupying great portions of city real estate, but the city is barred from levying property taxes on those buildings, which is standard practice in other localities. This deprives the city of much-needed revenue. Moreover, the city has no power to tax the paychecks of individuals who earn city wages but live in jurisdictions outside of the city's boundaries. And, perhaps, more bothersome is the fact that the President appoints all judges in the District. Thus, in a city that is majority–minority it is possible for the city's judiciary to consist of mostly white appointees as it was during the Reagan years (Price, 1998).

The particularities of the relationship between the District's organization and the federal government cannot be extricated from the racial composition of the city. The city has long had a substantial Black population that had been through deed and custom confined to certain parts of the city (Price, 1998). As Blacks were gaining political power in the District, electing Walter Washington as their first Black mayor in 1973, the city was beginning its financial decline, which continued through the 1990s.[4] The "hollow prize" problem would plague DC for the next 25 years, as the eroding of the tax base meant declines in city services, failing educational institutions, and increasing crime, leading to the city facing economic collapse. The more affluent parts of the city were able to stay afloat amid the chaos, but many white middle-class residents made their way to the neighboring suburbs of Montgomery and Prince George's Counties beginning around 1970.[5] Middle-class Black residents lagged behind, as restrictive covenants and capital kept them out of the surrounding suburbs as noted in the introduction of this volume. When housing restrictions were lifted, however, many of the District's better-off Black residents went to Prince George's County. The city, therefore, was left with mostly poor Black residents confined largely to areas east of the Anacostia River and who needed the most assistance.

Crime, underemployment, low wages, high rates of violent crime, drugs, the HIV/AIDS epidemic, high infant mortality, low-quality schools, mass incarceration, and poor health outcomes left a city long on problems and short on the ability to address them.[6] As the city's tax base was severely depleted, the neediest residents fell through the cracks. White Washingtonians who remained in the city were relatively wealthy by comparison to their Black counterparts and able to remain in enclaves that largely shielded them from this relative deprivation.

Blacks would continue, however, to make strides gaining more representation on the City Council and School Boards. Despite this political incorporation for Blacks, DC continued to hemorrhage population, as those with means continued moving out of the city. Blacks, however, maintained their numeric majority status and were still the most highly identified with Washington, hence its moniker as *the* "chocolate city." This fact, however, did not necessarily help DC's attempts to gain more independence of federal authority. This was particularly true after Mayor Barry's drug problem became public knowledge in 1990.[7] A Congress that was always skeptical of the city's ability to govern itself had more ammunition to deny the city statehood. By 1995, under the leadership of Newt Gingrich, the Committee on the District of Columbia was dissolved, which ended one avenue of the city's presence in Congress.

The aforementioned information begs the question, how did the District become a sanctuary city in the first place? The following section traces DC's relationship to the sanctuary city debates and its designation as a sanctuary city.

Federal Immigration Enforcement and Sanctuary Status in the District

Part of the answer to the above question is the history of the city itself. How DC has worked with the federal government has changed over time. During the first years of home rule,[8] the District, in particular native-born Black Washingtonians, sought increased independence from federal control. This desire was not separate from the spirit of determination that characterized the politics of many increasingly Black-dominated cities and localities in the post-civil rights era (Stone, 1989). In the interim, the city had to address the exigencies of changing circumstances such as high crime rates throughout the 1980s, an increasing immigrant population from Africa and Latin America, and changing federal immigration policy. These shifts in the city's fortunes have influenced its relationship with the federal government and are also part of the reason why the city has been invested in its sanctuary status for over 30 years. Therefore, this section tries to demonstrate the District's sanctuary status is as much as a political commitment as it is a local identity.

When Marion Barry took office in 1979, he inherited a city with an extremely complicated politics. First, the District was becoming demographically Blacker, yet Blacks were conspicuously absent in a number of the city's key leadership positions. What is more, the issue of statehood became increasingly difficult to defend amid the city's financial and criminal woes—problems that generally followed the flight of capital from the city. And, of course, the city's complicated relationship with the federal government. Yet, in 1984, Mayor Barry made DC a sanctuary city. The impetus for this move seemed to be an emphasis on community policing as the city faced rising crime rates (Cheh, 2012). By the 1990s, DC was identified as the murder capital of the United States, and community policing was considered a key crime-fighting strategy. Yet, it is difficult to coax a leery public to come forward and report crimes when they have to fear federal detention due to their immigration status.

Barry's 1984 executive order drew a distinct border between the duties of the MPD and immigration enforcement, which was the province of the federal government. Through this executive order, Barry clearly indicated MPD officers would not be used as quasi-immigration officials and would neither investigate an individual's immigration status nor detain these individuals on behalf of the federal government. It is well-documented that the District in the 1980s had a crime problem on their hands that was largely fueled by the introduction of crack cocaine and heightened by access to firearms. Federal immigration policy made it all the more difficult for city authorities to investigate crimes.

Prior to the passage of the IRCA in 1986, there were an estimated 4 million undocumented persons in the United States, and deportation was really the only tool the Immigration and Naturalization Service (INS) practiced. As a result, immigration raids were commonplace in areas densely populated with immigrants, and this predictably had a chilling effect on communities across the nation. The District was no exception. Barry's order made noncompliance with federal immigration enforcement the norm of the city from that date forward. He ordered city agencies not to check the immigration status of individuals applying for city services or in detention. The goal for Barry was public safety. If city officials were seen as being in collusion with the INS, it would have a chilling effect on the public, who were vital to the city's ability to manage crimes.

At the time the bipartisan bill was issued, it was clear mass deportations were ineffective for addressing undocumented immigration in the long term. Thus, IRCA was essentially a compromise that offered naturalization to those who had come to the United States without papers prior to 1982. It also made eligible for naturalization certain classes of agricultural laborers while requiring employers to verify the citizenship or visa status of all employees. This law, in effect, gave those currently living in the shadows a pathway to citizenship.

For the effectiveness of IRCA, the issue of undocumented immigration did not go away. While DC had been acquainted with immigration for at least a decade, it did not always offer the city's Latinx residents the best treatment. Barry's successor Sharon Pratt in 1992 reissued his initial order designating DC a sanctuary jurisdiction. While Mayor Pratt, nee Sharon Pratt Kelly, was in office, civil unrest in the Mt. Pleasant neighborhood in 1991 seemed to cause city leaders to revisit sanctuary status as a matter of policy and as a strategy for quelling unrest. Mt. Pleasant, a multiracial and multiethnic community with a large Latinx population, exploded after a Salvadoran immigrant was shot by a Black woman MPD officer. Following a Cinco de Mayo celebration, rookie Officer Angela Jewell attempted to arrest Daniel Enrique Gomez on a charge of public drunkenness. Officer Jewell alleged Mr. Gomez lunged at her with a hunting knife, and she shot him in the chest in self-defense. Latinx members of the community disputed the officer's account and said Mr. Gomez was hand-cuffed when shot. In response, residents filled the streets, and for two days, Latinxs and Blacks took to the streets. In order to quiet the disturbance, Mayor Kelly went to the northwest neighborhood and met with community leaders. Though Mayor Kelly may have been inclined to a pro forma reissue of Barry's executive order, the fallout of the riots made her decision easier.

After the riots, the US Commission on Civil Rights issued a report where they outlined the city's Latinx residents' primary concerns.[9] In sum, the city's Latinx residents felt disrespected and racially profiled by local police. Because many of the city's Latinx residents were undocumented, their mistreatment by police was underreported for fear they would be targeted by the INS. While Latinxs, mainly from El Salvador, had been moving to the area since the 1970s, they were in no way incorporated into the city's power structure. In fact, there were no Latinxs on the city council; this underrepresentation continues, as no Latinx person has been elected mayor or city council person (Jamison, 2016; López & Stepler, 2016).[10] Moreover, in the midst of a recession, Latinxs reported facing discrimination in their attempts to access city services. This event served as a catalyst and caused Mt. Pleasant residents to protest their maltreatment. As a result of this report, the Mayor's Office of Latino Affairs was created and more bilingual officers hired; the city began providing information on city services in Spanish and increased funding for organizations providing assistance to Latinx residents, such as legal services and economic development. At this juncture, the city's sanctuary status, already secured by Barry in the 1980s, became a mechanism to quiet racial tensions and send a signal, particularly to the city's residents that they were valued and protected members of the District community. This would not be the last time, however, the city's political leaders would return to its sanctuary status.

Concerns around undocumented immigration intensified after September 11, where the preoccupation with domestic security marked noncitizens as potential dangers. Of course, the problem with this "us versus them" mentality was that it was not easy to tell who belonged and who did not (Kinder & Kam, 2010). As a result, skin color and other markers of difference, such as religious regalia, were used to make decisions about who was an American and who was not. This preoccupation even made President Barack Obama suspect because of his name, his blackness, his father's Kenyan nationality, his Hawaiian birth certificate, and his alleged Muslim ties. All of these parts of the American demographic landscape became increasingly scrutinized in the war on terror.

As the INS became Immigration and Customs Enforcement (ICE) in the newly formed Department of Homeland Security (DHS) under President Bush, there was more attention paid to the Mexican border, though none of the 9/11 attackers were Mexican or in the country without authorization.[11] He also greatly expanded the use of detentions for deportable individuals and decreased the time to process individuals out of the country from approximately three months to approximately three weeks (Slevin, 2010). The framework for deportations he created in the DHS would be picked up under President Obama.[12]

As previously mentioned, Secure Communities[13] was a DHS program designed to foster cooperation between local law enforcement and ICE in identifying noncitizens. Of particular importance were "Level 1" offenders who are the most serious criminal offenders charged with major narcotics and violent offenses. Secure Communities would have local police departments submit the fingerprints of detainees in order to find deportable individuals; this means that fingerprints were submitted both to criminal databases, like CODIS, as well as immigration databases like IDENT. If the fingerprints submitted produced a match, ICE would issue a detainer to local authorities requiring jails to hold on to arrestees suspected of violations of immigration law until ICE could determine whether these persons should be transferred to a federal facility or released from custody.

Recall that when Secure Communities began, DHS entered into memoranda of agreement with local authorities. This meant each local jurisdiction had its own relationship to the federal program and could potentially set boundaries limiting federal authority. DC entered into one of these memoranda of agreement with the federal government despite the seemingly optional nature of the program. Participation in the program was a violation of Executive Order 84–41, a city policy that forbade public service officials like emergency medical technicians, MPD officers, and the DC Fire Department from inquiring about an individual's immigration status.[14] As participants in the Secure Communities program, the MPD would share fingerprints of all arrestees, regardless of offense, with ICE officials. Therefore, when the city voluntarily entered into the Secure Communities program, it was in contradiction with the long-running norm of nonenforcement of federal immigration law.

This process, while it did not necessarily transform local police into immigration officers, gave them little discretion in terms of what information they turned over to DHS. Since all fingerprints were provided, even those booked on the most minor offenses were at risk of deportation regardless of DHS's stated priorities with "Level 1" offenders. Moreover, the program was relatively indiscriminate, and individuals who were legal permanent residents could be flagged by the identification system, which put them at risk for unlawful, extended detentions in jail. Moreover, because a flag by the system led to an automatic hold on a person, individuals were essentially imprisoned though they had not been convicted of any crime. In short, automatically supplying ICE with the fingerprints of arrestees violated a more than 30-year-long standing policy in the city.

Criticism of the District's participation in Secure Communities led to the withdrawal of the city from the memorandum of agreement with DHS. Not long after, DHS withdrew all memoranda of agreement in favor of making the program mandatory for all jurisdictions across the country. In order to preempt Secure Communities' implementation, Mayor Gray signed order 2011-174 in October 2011. One of the most important provisions of the order was limiting federal access to the District's jails. According to the order, the city would not provide DHS with rosters of undocumented inmates. And unless ICE was investigating a criminal matter or had probable cause, the District would not make inmates available to immigration officials for interviews, and the city was not going to be involved in enforcement of civil violations of immigration statutes. As it stands, this latest assertion of the city's sanctuary status was a response to federal overreach in District affairs.

What this section has outlined is roughly three regimes of sanctuary city policy that served the needs of the city on several dimensions. When the policy was first issued in the 1980s, the city was in the middle of an extended period of high crime. It seems the policy was as much about protecting undocumented persons as it was about enhancing public safety. In the 1990s, the city was experiencing the growing pains during this period of immigration, and the policy, already several years old, was reissued in an effort to stave off more political unrest. In its latest iteration, sanctuary policy is about protecting undocumented people along with the city's sovereignty, financial, and ethical interests.

Sanctuary policy is standard operating procedure; this comports with the city's renaissance that is spurred by a bustling "back to the city" movement. For now, the city seems to have left the economic and criminal strife of prior decades in its rear view; it is also the case that many native-born Black and immigrant residents have been left behind (Hyra, 2015). For example, in spring 2017, there was a lot of attention given to the plight of missing Black children. First covered in *The Root*, the story gained widespread attention and underscored the fact that Blacks and others remain marginalized. What was felt locally was the widening racial divide in the city. A District town hall to address the matter was standing room only, and not a single white person was in attendance. This lack of white representation highlighted the many ways in which Black DC residents feel ignored in their own city, a city that was bolstered in the lean years by their presence, but now seemingly accelerates their exit through exorbitant housing prices and rising taxes (Hyra, 2015).[15] If it is the case that the District is a safe haven for some but not others, then what does it mean for how Black residents think about immigration in the city?

Blacks, Immigration, and Public Opinion

The coalition and competition models have been the dominant frames for understanding interminority relations (Bobo & Hutchings, 1996; McClain et al., 2006; Pastor & Marcelli, 2003; Shinault & Seltzer, 2017). The competition model argues the extent to which individuals view themselves as competing with immigrants for employment opportunities; they will tend to view immigration negatively (Citrin, Green, Muste, & Wong, 1997; Gay, 2006). This is particularly true for the native-born who have the fewest skills and are in more direct competition with the undocumented persons (Catanzarite, 2000; Waldinger, 1997). For native-born Blacks, this sense of competition can be especially acute given their proximity to immigrants spatially and in terms of skill.

Powers (2005) demonstrates how employer preferences for immigrant labor become racialized. Employers prefer to hire immigrants because they are easier to exploit but suggest native-born Black workers are stereotypically less committed to hard work. In this case, immigrants do not "take jobs" so much as employers give them jobs because they are an easier workforce to manage. Moreover, research suggests immigrants and native-born Blacks and whites are not even in the same job markets. Rather, low-skilled Blacks and whites are placed in different positions in the same industry and have ceased to do the lowest-wage, lowest-skilled work immigrants are subjected to (Betancur, 2005; Torres, Popke, & Hapke, 2006). What is more, there is evidence that suggests that not only are the native-born not vying for the same positions as immigrants, the jobs that immigrants do take are ones that used to be available to the native-born seasonally but are now less available, as immigrants are in these positions on a more permanent basis.

Jobs, however, are only one part of the story. Group threats are activated as groups live in proximity to others. Gay (2006) demonstrates that Blacks are more likely to live in proximity to immigrants and, as such, view their position as more precarious in relationship to immigrants and have more negative opinions of immigrants and immigration. Nteta (2013) also finds evidence that Blacks are supportive of restrictive immigration when taking into account their class status. Those Blacks who are working class were most supportive of identification cards, creating an immigrant database, and decreasing the numbers of immigrants allowed into the county. These feelings of threat and insecurity cannot be separated from innumeracy. To the extent that a group *overestimates* the presence of "the other," there is a tendency to feel more threatened (Key, 1984; Rocha & Espino, 2009). Generally speaking, individuals are not proficient at estimating the presence of others, and this often leads to exaggerating the presence of "others" (Brader, Valentino, & Suhay, 2008).

Still, there is evidence that Blacks are less hostile with regard to immigrants than their White counterparts (Cummings & Lambert, 1997; Thornton, Taylor, & Chatters, 2012). Thornton and Mizuno (1999) show that Blacks view themselves as being more proximate to immigrant groups than to fellow White citizens. Further, Diamond (1998) shows that Blacks do not necessarily favor restriction despite the belief that they face the most competition from immigrants. Where the opinions of Blacks and Whites have been explicitly compared, Blacks "are, in fact, consistently more permissive on immigration than whites," which suggests a need to take into account group identity rather than individual self-interest (Brader, Valentino, Jardina, & Ryan, 2010, p. 1).

Part of the uniqueness of Black politics, generally, and Black public opinion, specifically, is the centering of the group in making individual political decisions. Popularized by Dawson (1994), the idea of linked fate is that group well-being becomes a cognitive shortcut for deciding political matters. This focus on group well-being is a proxy for self-interest and helps individuals sort through the range of political options. This matters for opinions on immigration because much of the debate around immigration is preoccupied with notions of race. Much of the rhetoric around immigration is rooted in racialized, if not outright racist, language—so much so that the term "immigrant" is often thought to apply only to communities of color and has become hyper-identified with Latinx.

As a consequence, it is difficult for Blacks, in the main, to tie their group consciousness with this racial rhetoric. This is not because Blacks are always altruistic (Sawyer, 2005) so much as they do not want to align themselves with a worldview that would also oppress and subjugate their group (Carter & Pérez, 2016). In short, the racial logic that leads people to treat all Latinxs as (undocumented) immigrants and therefore not "real Americans" is the same racial logic that suggests Blacks are not "real Americans" and are not necessarily entitled to the same protections under the law (Carter, 2007; Carter & Pérez, 2016). This can be dangerous for native-born Blacks and immigrant Blacks also. There is evidence to suggest that immigrant Blacks are not generally seen as different from native-born Blacks for longer than a generation (Waters, 2009). This means those Black immigrants who may enjoy preliminary benefits because they are seen as better than native-born Blacks cannot transfer those benefits to their children. Similarly, because Black communities are surveilled to a greater degree than others, it is also the case that unauthorized immigrants are more likely to be adversely affected by an aggressive immigration enforcement regime (Morgan-Trostle, Zheng, & Lispcombe, 2016). Blacks have more engagements with the police, to the extent that local authorities are allowed to function as quasi-immigration officials, which can have disastrous consequences on the health and safety of immigrants who live in Black communities (Lawston & Escobar, 2009). In this way, Black resistance to supporting immigration restriction may be less about being in solidarity with immigrants rather than being in cahoots with potential bigots.

A place like DC where many of the immigrants are African and Caribbean as well as Latinx changes the narrative of this conversation a bit. Much of the national conversation about immigration is hyper-focused on Latinx immigration but ignores immigrants of the Black diaspora. In this city, however, the blackness of immigrants has to be a primary consideration.

Methodology

I evaluate public opinion from a variety of sources in order to assess the opinions of Washingtonians in particular and Black people in general. Therefore, this work relies on descriptive analyses of several surveys conducted by different organizations with varying sample populations. I conduct a descriptive analysis of the 2017 *Washington Post*/University of Maryland Poll ($n = 914$) to suggest how DC residents might feel about the use of local police for immigration enforcement—a key issue in the development of sanctuary cities. I also conduct a meta-analysis of a McClatchy-Marist Poll (2017) that asks specifically about sanctuary cities; there are 865 respondents included in this survey. Finally, I utilize a regression analysis of *Washington Post's* DC Poll (2006) of 1,350 adult DC residents. This survey, however, only asks one item regarding the perception of immigrants in the area. Given the theoretical frames addressed above, I hypothesize the following:

H_1: Blacks will express more pro-immigrant sentiment than their white counterparts.

H_2: Blacks will be more in favor of immigration reform rather than immigration enforcement.

H_3: Blacks will be more supportive of sanctuary cities than whites.

With regard to Hypothesis 2, it is important to explain what I see as the differences between immigration reform and immigration enforcement. While it can be argued that any type of overhaul of the federal immigration system is reform of some kind, there seems to be a clear dichotomy in the literature between these two perspectives. Generally speaking, the current immigration regime would prescribe deportation for those in the United States without authorization. Yet, when discussing "immigration reform," deportation seems to be the option of last resort that should be reserved for those who represent a danger to the public. Thus, when I speak of "immigration reform," I am, in part, hamstrung by the way the items are asked. But, more importantly, the term "reform" suggests approaching immigration differently as in the case of the Dreamers or those who are protected by Deferred Action for Childhood Arrivals (DACA), which allowed those who entered the country as minors who were in good standing to remain in the country. The Obama administration proposed this policy be extended to parents, but the measure stalled. Under the Trump administration, DACA has been discontinued. While I cannot say with certainty how respondents received this question, "immigration reform" is posed as the opposite of "border enforcement" and suggests, perhaps, a more liberal alternative to keeping individuals out of the country. While this is imperfect, it is important to acknowledge the differences these answer choices present to respondents.

There are a number of data limitations confronting the specificity of this work. First, little data asks about "sanctuary cities" specifically and smaller, regional surveys that examine the opinions of adults, Washingtonians rarely ask about immigration at all. Moreover, given the recent collection of much of this data, they are yet to be made publicly available. As a consequence, only the most rudimentary analysis can be completed. That said, descriptive information is useful, as it can give a sense of what to look for and can be suggestive of what variables may be related to each other. Therefore, working across data sources can be indicative of a set of relationships, if not conclusive.

In spring 2016, *The Washington Post*, in partnership with the University of Maryland, conducted a survey on the state of Maryland politics and included items about immigration ($n = 914$). While this survey is limited to Maryland residents, it can give us some useful insights into the District, as they are part of a larger metropolitan area. DC, Maryland, and Northern Virginia, known colloquially as the DMV, is composed of the District and several counties in Maryland, particularly Prince George's County and Montgomery County, which border the District and Northern Virginia. The borders between these states and the District is fairly porous as they are interconnected via Washington Metro transit and a complex interstate system that encourage workforce participation and commercial activity across boundaries. In addition, the federal government, which is primarily located in the District is the region's major employer.

What is more, when the District began its downward tumble in the 1980s and 1990s, the suburbs of Maryland and Virginia were the primary receiving contexts for these relocations. By the late 1990s, reducing areas of concentrated poverty became a priority of federal and local authorities. This made the dispersion of poverty and relocation from the central city to the suburbs a reality for many of the city's poorest residents (Hartung & Henig, 1997). In the District, as in other major cities, this was achieved through housing vouchers for rental assistance. In fact, DC was overrepresented in the region in terms of public housing. Therefore, when the federal government began providing vouchers for relocation, the suburbs were unopposed to being recipients of this additional rental income (Hartung & Henig, 1997). Those DC residents tended to move to Prince George's and Montgomery Counties, where there are a large number of Black people already residing, and helped to make Virginia more diverse (Pope, 1995); they estimate "that about 61% of recent voucher and certificate recipients in Virginia are Black" (Hartung & Henig, 1997, p. 409). As DC residents were being channeled and integrated into the near suburbs of Maryland and Virginia, I argue that the identity of the DMV became more cosmopolitan. Consequently, it is not uncommon to find individuals with interpersonal attachments to one or more of these localities. For these reasons, I think it appropriate to use this data as a proxy, not a perfect measure, for District attitudes.

Results

Immigration Reform

Immigration reform as a concept can have a number of meanings, as discussed above. I was limited to the questions as asked by the survey outfit. Therefore, I chose a proxy measure that asked individuals about using local law enforcement as part of an immigration enforcement regime. While this is an imperfect measure, this was a common proposal as Secure Communities demonstrated, and some localities are pushing for a more pronounced role for local law enforcement in immigration enforcement (Armenta, 2012). For these reasons, I utilized the item that asks, "If local police become more active in identifying undocumented immigrants for potential deportation, do you think this will improve compliance with immigration laws, or not?" A majority of Blacks (63%) do not believe local police involvement will improve compliance with immigration law. The same is true for a majority of whites, though there is an 11-point difference between these communities. This may not be all that surprising given these communities' different relationships to police authority (Brunson, 2007). I also looked at ideology, which is a major driver of immigration opinion. As you see, ideological liberals do not believe police involvement improves compliance (See Figure 3.1).

When looking by region, with particular attention to Prince George's County, a Black majority county in close proximity to the city, 66% of the county's residents do not believe police involvement will improve conditions.

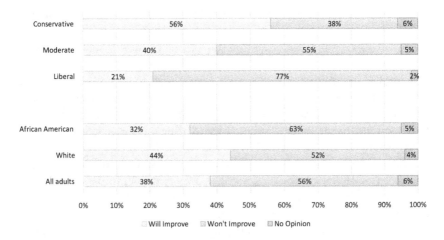

FIGURE 3.1 If local police become more active in identifying undocumented immigrants for potential deportation, do you think this will improve compliance with immigration laws, or not?

Similarly, 61% of Montgomery County residents believe police improvement will not improve the situation. Montgomery County, which also shares a border with the District, is a racially and ethnically diverse county despite being majority white.

Furthermore, Marylanders were asked about the effect the fear of deportation has on public safety. There was near uniformity across racial groups on this question. All groups believe fear of deportation will put a damper on the reporting of crimes. Public safety was a primary motivator of city decisions to create "sanctuary cities," and the fact that the public agrees with this idea suggests a clear understanding of the stakes in a more enforcement-driven regime. It is worth noting that this agreement was also found across the Maryland region.[16] The belief that immigration enforcement is at odds with the goal of public safety is important when considering what types of policies District residents may be in favor of (see Figure 3.2).

In short, Marylanders do not feel there is a place for local law police forces in the enforcement of federal immigration policy. When asked, 84% of Blacks believe the identification of undocumented persons should be left to federal authorities. Among whites, 62% feel the same. Prince George's County (84%) residents firmly believe immigration should be left to federal authorities, and the same can be said for Montgomery County residents. This deferral to federal authorities on the part of Blacks makes sense given

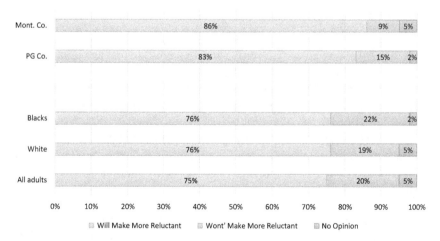

FIGURE 3.2 If local police become more active in identifying undocumented immigrants for potential deportation, do you think this will make undocumented immigrants reluctant to inform police of crime, or not?

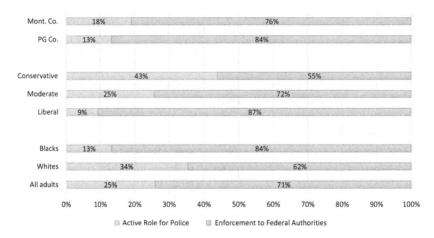

FIGURE 3.3 Should local police take an active role in identifying undocumented or illegal immigrants, or should enforcement be left mainly to the federal authorities?

the importance of the federal government in the enforcement of equity for Blacks. While Blacks cannot claim to have experienced fairness at all levels, generally the federal government has been more open to Black inclusion (see Figure 3.3).

Sanctuary Cities

Given the data limitations of the Washington Post/University of Maryland poll, there were no items asking specifically about "sanctuary cities." As a result, I looked at a February 2017 McClatchy-Marist national poll asking respondents (n = 1,073) specifically about the term "sanctuary cities" and their opinions on the appropriateness of these arrangements (see Table 3.1). Analysis provided by McClatchy-Marist demonstrates that roughly six out of ten Blacks favor the idea that "sanctuary cities are needed to provide services to undocumented immigrants while they are in this country"; only 45% of whites feel this way by comparison. Education slightly moderates White opinion, as those with a college degree are more supportive of sanctuary cities (53%).

When asked whether designated sanctuary cities should face decreases in federal funding (see Table 3.2), Blacks were most opposed to this idea (70%), followed by Latinxs (59%) and whites (51%) (McClatchy-Marist, 2017).[17] Given the hyper-identification of Latinxs with the idea of undocumented immigration

TABLE 3.1 "Sanctuary City" is a Term Used to Describe US Cities which Do Not Enforce Immigration Laws and Allow Undocumented Immigrants to Live there and, in Many Cases, Receive Services. Which Comes Closer to Your Opinion?

	Undocumented Immigrants Should Be Deported so There Is No Reason to Have Sanctuary Cities (%)	Sanctuary Cities Are Needed to Provide Services to Undocumented Immigrants While They Are in this Country (%)	Unsure (%)
White	44	45	11
Black	32	59	8
Latinx	28	68	4
White college grad	39	53	8
White no college	48	40	12

Source: Data from the McClatchy-Marist Poll National Tables.

Note. Interviews conducted February 15–19, 2017; *n* = 1,073; Margin of error ±3%.

TABLE 3.2 Do You Support or Oppose the Federal Government Cutting Funds to Cities that Provide Sanctuary for Undocumented Immigrants?

	Support (%)	Oppose (%)	Unsure (%)
White	45	51	5
Black	20	70	10
Latinx	36	59	5
White college grad	39	58	3
White no college	49	46	6

Source: Data from the McClatchy-Marist Poll National Tables.

Note. Interviews conducted February 15–19, 2017; *n* = 1,073; Margin of error ±3%.

(Chavez, 2013), I find it interesting that Blacks are the most opposed to cutting federal funds to cities in response to this matter. Black support may be conditioned by self-interest. The fact that they remain residents in a number of designated sanctuary cities, like Baltimore, could be driving this sensibility. It could also be the long history of activism around civil rights and social justice that included providing a safe haven for those fleeing enslavement or the oppression of the South. Without more probing questions it is difficult to say, however, I think it is useful to understand how Blacks position themselves relevant to the issue of sanctuary cities.

Lastly, on the question of whether immigrants should be allowed a pathway to citizenship provided they meet certain requirements, such as paying fines, having jobs, and learning English, Blacks (81%), whites (81%), and Latinxs (85%) are firmly in support of this policy. It is difficult, however, to get too excited about this result. Given the nature of the question wording, we are not exactly sure what respondents have answered. Do they want immigrants to do all three of the above things (pay fines, speak English, and have a job) or would they be fine with immigrants completing one or two of the three options? Moreover, while these proposals appear reasonable, they still can be viewed as putative. Making English proficiency a marker of belonging though it is not the official langue of the United States is one of those national identity measures that are not necessarily value- or race-neutral. Undoubtedly, all of these proposals are punishments and place the burden of belonging on immigrants who are ostensibly auditioning for membership if they complete these tasks. Therefore, one cannot draw too many conclusions from these findings. However, it has been found in other sources that a pathway to citizenship is the preferred option for most Americans. Again, how that is supposed to happen is unclear, but it is an option people are open to. It is reasonable, therefore, to see if similar attitudes are found among DC residents.

Effect of Immigrants on Community

The *Washington Post* DC poll focuses on a range of city issues, such as mayoral approval and satisfaction with city services. Perceptions of service delivery is one place to begin looking at whether there is racial convergence or divergence (Schafer, Huebner, & Bynum, 2003; Weitzer, 1999). Generally, you would expect the city population that is most vulnerable and has most engagement with bureaucrats to have a poor view of those services (Schram, Soss, Fording, & Houser, 2009; Watkins-Hayes, 2011). Yet, when looking at Black and White Washingtonians, they basically have the same opinions of police, 911, care for the poor, and education. These views, however, tend to be rather negative. My guess is that these negative attitudes may have to do more with a generally poor attitude of city governance more generally as there are parts of the city that do not have a hospital, as is the case in the southeast quadrant of the city. There is no reason to believe residents, given the deep class divisions of the city, have the same experience with city service delivery. The only exception was parks and recreation, with most residents being pleased with the quality of these facilities. This is heartening given the racial distribution across the city's eight wards. For example, Ward 8 is over 90% Black and Ward 3 is one of the whitest and most expensive enclaves in the city (see Table 3.3).

For my dependent variable, I relied on the question, "Generally speaking, do you think the growing number of immigrants from other countries has

TABLE 3.3 Ward Residence by Race

	White	Black	White Latinx	Black Latinx	Latinx (no race)	Asian	Other Race	Total
Ward 1	41	29	3	0	1	1	7	82
	10.8%	7.2%	37.5%		50%	20%	11.7%	
Ward 2	56	16	1	2	0	0	3	78
	14.7%	4.0%	12.5%	33.3%			5%	
Ward 3	147	13	1	0	0	2	10	173
	38.7%	3.2%	12.5%			40%	16.7%	
Ward 4	47	7	0	0	1	2	12	132
	12.4%	1.7%			50%	40%	20%	
Ward 5	22	86	1	1	0	0	5	115
	5.8%	21.3%	12.5%	1.7%			8.3%	
Ward 6	59	43	1	0	0	0	9	112
	15.5%	10.7%	12.5%				15%	
Ward 7	6	82	0	1	0	0	8	97
	1.6%	20.3%		1.7%			13.3%	
Ward 8	2	64	1	2	0	0	6	75
	0.5%	15.9%	12.5%	33.3%			10%	
Total	380	403	8	6	2	5	60	864

Source: Data from the Washington Post Poll #2006–117934: DC Elections/Quality of Life/ Education/Redevelopment.

been (good) for your community, (bad) for your community, or hasn't it made much difference?" (see Table 3.4) The variable is coded from bad (1), hasn't made much difference (2), to good (3). Given the issues discussed earlier around perceptions of Blacks' general economic well-being along with their considerations of their own group well-being, I included controls for their sense of whether redevelopment is good for their group and the ward they live in. Moreover, I tested whether education moderates the effect of race on Blacks' response to the question. I would expect more education would lead one to have more liberal attitudes with respect to immigration. Education has been shown to moderate attitudes across domains, and I want to control for this here. Similarly, I included an interaction for Black and male given the gendered dimensions of policy opinions.

Generally, most Washingtonians believe that immigrants haven't made much difference. In the model, however, very few of the predictors were significant with the exception of education, party identification, and whether a person resides in Ward 1. Starting with race, there were no effects. Blacks were more likely to believe immigrants have had no effect on their community. This positive result was also found for whites; in both cases, however, the results were insignificant. Asians were the reference category. This response, however, does not give us much to interpret. This can be understood in a variety

TABLE 3.4 Generally Speaking, Do You Think the Growing Number of Immigrants from Other Countries Has Been (Good) for Your Community, (Bad) for Your Community, or Hasn't Made Much Difference?

	Coefficient	Standard Error
Constant	1.823★★★	0.343
White	0.023	0.240
Male	0.062	0.076
Black	0.060	0.047
Latinx	0.148	0.278
Redevelopment good for whites	0.069	0.103
Redevelopment good for Blacks	0.042	0.047
Education	0.084★★	0.038
Black* education	−0.039	0.045
Black* male	−0.127	0.106
Ward 1	0.169^	0.091
Ward 2	−0.066	0.091
Ward 3	0.094	0.076
Ward 4	0.059	0.077
Ward 5	−0.020	0.080
Ward 6	−0.013	0.080
Ward 7	0.028	0.090
Democrat	0.051	0.075
Republican	−0.338★★★	0.117
Black* Republican	0.115	0.195
Black* Democrat	−0.159	0.141
Adj. R square	*0.162*	
N	740	

★★★ $p < 0.001$; ★★ $p < 0.01$; ★ $p < 0.05$; ^ $p < 0.10$.

Source: Data from the Washington Post Poll #2006–117934: DC Elections/Quality of Life/ Education/Redevelopment.

of ways. Does this mean individuals across groups think the same way about immigration? Or are they simply unbothered by the appearance of multilingual advertisements, city mailers, and other types of indicators of a growing immigrant population? This insignificant result is reason to believe that other things may matter more than race in this context. This is seen with the questions regarding whether redevelopment is seen as being good for Blacks. To the extent that a respondent believes redevelopment to be good for Blacks, they are more positive about the effect of immigrants in their community. This is also true if a person believes redevelopment to be good for whites. In either case, it suggests positive economic outlooks can overcome potentially negative feelings about immigrants.

The fact that education is a significant predictor is in line with much of the research that shows those with more education to be more liberal on immigration and a host of other issue areas (Zaller, 1992). This area has a high concentration of individuals with college degrees, which suggests a more liberal city overall. In this case, those with higher education levels are more positive in their feelings about immigrants. However, when race is interacted with education, there is a negative coefficient, which suggests more education leads to a less positive outlook on immigrants for Blacks. It is uncertain why this outcome arises, given that higher-status individuals should be better able to navigate these changing demographics. Despite the negative sign, however, this coefficient is insignificant. When looking at party identification, being a Republican is related to having a more significantly negative opinion about the effect of immigrants on the community. This is consistent with the findings cited earlier and other work that shows the partisan nature of immigration opinions.

Residence in Ward 1 (in comparison to Ward 8) is also a significant finding in this work. While Ward 1 is the smallest of the eight wards, it is one of the more densely populated areas of the city. It consists of popular neighborhoods like Mt. Pleasant and Park View, which have a large representation of immigrants, particularly from Central America. Therefore, it stands to reason why those who live in this area would be more positive toward immigrants. Though the question asks about immigrants, in general, it is difficult to disentangle what "immigrant" means in the context of DC. In many cases, the default immigrant is characterized as "Latino," but there is also a concentration of Eastern and Western Africans in this city and metropolitan areas. That said, this provides some evidence that interaction or proximity to the "other" does not necessarily lead one to have a negative opinion of presumed outsiders. As the Districts leaders remain steadfast to its status as a sanctuary city, even in the face of more stringent federal guidelines, it does not appear that they will get much pushback from native-born Black residents. All of this bodes well for the long-term health of the city and perhaps for building bridges between the native-born Black community and immigrants.

Conclusion

This chapter began with a discussion of what sanctuary cities mean for their Black residents. I initially conceived of and thought of this research project in an either/or manner—that either the city is a sanctuary for all people, including native-born Blacks, or it cannot be a sanctuary at all. This question, however, is far more complex, as Blacks exhibit a range of sensibilities around immigration, not only sanctuary cities. And while there is much that needs to be done about the treatment of native-born Blacks in the District, as well as the nation as a whole, I think the sanctuary status of the District is possible, in part, through the activism of Black people.

Not only are Black elites interested in creating a welcoming city for immigrants, in some places, there are active efforts to bring immigrants to the city, as is the case with Detroit and Baltimore, which have experienced population decline (Arthur, 2017; Economist, 2015). Still, creating spaces for newcomers even when that same space feels less than inclusive to native-born Blacks is as much about elite politics as it is about Black politics more generally. Native-born Blacks have generally supported a political agenda that has opened up the public sphere to others, not simply those who look like them. In this way, sanctuary status in majority Black cities seems to comport with a Black political agenda. Indeed, revising immigration quotas in 1965 is as much about civil rights politics as voting rights. Thus, what we see in DC may be an extension of Blacks politics, which have made DC the inclusive space that it is for so many people. Though not explored in depth here, the Black community in DC is not monolithic and is not universally poor. Yet, it would be misleading to suggest Blacks in the city are at the receiving end of the city's largesse. As of 2015 in DC, the median household income was $41,522 for Blacks and $120,405 for whites.[18] The realities of these disparities cannot be ignored. Therefore, when we reside in a city where White households earn roughly three times that of their Black counterparts, it becomes necessary to interrogate what a "sanctuary city" is and what it means for localities to make these pronouncements.

While "sanctuary city" refers to a particular set of institutional arrangements with respect to the federal government around immigration enforcement, what undergirds this term is a set of ethical considerations around a people's humanity. While much of the moral and ethical considerations have been lost in the overwrought political conversation that does not even reflect the public's desire for a pathway to citizenship, it is necessary to keep this at the fore, as the city decides who it wants to be in the coming years. For sure, redevelopment of the city has been a boon for many, but Blacks have largely lagged in most measures of economic and physical well-being. For example, as of 2012, Blacks in the District had one of the highest infant mortality rates in the country (Vinik, 2015) and the Civil Rights Movement has arguably given more to White women than it has to Black people. Currently, White women earn more than Black men *and* women (AAUW, 2017).

Yet, there needs to be more discussion about how DC in particular and this nation in general can be a safe space for Black people. To be clear, achieving this safe space cannot come at the expense of doing the right thing for all of the District's residents. It is certainly a necessary measure, as undocumented immigrants from the African diaspora need these protections. At the same time, it is necessary to acknowledge that Black immigrants are not safe because they are also Black. Therefore, protecting one identity (i.e., immigration status) while ignoring another that is also vital for community safety (i.e., blackness) is a losing proposition; this, by definition, makes this place not a sanctuary for all residents and their multiple identities. It is not enough for the city to simply declare itself a sanctuary and not think of the many identities that make its residents unsafe. It is also important that this city send a clear message to its Black citizens that they matter too and this place they call home will continue to be so until they say otherwise. By reading the experience of the city's native-born Black residents into this conversation, it is my intention to broaden the conversation of sanctuary cities to incorporate native-born Blacks, and other marginalized groups, who are often forgotten in the city's renaissance.

Notes

1 I use native-born Black throughout the text to refer to those Black people who are born in the United States and who have at least three generations of ancestors born in the United States. This is not to be divisive. Rather, it is to be specific. The District, and larger region, is home to a number of Black communities from throughout the Diaspora, particularly Nigeria, Ghana, Ethiopia, and Egypt. This distinction is meant to capture the unique relationship of those Black people born in the United States and who have descended from those formerly enslaved in this country.
2 The memoranda, signed by 39 states, had the same language. A template of the memorandum can be found at https://www.ice.gov/doclib/foia/secure_communities/securecommunitiesmoatemplate.pdf. Inconsistencies between states were most pronounced in the termination clauses negotiated with the federal government. Secure Communities became more contentious as states such as Illinois and localities like San Francisco County, California, attempted to abandon the partnership with the federal government. The Obama administration eventually discontinued the memoranda citing the supremacy of federal authority.
3 The 23rd Amendment (1961) granted DC residents the right to vote in presidential elections and allowed the city two electors in the Electoral College. The number of electors, however, cannot exceed the number of electors allocated to the least populous state. Therefore, DC has three electors.
4 Washington had a long career in public service and was first appointed mayor in 1967. He was elected when the first elections were held in 1973 and remained mayor until 1978, when he was defeated by Marion Barry.
5 In 1950, there were roughly 982,000 people living in DC. By 1980, there were only about 635,000 residents in the District (US Census). In 1991, the District became the nation's murder capital with a record number of homicides (District Crime Data at a Glance, Metropolitan Police Department). Currently, the city has about 681,170 residents (2015 American Community Survey) and violent crimes have trended downward.
6 Another contributing factor to the city's misery was the uneven rollout of the METRO system. The system first completed lines from the wealthy Maryland and Virginia suburbs to the wealthier parts of the city center to allow workers to get to their downtown employers before completing lines running in poorer parts of the city. As a result, these areas were left with fewer transportation options.
7 Marion Barry had a long career prior to this incident. He was a civil rights activist and became a member of the board of education and council person before being elected mayor in 1979. Mayor Barry also established a summer works program that allowed eligible District teens to be employed. He is also credited with helping minority owned businesses gain city contracts. In short, Mayor Barry's early terms demonstrated competent leadership. He was reelected to an additional term in 1995 and went on to serve Ward 8 as a councilman when elected in 2000.

8　Prior to 1973, all of the decisions for the District were made by Congress. Via the Home Rule Act (1973), DC residents were allowed to elect a mayor and city council. As a result, home rule devolved some of the responsibilities for decision-making from the federal government to the DC government.

9　To access the complete report on Mt. Pleasant as well as the recommendations made by the Commission, please visit http://files.eric.ed.gov/fulltext/ED359294.pdf.

10　There have been Latinxs elected commissioners and school board members. Much of this is due to the lack of political power wielded by Latinxs in the city. Relative to Blacks and Whites in the District, significantly fewer Latinxs are voting eligible. Further, the Latinx community is dispersed across the city and is not a majority in any ward in the city. For a more detailed discussion, see "New Americans in Washington, D.C.: The Political and Economic Power of Immigrants, Latinxs, and Asians in our Nation's Capital" at https://www.americanimmigrationcouncil.org/research/new-americans-washington-dc.

11　The responsibilities and duties of INS were absorbed by ICE when the DHS was created in 2003.

12　Current Secretary of the DHS, General Kelly, previously served under President Obama and seems to have stepped up efforts to deport undocumented persons, though he has stopped short of deporting the over 750,000 persons covered by Deferred Action for Childhood Arrivals. In particular, Kelly's tactics of detaining individuals at schools and courthouses has received the greatest level of scrutiny. Despite Kelly switching roles to become Trump's second Chief of Staff (effective July 31, 2017), there is no reason to believe the Trump administration will stem its hostility toward immigration.

13　Secure Communities ran from 2008–2014. It was replaced by the Priority Enforcement Program (PEP) in 2015. PEP was enacted to address many of the issues of Secure Communities. Primarily, it focused on the most dangerous criminals who have already been convicted of a crime. This narrowing of requirements meant the federal government relied less on *immigration detainers* and requests for continuing custody, and more on notifications of release. Thus, PEP was seen as an improvement on DHS guidelines for violations of immigration law. PEP was discontinued in 2017 after the election of Donald Trump. For a more detailed comparison of PEP and Secure Communities, please visit ww.ice.gov/pep.

14　In 2003, Chief Ramsey of the MPD made it clear that officers were barred from asking about individuals' immigration status, and they certainly were not to use that information in order to inform federal authorities. Additionally, officers could not use law enforcement database checks to find out a person's status.

15　DC is one of the most expensive cities in the United States. The median rent for a one-bedroom apartment in the District is $2,000.

16　Though I do not have any specific hypotheses about ideology, ideology has shown to have a relationship with immigration opinions. Inclusion here is to show another potential cleavage besides race; for a more robust discussion of ideology and immigration attitudes, see Pantoja (2006), Chandler and Tsai (2001), Wilkes, Guppy, and Farris (2008). Party identification was the notable exception here. Those identified as Republican were not as enthusiastic in their belief that fear of deportation would dampen crime reporting. Still, 58% of those identified as Republican did say fear of deportation would make immigrants less likely to report crimes.

17　For the complete tables produced by McClatchy-Marist, please go to http://marist poll.marist.edu/wp-content/misc/usapolls/us170215/McClatchy-Marist%20Poll_National%20Nature%20of%20the%20Sample%20and%20Tables_Immigration_February%202017.pdf#page=3.

18　The median for the city at large was $75,628. For Latinxs, this income is approximately $65,000 and for Asians $94,000 (source: http://www.city-data.com/income/income-Washington-District-of-Columbia.html).

References

Aguilar, C. (2005, July 21). Ramsey Reaffirms a Ban on Citizenship Questions to Ease Immigrants' Fear. *The Washington Post*. Retrieved August 2, 2018, from http://www.washingtonpost.com/wp-dyn/content/article/2005/07/20/AR2005072000806.html.

American Association of University Women. (2017). The simple truth about the gender pay gap. Retrieved from 1http://www.aauw.org/research/the-simple-truth-about-the-gender-pay-gap/

Armenta, A. (2012). From sheriff's deputies to immigration officers: Screening immigrant status in a Tennessee jail. *Law & Policy, 34*(2), 191–210.

Arthur, A. (2017, May 2). Illegal immigrants get off easy in Baltimore. *The Baltimore Sun*. Retrieved from http://www.baltimoresun.com/news/opinion/oped/bs-ed-baltimore-immigration-enforcement-20170502-story.html

Bernal, R. (2017, May 22). Sessions issues narrow definition of "sanctuary city". *The Hill*. Retrieved from http://thehill.com/latino/334642-sessions-issues-narrow-definition-of-sanctuary-city

Betancur, J. J. (2005). Framing the discussion of African American-Latino relations: A review and analysis. In S. Oboler, & A. Dzidzienyo (Eds.), *Neither enemies nor friends: Latinos, Blacks, and Afro-Latinos* (pp. 159–172). New York, NY: Palgrave Macmillan.

Bobo, L., & Hutchings, V. L. 1996. Perceptions of racial group competition: Extending Blumer's theory of group position to a multiracial social context. *American Sociological Review, 61*(6), 951–972.

Bonacich, E. (1972). A theory of ethnic antagonism: The split labor market. *American Sociological Review, 37*(5), 547–559.

Brader, T., Valentino, N. A., Ryan, T. J., & Jardina, A. (2010). The racial divide on immigration opinion: Why African Americans are less threatened by immigrants. *Proceedings from the Annual Meeting of the American Political Science Association*, Washington, DC.

Brunson, R. K. (2007). Police don't like black people: African American young men's accumulated police experiences. *Criminology and Public Policy, 6*(1), 71–101.

Brader, T., Valentino, N. A., & Suhay, E. (2008). What triggers public opposition to immigration? Anxiety, group cues, and immigration threat. *American Journal of Political Science, 52*(4), 959–978.

Carter, N. M. (2007). *The black/white paradigm revisited: African Americans, immigration, race, and nation in Durham, North Carolina*. Duke University.

Carter, N. M., & Pérez, E. O. (2016). Race and nation: How racial hierarchy shapes national attachments. *Political Psychology, 37*(4), 497–513.

Catanzarite, L. (2000). Brown-collar jobs: Occupational segregation and earnings of recent-immigrant Latinos. *Sociological Perspectives, 43*(1), 45–75.

Casselman, B., Casteel, K., & Koeze. E. (2017, July 28). Sessions in cracking down on sanctuary cities again. *FiveThirtyEight*. Retrieved from https://fivethirtyeight.com/features/sessions-is-cracking-down-on-sanctuary-cities-again/

Chandler, C. R., & Tsai, Y. M. (2001). Social factors influencing immigration attitudes: An analysis of data from the general social survey. *The Social Science Journal, 38*(2), 177–188.

Chavez, L. (2013). *The Latino threat: Constructing immigrants, citizens and the nation*. Palo Alto, CA: Stanford University Press.

Cheh, M. M. (2012). Threading the needle: Constitutional 2ays for local governments to refuse cooperation with civil immigration policies. *UDC/DCSL Law Review, 16*, 123–140.

Chen, M. H. (2016). Trust in immigration enforcement: State noncooperation and sanctuary cities after Secure Communities. *Chicago-Kent Law Review, 91*(3), 13–57.

Citrin, J., Green, D. P., Muste, C., & Wong, C. (1997). Public opinion toward immigration reform: The role of economic motivations. *The Journal of Politics, 59*(3), 858–881.

Cummings, S., & Lambert, T. (1997). Anti-Hispanic and Anti-Asian sentiments among African Americans. *Social Science Quarterly, 78*(2), 338–353.

Dawson, M. C. (1994).*Behind the mule: Race and class in African-American politics*. Princeton University Press.

Diamond, J. (1998). African-American attitudes towards United States immigration policy.*International Migration Review,32*(2), 451–470.

Dvorak, P. (2015, October 15). From chocolate city to latte city: Being black in the new D.C. *The Washington Post.* Retrieved from https://www.washingtonpost.com/local/from-chocolate-city-to-latte-city-being-black-in-the-new-dc/2015/10/15/c9839ce2-7360-11e5-9cbb-790369643cf9_story.html?utm_term=.d72ef7094851

Fauntroy, M. K. (2003). *Home rule or house rule? Congress and the erosion of local governance in the District of Columbia.* Lanham, MD: University Press of America, Inc.

Flores, L. A. (2003). Constructing rhetorical borders: Peons, illegal aliens, and competing narratives of immigration. *Critical Studies in Media Communication, 20*(4), 362–387.

Gay, C. (2006). Seeing difference: The effect of economic disparity on black attitudes toward Latinos. *American Journal of Political Science, 50*(4), 982–997.

Hartung, J. M., & Henig, J. R. (1997). Housing vouchers and certificates as a vehicle for deconcentrating the poor: Evidence from the Washington, D.C., metropolitan area. *Urban Affairs Review, 32*(3), 403–419.

Hing, J. (2011, August 9). DHS tells states: We don't need your approval for secure communities. *Colorlines.* https://www.colorlines.com/articles/dhs-tells-states-we-dont-need-your-approval-secure-communities

Huntington, S. P. (1993). The Clash of Civilizations? *Foreign Affairs, 72*(3), 22–49.

Hyra, D. (2015). The back-to-the-city movement: Neighborhood redevelopment and processes of political and cultural displacement. *Urban Studies, 52*(10), 1753–1773.

Jamison, P. (2016, November 7). The rising tide of Latino political power detours around D.C. *The Washington Post.* https://www.washingtonpost.com/local/dc-politics/the-rising-tide-of-latino-political-power-detours-around-dc/2016/11/06/0bb8777e-a202-11e6-8d63-3e0a660f1f04_story.html?utm_term=.5938f11cdf37

Jeong, G., Miller, G. J., Schofield, C., & Sened, I. (2011). Cracks in the opposition: Immigration as a wedge issue for the Reagan coalition. *American Journal of Political Science, 55*(3), 511–525.

Jones-Correa, M. (Ed.). (2001). *Governing American cities: Inter-ethnic coalitions, competition, and conflict.* New York, NY: Russell Sage Foundation.

Key, V. O. (1984). *Southern politics in state and nation.* Knoxville, TN: University of Tennessee Press.

Kinder, D. R., & Kam, C. D. (2010). *Us against them: Ethnocentric foundations of American opinion.* Chicago, IL: The University of Chicago Press.

Lawston, J. M., & Escobar, M. (2009). Policing, detention, deportation, and resistance: Situating immigrant justice and carcerality in the 21st century. *Social Justice, 36*(2), 1–6.

Lee, E. (2002). The Chinese exclusion example: Race, immigration, and American gatekeeping, 1882–1924. *Journal of American Ethnic History, 21*(3), 36–62.

López, G., & Stepler, R. (2016, January 19). *Latinos in the 2016 election: District of Columbia.* Washington, DC: Pew Research Center. http://www.pewhispanic. org/fact-sheet/latinos-in-the-2016-election-district-of-columbia/#hispanics-in-the-district-of-columbias-eligible-voter-population

Massey, D. S., & Pren, K. A. (2012). Unintended consequences of US immigration policy: Explaining the post⊠1965 surge from Latin America. *Population and Development Review, 38*(1), 1–29.

McClain, P. D., Carter, N. M., DeFrancesco Soto, V. M., Lyle, M. L., Grynaviski, J. D., Nunnally, S. C., … Cotton, K. D. (2006). Racial distancing in a southern city: Latino immigrants' views of black Americans. *The Journal of Politics, 68*(3), 571–584.

McClatchy-Marist Poll. 2017. *McClatchy-Marist Poll of 1,073 National Adults.* Retrieved from http://maristpoll.marist.edu/wp-content/misc/usapolls/us170215/McClatchy-Marist%20Poll_National%20Nature%20of%20the%20Sample%20and%20Tables_Immigration_February%202017.pdf#page=2.

Mehan, H. (1997). The discourse of the illegal immigration debate: A case study in the politics of representation. *Discourse & Society, 8*(2), 249–270.

Morgan-Trostle, J, Zheng, K., & Lipscome, C. *The state of black immigrants, Part II: Black immigrants in the mass criminalization system.* New York, NY: Black Alliance for Just Immigration and NYU School of Law Immigrant Rights Clinic, 2016. Retrieved from http://www.stateofblackimmigrants.com/assets/sobi-deportation-sept27.pdf

Nteta, T. (2013). United we stand? African Americans, self-interest, and immigration reform. *American Politics Research, 41*(1), 147–172.

Pantoja, A. (2006). Against the tide? Core American values and attitudes toward U.S. immigration policy in the mid-1990s. *Journal of Ethnic and Migration Studies, 32*(3), 515–531.

Pastor, M., & Marcelli, E. (2003). Somewhere over the rainbow? African Americans, unauthorized Mexican immigration, and coalition building. *The Review of Black Political Economy, 31*(1–2), 125–155.

Pope, A. A. (1995). *Section 8 certificate and vouchers: Where are they going?* Washington, D.C.: Washington Metropolitan Council of Governments.

Powers, R. S. (2005). Working it out in North Carolina: Employers and Hispanic/ Latino immigrants. *Sociation Today, 3(2).* This is a web-based journal. Here is the URL http://www.ncsociology.org/sociationtoday/v32/powers.htm

Price, T. Y. 1998. White public spaces in black Places: The social reconstruction of whiteness in Washington, D.C. *Urban Anthropology and Studies of Cultural Systems and World Economic Development, 27*(3/4), 301–344.

Reel, M. (2013, May 25). D.C. prosperity bypasses Barry Farm. *The Washington Post.* Retrieved from http://www.latimes.com/nation/immigration/la-na-virginia-immigration-20140804-story.html

Rocha, R. R., & Espino, R. (2009). Racial threat, residential segregation, and the policy attitudes of Anglos. *Political Research Quarterly, 62*(2), 415–426.

Rodriguez, C. M. (2007). The significance of the local in immigration regulation. *Michigan Law Review, 106*, 567–642.

Sawyer, M. Q. 2005. *Racial politics in post-revolutionary Cuba.* Cambridge, England: Cambridge University Press.

Schafer, J. A., Huebner, B. M., & Bynum, T. S. (2003). Citizen perceptions of police services: Race, neighborhood context, and community policing. *Police Quarterly, 6*(4), 440–468.

Schram, S. F., Soss, J., Fording, R. C., & Houser, L. (2009). Deciding to discipline: Race, choice, and punishment at the frontlines of welfare reform. *American Sociological Review, 74*(3), 398–422.

Shinault, C. M., & Seltzer, R. A. (2017). Crossing the Mason Dixon versus the Rio Grande: Evaluating the effect of race on attitudes toward immigration policy. *Challenging the Legacies of Racial Resentment: Black Health Activism, Educational Justice, and Legislative Leadership, 18,* 41–66.

Simon, R. (2014, August 4). Amid border crisis debate, many new immigrants land in D.C. area. *The LA Times.* Retrieved from http://www.latimes.com/nation/immigration/la-na-virginia-immigration-20140804-story.html

Slevin, P. (2010, July 26). Deportation of illegal immigrants increases under Obama administration. Retrieved August 2, 2018 from http://www.washingtonpost.com/wp-dyn/content/article/2010/07/25/AR2010072501790.html.

Stone, C. N. (1989). *Regime politics: Governing Atlanta, 1946–1988.* Lawrence, KS: University of Kansas Press.

The Economist. (2015, February 5). Rolling out the welcome mat: Two cities hope that embracing immigrants can reverse their decline. Retrieved from https://www.economist.com/news/united-states/21642226-two-cities-hope-embracing-immigrants-can-reverse-their-decline-rolling-out-welcome

Thornton, M. C., Taylor, R. J., & Chatters, L. M. (2013). African American and black Caribbean mutual feelings of closeness: Findings from a national probability survey. *Journal of Black Studies, 44*(8), 798–828.

Thornton, M. C., & Mizuno, Y. (1999). Economic well-being and black adult feelings toward immigrants and whites, 1984. *Journal of Black Studies, 30*(1), 15–44.

Torres, R. M., Popke, E. J., & Hapke, H. M. (2006). The South's silent bargain: Rural restructuring, Latino labor and the ambiguities of migrant experience. In H. A. Smith, & O. J. Furuseth (Eds.), *Latinos in the new South: Transformations of place* (pp. 37–67). Burlington, NJ: Ashgate Publishing Company.

Viladrich, A. (2012). Beyond welfare reform: Reframing undocumented immigrants' entitlement to health care in the United States, a critical review. *Social Science & Medicine, 74*(6), 822–829.

Villazor, R. C. 2008. What is a sanctuary? *Southern Methodist University Law Review, 61,* 133–156.

Vinik, D. (2015, May 5). Washington, D.C. has the highest infant mortality rate of 25 rich world capitals. *New Republic.* Retrieved from https://newrepublic.com/article/121719/washington-dc-highest-infant-mortality-rate-rich-world-capitals

Waldinger, R. (1997). Black/immigrant competition re-assessed: New evidence from Los Angeles. *Sociological Perspectives, 40*(3), 365–386.

Washington Post. 2006. *Washington Post Poll: DC--Elections/Quality of Life/Education/Redevelopment, Jul, 2006* [USWASH2006-117934, version 2]. TNS Intersearch [producer]. Cornell University, Ithaca, NY: Roper Center for Public Opinion Research, Roper Express [distributor]. Retrieved from https://ropercenter.cornell.edu/CFIDE/cf/action/catalog/abstract.cfm?type=&start=&id=&archno=USWASH2006-117934&abstract=

Waters, M. C. (2009). *Black identities: West Indian immigrant dreams and American realities.* Cambridge, MA: Harvard University Press.

Watkins-Hayes, C. (2011). Race, respect, and red tape: Inside the black box of racially representative bureaucracies. *Journal of Public Administration Research and Theory, 21*(suppl_2), i233–i251.

Weitzer, R. (1999). Citizens' perceptions of police misconduct: Race and neighborhood context. *Justice Quarterly, 16*(4), 819–846.

Wilkes, R., Guppy, N., & Farris, L. (2008). "No thanks, we're full": Individual characteristics, national context, and changing attitudes toward immigration. *International Migration Review, 42*(2), 302–329.

Wilson, J. H. (2008). African-born blacks in the Washington, D.C., Metro Area. *Population Research Bureau.* http://www.prb.org/Publications/Articles/2008/blackImmigrantsdc.aspx

Yon, R. (2010). The declining significance of race: Adrian Fenty and the smooth electoral transition. In A. Gillespie (Ed.), *Whose Black politics? Cases in post-racial Black leadership.* New York: Routledge Press.

Zaller, J. R. (1992). *The nature and origins of mass opinion.* Cambridge, England: Cambridge University Press.

4

THE THREE DIMENSIONS OF POLITICAL INCORPORATION

Black Politics in a Majority-Minority City

Andrea Benjamin

At the turn of the twentieth century, scholars turned their eyes to the city of Durham, NC. W.E.B DuBois, Booker T. Washington, and E. Franklin Frazier all visited Durham and wrote about the potential for Blacks in the city (Franklin, 1925; Washington, 1911). Of his visit, DuBois (1912) said,

> Today there is a singular group in Durham where a Black man may get up in the morning from a mattress made by Black men, in a house which a Black man built out of lumber which Black men cut and planed; he may put on a suit which he bought at a colored haberdashery and socks knit at a colored mill; he may cook victuals from a colored grocery on a stove which black men fashioned; he may earn his living working for colored men, be sick in a colored hospital, and buried from a colored church; and the Negro insurance society will pay his widow enough to keep his children in a colored school. This is surely progress.

All of this attention was for good reason. The city is home to one of the oldest and most influential Black mutual insurance companies, the NC Mutual Insurance Company, which was founded in 1898 (Anderson, 2011; Brown, 2008). The teachers who taught at the city's first Black high school were trained at the first liberal arts college for African Americans in the country, which opened in 1910—now North Carolina Central University (Brown, 2008). Political scientist Bill Keech notes that only 50 Blacks were registered to vote in 1929 in the city of Durham, and by 1939, that number was 3,000, which represented a little more than 25% of eligible Black voters (1968, p. 27).[1] Despite not being able to vote in any elections at the beginning of the twentieth century, Blacks in the city of Durham were doing quite well translating their preferences into political outcomes (Brown, 2008; Walton, 1972). As a result of all of these amenities,

Blacks in the city of Durham had all the things they might need to eventually become active participants in the political arena in the city.

Today, Durham, NC, looks like many cities that have recently welcomed new residents. In addition to an increase in the number of immigrants calling Durham and other "new" destinations home, there are also native-born Black and White Americans who are migrating across the country to Durham, thanks to economic growth the city has experienced in the last 15 years (Florida, 2002; McClain et al., 2006). Of the 40 cities with the highest percentage of Black population, 27 of them are in the South, and Durham is ranked 39 out of 40 when we consider metropolitan statistical areas with the highest percent Black (Pattillo, 2017). The history of Black Politics in the city of Durham, coupled with the rapid increase in the Latinx population in the context of rapid economic development makes this an important place to study racial politics.

In 1935, Black leaders in the city founded the Durham Committee on the Affairs of Negros (now called the Durham Committee of the Affairs of Black People, DCABP) (Anderson, 2011; Keech, 1968). Keech (1968) demonstrated that endorsements from DCABP explained the city's Black vote choice fairly well; the organization's endorsements helped give endorsed candidates an edge by unifying the Black vote. The unity of the Black vote was necessary during these early years, and the DCABP is credited with helping to incorporate Blacks into the political arena in Durham (Keech, 1968). The same remains true today, as I show in my book, *Racial Coalition Building in Local Elections: Elite Cues and Cross-ethnic Voting*, there still exists a strong relationship between co-ethnic cues, such as endorsements, and the outcome of the collective Black vote, and this relationship exists for Latinx voters, though it is not as strong (Benjamin, 2017). Endorsements serve as a signal to voters about which candidates will represent Black and Latinx communities well, thus ensuring some measure of political incorporation for these groups. In this chapter, I return to the concept of political incorporation. In the fall of 2015, the DCABP endorsed only one Black candidate in the race for city council, but he was not elected. The city did send one new Black representative to the city council, but many Blacks in the city did not prefer this candidate. Using data from an exit poll conducted after the city council race, I show that although Black descriptive representation went up in 2015, this happened without Black support. While Blacks in Durham have achieved political incorporation, as political scientists have traditionally measured it, the 2015 election demonstrates why we need to rethink the process of political incorporation in this context. In doing so, we can better understand why Blacks in Durham (and many other places) still face political and economic challenges in the city despite making strides in the local arena.

I am not the first scholar to revisit political incorporation. Political scientists Luis Fraga and Ricardo Ramirez offered a new way to think about this concept with regards to Latinx politics in California (2003). They define political incorporation "as the extent to which self-identified interests are articulated, represented, and met in public policymaking. Political incorporation has three descriptive dimensions: electoral, representational and policy based." (Fraga & Ramirez, 2003, p. 304). Given the traditionally overlooked complexities that arise from gentrification and immigration, I rely on the three-part conceptualization of political incorporation suggested by Fraga and Ramirez to assess Black incorporation in Durham. Rather than assuming that electoral success guarantees policy outcomes, I argue that it is conceptually and theoretically necessary to distinguish between the three types of incorporation. *Electoral incorporation* is the process of electing the groups preferred candidate into office. *Representational incorporation* is manifested by a candidate in office that descriptively represents the group. *Policy incorporation* is the ability to generate policies that benefit the group. By disentangling these three processes, we can ascertain a more nuanced evaluation of the success of any group at a given stage, recognizing that groups may find success at one stage but not others. Electoral incorporation is likely a necessary but not sufficient factor in understanding the everyday outcomes for Black people in many cities like Durham because representational incorporation can happen without unified support from a group but still lead to policies that benefit that group. Finally, policy incorporation can come from places other than the city council—community groups and organizations can also demand policy changes that might benefit groups in the city. Given the lessons learned from rendering a more holistic conception of political incorporation, I ask what electoral, representational, and policy incorporation mean for Latinx communities in "new destinations."

Political Incorporation

In *Protest Is Not Enough*, Browning, Marshall, and Tabb (1984) consider *how* political incorporation for racial minorities occurs and ask whether incorporation makes any substantive difference. In their classic book, they consider ten different cities in northern California from the early 1960s into the early 1980s. These authors have a very specific definition for political incorporation: "political incorporation concerns the extent to which group interests are effectively represented in policy making." (Browning et al., 1984, p. 25). They insist on going beyond simple representation to consider the policy implications of diversity on local governments because for these authors, descriptive representation ought to lead to substantive representation. In short, it is not just Black and Latinx descriptive representation on the local governing body—they need to be able to make policy that benefits their constituents. While whites do have the capacity to represent the interests of Black and Latinx Americans, Browning et al. (1984) are interested in significant Black and Latinx participation in the dominant governing coalition. It is here that the policy outputs should benefit Blacks and Latinxs the most. Yet, as they find in their study, this is not always the case.

Inherent in this definition of political incorporation is the assumption that electoral incorporation assures representational incorporation, which leads to policy incorporation for Black and Latinx residents. For Browning and his colleagues, incorporation is measured by a scale that ranges from "0" when there are no minorities serving in the local government to "1 or 2" when minorities have been elected to the council but not in the dominant coalition, to "3 or 4" when minorities are minor players in the dominant coalition to "5 or more" when minorities are significant partners in the coalition. When a minority actually holds the mayor's office, Browning et al. (1984) score "incorporation" at its highest value "9." According to the authors, marginalized racial groups, Democrats, and liberals are all necessary actors who must engage the electoral process for the political incorporation of minority interests to come to fruition.

The authors identify four routes to incorporation, and they focus on whether minorities are able to get elected into office. The first route is the *biracial electoral alliance*. With this strategy, minority elites form an equal partnership with white liberal elites, and together they are able to take control of the city government. The second route, *co-optation*, also relies on biracial coalitions, but instead of being equal partners, minorities are junior partners relative to whites. The third route is *protest* coupled with electoral strategies. Here, there is a limited use of the biracial coalition. Finally, the fourth route is *weak minority mobilization*. Here, minorities are unorganized are unable to contend for power in the local government. Once they categorize the ten cities, the authors then turn to the policy outputs.

The Impact of Incorporation

In the second half of the book, Browning et al. (1984) examine if getting minorities into office had an effect on whether policies supported by Black and Latinx residents were enacted in city government. They determine the extent to which minority representation benefits minorities on a series of policies: the creation of police review boards; city selection of minority contractors; appointments of minorities to city commissions; and employment of minorities in city government. They find that on all of these measures, minorities fared better after they had been incorporated into city government than they did before. Initially, then, it seemed that electoral incorporation did lead to policy incorporation.

In Browning, Marshall, and Tabb's (1997) later work, *Racial Politics in American Cities*, they examine the effects of incorporation in a broader set of cities, but this time they are less optimistic. They find that political incorporation increased minority city employment, but it only slightly decreased police misconduct; in cities with higher levels of incorporation, they found an increase in minority appointments but found a weak effect on minority business ownership. Essentially, they show that full electoral incorporation does not lead to full policy incorporation. This is very similar to what Keech (1968) found in Durham in the 1960s. The vote, while important, did not guarantee substantive changes in the lives of Blacks in the city. Keech recommended "demonstrations and boycott" as a route to real change (1968, p. 105). Much like what Browning et al. (1984) found, *both* electoral and nonelectoral strategies were most effective. Now that we have a better understanding of the three parts of political incorporation (electoral, representational, and policy), we turn to Black political incorporation in Durham.

Political Incorporation in Durham

After the founding of what is now called DCABP in 1935, the organization began to work to improve the lives of Blacks in Durham. The organization set up subcommittees to address issues like education, housing, and of course, politics. In 1953, the first Black city council member was elected. When R.N. Harris joined the council, he did so with the support of the DCABP and the white liberal Voters League for Better Government (Anderson, 2011). Harris relied on a biracial electoral alliance to get into office. The second Black council member was elected in 1967 (Keech, 1968). According to Browning, Marshall, and Tabb's (BMT) incorporation scale, Durham was a solid "2." It would take 22 more years to elect the first Black mayor in Durham. When Chester Jenkins was elected in 1989, the city saw the highest turnout in the city's municipal election history. His win is attributed to the DCABP (Anderson, 2011). Mayor Jenkins only served one two-year term.

In 2001, William V. "Bill" Bell became the second Black mayor of Durham, and he was reelected eight times. When Mayor Bell was elected for the first time, it was the first election under the new council structure that reduced the size of the council from 13 to 7 (Flanigan, 1998). Voters approved the reduction of the council in 1998, and in 1999, they elected the last set of councilmembers under the larger system. That council was majority Black (8–5). In the eight city councils between 2001 and 2017, Black representatives have been a majority for six of the councils. Under Mayor Bell, the city of Durham has consistently been a "9" on the BMT scale of political incorporation. Though the councils in 2011 and 2013 were not majority Black, in 2015, the city council was represented by a majority of Black councilmembers once again. While a unified vote was needed to elect the first Black council members and the first Black mayor, this bloc vote might be necessary but *still* insufficient for electoral, representational, or policy incorporation even in a city where Blacks have historically garnered plenty of political success.

Blacks in Durham achieved full political incorporation by the Browning et al.'s (1984) standard in 2001. Yet, the data show that this has not had the type of impact scholars had hoped. According to a report by diversitydata.org (n.d.), low-income Blacks in Durham are more likely to have high-interest loans; despite the economic growth in Durham, Blacks are a little less likely to own homes than they did ten years ago, while white homeownership has increased in the same time period; whites are 24% more likely to own homes in Durham. Both Blacks and whites are equally likely to spend more than 30% of their income on housing, but the poverty rate for Blacks is 19%, compared to only 8% for whites.

Unfortunately, the Latinx population in the city fares worse than Blacks on each of these dimensions (diversitydata.org, n.d.). The Latinx poverty rate (19.2%) is higher than the poverty rate in North Carolina (17.4%) and the country (13.5%) (Willets, 2017b). Even more troubling is that almost half of the city's population that lives under the poverty rate is Black (48.7%) (Willets, 2017b). The county estimates that there are more than 800 evictions a month in Durham County in the 2015–2016 fiscal year (Willets, 2017a). In this way, the day-to-day lives of many Blacks in the city of Durham are not necessarily better under a Black mayor and majority Black council.

There is some good news. According to the US Census Bureau, 8,303 of the 21,339 businesses in the city are minority owned (39%). And, in 2016, the city hired its first African American female police chief. Under her watch, Blacks are still more likely to be searched than whites, but the total number of searches for Blacks has been cut by almost 45% (Bridges, 2017).

The extant literature gives us guidance on the overall outcome of political incorporation but cannot explain the set of outcomes we observe in Durham. In order to fully understand and measure Blacks' political prowess at the local level, we have to determine what happens when a Black candidate is elected without the support of Black voters. What's more, endorsements from the DCABP were key to earlier electoral and representational incorporation, but this was not the case in 2015. Does this outcome equate to electoral incorporation or representational incorporation? And can policy incorporation still come from this situation?

The following set of analyses examine the extent to which Blacks' preferences were translated into electoral, representational, and policy incorporation. I use the 2015 City Council Election as an illustrative case to study the three dimensions of political incorporation because while the Black vote was unified, they preferred a different set of candidates. Perhaps counterintuitively, they did achieve representational incorporation—which can be thought of as a form of descriptive representation. Through this representational incorporation, they achieved some policy incorporation, as the policies enacted by the new council benefit Blacks.

The 2015 City Council Election

Durham's citizens are represented through a council–manager government structure featuring a six-member city council that is led by the mayor. The mayor serves two-year terms, while the city council serves four-year terms; the city council elections occur every 2 years. The city council is comprised of three ward seats and three at-large seats. Ward seats only require the councilmember to live in the specific ward, and all voters cast a ballot for all councilmembers campaigning for office.

In 2015, Mayor William V. "Bill" Bell was easily reelected. In the sample, both Black and White voters supported him (73% of Blacks and 82% of whites), so this chapter focuses on the city council election, which was more competitive. The three at-large city council seats were open. Initially, ten candidates, including one incumbent running to keep his seat, filed to run for office.[2] During the primary election, voters were allowed to select up to three candidates. The six candidates who received the most votes advanced to the general election.

The City Council Candidates

Steve Schewel, a white candidate, won reelection and also received the largest number of votes (15,011 or 28.07%). Schewel is a registered Democrat, and self-identifies as progressive[3] (Reed, 2015d) He was the only incumbent in this race. He founded the Independent Newspaper—the INDY Week, which he sold in 2012. Schewel included economic development, open areas/parks and affordable housing as his top three issues (Reed, 2015d). He received the endorsement from the DCABP.

Jillian Johnson, a Black candidate, won a seat on the council and received the second most votes in the election (12,497 votes or 23.37%). She moved to Durham around 2001. She is a registered Democrat and identifies as progressive (Reed, 2015b). Johnson works as a nonprofit administrator for the Southern Vision Alliance. She has worked on criminal justice campaigns in Durham, Orange, and Alamance counties to monitor racially biased traffic stops (Reed, 2015b). Johnson also worked on housing committees that addressed affordable housing and gentrification and included affordable housing, crime, and economic development/jobs as her top three issues (Reed, 2015b). She did not receive an endorsement from the DCABP.

Charlie Reece, a white candidate, also won a seat on the council with the third most votes (9,680 votes or 18.10%). He has lived in Durham for 9 years and is a registered Democrat. He self-identifies as progressive (Reed 2015c). Reece works as an attorney at General Counsel, Rho, Inc. He included affordable housing, crime, and economic development/jobs as his top three issues (Reed 2015c). Reece did not receive an endorsement from the DCABP.

Mike Shiftlett, a white candidate, did not win a seat on the council. He received 7,376 votes (13.79%). He has resided in Durham for 31 years and is registered as an unaffiliated voter (Reed 2015e). Shiftlett is a retired president of American Labor, a clinical lab equipment company. He listed transparency, youth development, and the light rail/affordable housing as his most important issues (Reed 2015e). Shiftlett received the endorsement from DCABP.

Ricky Hart, a Black candidate, also did not win a seat on the council. He received 5,844 votes (10.93%). He has been a lifelong resident of Durham and is a registered Democrat. Hart is employed at Orange County Child Support Services (Reed, 2015a). He lists economic development/jobs, crime, and transparency as his top three issues (Reed, 2015a). Hart received the endorsement from the DCABP.

Finally, Robert Stephens, a Black candidate, did not win a seat on the council. He received 2,925 votes (5.47%). He has lived in Durham for 1 year and is employed as the Director of Alumni Teacher Leadership for Teach for America. Stephens is a registered Democrat (Reed, 2015f). His main focus is police accountability and economic equality (People's Alliance, 2015). He listed affordable housing, crime, and economic development as his top issues (Reed, 2015f). He received did not receive an endorsement from the DCABP. Table 4.1 provides a brief summary of each candidate.

TABLE 4.1 Summary of Candidate Characteristics

Candidate	Race	Lived in Durham	Affiliation	Experience	Issues	Endorsements
Schewel (Incumbent)	White	45 years	Democrat and progressive	Former schoolboard member, current council member	Affordable housing, parks, police department/crime	INDY Week, Friends of Durham, People's Alliance, DCABP
Johnson	Black	16 years	Democrat and progressive	Worked on criminal justice campaigns and housing committees	Affordable housing, police department/crime, economic development	INDY Week, People's Alliance
Reece	White	9 years	Democrat and progressive	Advocate for the Fostering Alternative Drug Enforcement Coalition	Affordable housing, police department/crime, economic development	INDY Week People's Alliance
Shiflett	White	31 years	Unaffiliated voter	Emergency Preparedness Committee, Partners Against Crime, and the Community Schools Initiative	Light rail, affordable housing	Friends of Durham DCABP
Hart	Black	Lifelong resident	Democrat	Former Chairman of the Durham Human Relations Committee	Police department/crime, economic development	Friends of Durham DCABP
Stephens	Black	1 year	Democrat and progressive freedom fighter	Community organizer for Durham's Black Lives Matter movement	Affordable housing, police department/crime	None

Data and Methods

The Durham general election for city council took place in the fall of 2015. The mayoral election was at the top of the ballot, followed by the city council. Overall, voter turnout was low (10.80%) in the general election. Low turnout is common in local off-cycle elections (Hajnal & Trounstine, 2005). In the city council election, voters were allowed to select up to three candidates, with the top three candidates winning the three at-large seats.

Students at the University of North Carolina at Chapel Hill conducted the Durham Votes 2015 exit poll on election day; they identified themselves as students and asked every other voter if they would be willing to complete an exit poll as they exited the polling station. The students worked in pairs and were stationed at the polling stations from the time the polls opened until the polls closed.[4] In the end, the students collected 343 responses from voters. In addition to questions about the mayoral election, the exit poll also asked voters, "In the Durham City Council Election, which three (3) candidates did you vote for?" The dependent variable is a measure of all votes for that candidate, regardless of first, second, or third choice. Voters were also asked about their awareness of the endorsements offered by the local political action committees.

Finally, the exit poll asked voters various demographic questions, including those on partisanship, ideology, gender, race/ethnicity, educational attainment, household income, and which issue was "most important in the election to [them] in deciding how [they] voted." In the analyses, party is a dichotomous variable where 1 = Democrat, 0 = Republican, and Other. Liberal is a dichotomous variable where 1 = Very Liberal or Liberal, 0 = Not Liberal. Black is a dichotomous variable where 1 = Black, 0 = Not Black. Female is a dichotomous variable where 1 = Female, 0 = Not Female. Age is a continuous variable between 20–96. Education is a categorical variable, where lower values indicate less education and higher values indicate more education (i.e., less than high school; high school graduate; some college/technical school; college degree(s); some graduate school; and graduate degree(s)). Income is a categorical variable, where lower values indicate less income and higher values indicate more income (i.e., just under $20,000; $20,000 to $39,999; $40,000 to $59,999; $60,000 to $79,999; $80,000 to $99,999; $100,000 to $149,999; $150,000 to $250,000; and more than $250,000).

The Demographic Make-Up of Durham Voters

Table 4.2 compares the population of Durham, the exit poll sample, and registered voters in the city of Durham. According to the US Census Bureau, Durham's population in 2010 was 228,000 people. The racial breakdown was 37% white, non–Hispanic, 41% Black, 5% Asian, and 14% Latinx. According to the Durham County Board of Elections, there were 178,959 registered voters in 2015. However, the racial breakdown of registered voters—whites comprise

TABLE 4.2 Demographics for Durham, NC Exit Poll Sample, and Registered Voters

Demographics	Durham	Durham Votes 2015 Exit Poll Sample	Registered Voters (Durham Board of Elections)
Total population	228,000 (census)	343	178,957
White	37% (census)	42%	82,483 (46%)
Black	41% (census)	50%	75,161 (42%)
Latinx	14% (census)	3.5%	5,180 (3%)
Asian	5% (census)	2%	4,950 (3%)
Native American	0.05% (census)	1.5%	501 (less than 1%)
Mean household income	$48,241 (census)	$60,000–$79,000	NA
Education (BA or higher)	46.6% (census)	88%	NA
Partisanship	59.3% (Board of Election)	79%	106,211 (59.3%)

Source: Data from US Census Bureau, Durham Votes 2015 Exit Poll, & Durham County Board of Elections.

46% of registered voters, Blacks comprise 42%, Latinx and Asian Americans each comprise almost 3% of registered voters—did not quite match population demographics (Durham County Board of Elections).[5]

The exit poll sample does a good job matching registered voters in Durham in terms of race and ethnicity: 42% white, 50% Black, 3.5% Latinx, 2% Asian American, and 1.5% Native American. The sample is highly educated, with 88% indicating they have a college degree or higher. They are financially well off, with 60% indicating a household income of more the $60,000 a year. The mean age is 48, and there are more women than men in the sample (57%). Finally, the sample is liberal, with 70% selecting somewhat or very Liberal for their ideological beliefs, and 79% identify as Democrats.

Results

Distinctive Black Voting in Durham

Did the candidates who Blacks supported gain a seat on the council? In order to explore levels of electoral incorporation among Blacks, I estimate a logistic regression model of overall support for each candidate (whether the voter selected the candidate as his or her first, second, or third choice). This analysis will help us determine whether Blacks' candidate preferences translated into successful election outcomes.

First, I assess candidate support among all voters in the sample. The results for logistic regression models are difficult to interpret, so I present both the regression output as well as figures of the predicted probability of support for the candidate (Table 4.3). Figures 4.1–4.6 show that for five of the candidates, Shiftlett being

TABLE 4.3 Support for City Council Candidates Among All Voters

Variables	Schewel (SE)	Johnson (SE)	Reece (SE)	Shifflett (SE)	Hart (SE)	Stephens (SE)
Constant	−0.08 (0.65)	−0.02 (0.62)	0.22 (0.63)	0.18 (0.59)	−2.83*** (0.81)	−1.37+ (0.78)
Political						
Party	0.44 (0.36)	0.45 (0.34)	1.04** (0.36)	−0.69+ (0.32)	0.19 (0.42)	−0.30 (0.42)
Liberal	0.92** (0.30)	0.54+ (0.29)	0.34 (0.31)	−0.16 (0.28)	−0.57+ (0.34)	−0.54 (0.36)
Demographics						
Black	−1.14*** (0.31)	−1.03*** (0.29)	−1.92*** (0.30)	0.35 (0.27)	2.56*** (0.37)	0.89* (0.37)
Female	−0.28 (0.28)	0.34 (0.27)	−0.05 (0.27)	0.07 (0.26)	0.68* (0.32)	0.49 (0.35)
Age	1.02 (0.73)	−1.52* (0.67)	−1.04 (0.68)	0.80 (0.64)	2.43** (0.83)	−1.81* (0.89)
Education	0.48 (0.57)	0.97+ (0.55)	−0.09 (0.58)	−0.90+ (0.53)	−1.48** (0.64)	0.32 (0.70)
Income	0.04 (0.55)	0.09 (0.53)	−0.04 (0.55)	0.18 (0.51)	1.21* (0.63)	−0.15 (0.67)
Log likelihood	−158.62	−170.28	167.29	−184.37	−130.50	−121.18
N	290	290	290	290	290	290

Source: Data from Durham Votes 2015 Exit Poll.

Note. SE = *standard errors.*

*** $p < 0.001$; ** $p < 0.01$; * $p < 0.05$; + $p < 0.10$ for a two-tailed test.

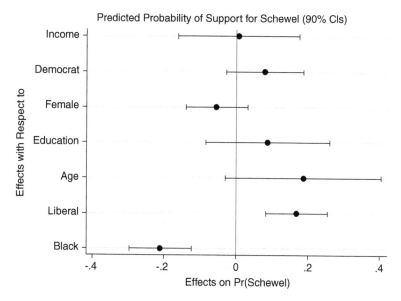

FIGURE 4.1 Predicted Probability of Support for Schewel

Source: Data from Durham Votes 2015 Exit Poll.

Note. See Table 4.3, Column 1.

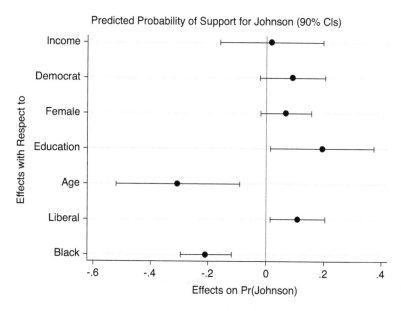

FIGURE 4.2 Predicted Probability of Support for Johnson

Source: Data from Durham Votes 2015 Exit Poll.

Note. See Table 4.3, Column 2.

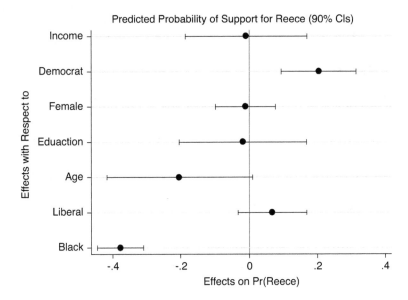

FIGURE 4.3 Predicted Probability of Support for Reece

Source: Data from Durham Votes 2015 Exit Poll.

Note. See Table 4.3, Column 3.

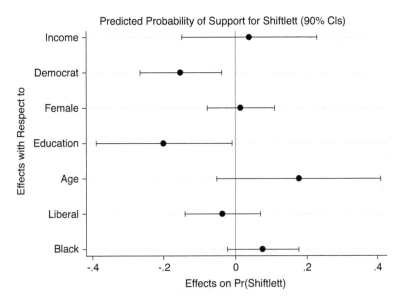

FIGURE 4.4 Predicted Probability of Support for Shiftlett

Source: Data from Durham Votes 2015 Exit Poll.

Note. See Table 4.3, Column 4.

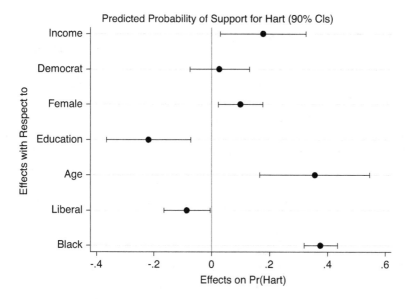

FIGURE 4.5 Predicted Probability of Support for Hart

Source: Data from Durham Votes 2015 Exit Poll.

Note. See Table 4.3, Column 5.

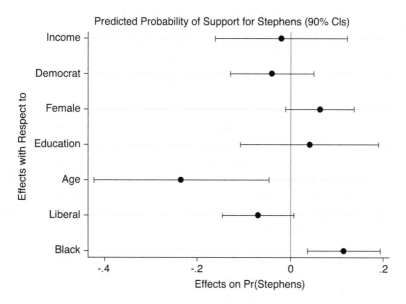

FIGURE 4.6 Predicted Probability of Support for Stephens

Source: Data from Durham Votes 2015 Exit Poll.

Note. See Table 4.3, Column 6

the exception, Black voters had a distinctive set of preferences from white voters in Durham. Blacks in the sample were less likely to vote for Schewel, Johnson, and Reece. Alternatively, they were more likely to vote for Hart and Stephens.

Both Hart and Stephens are African American, so this result is consistent with other studies that show that minorities support co-ethnic candidates at high rates (Bullock & Campbell, 1984; Hero, 1992). Although Johnson, who is also Black, won a seat on the council, she did not enjoy support from Black voters. When I interviewed Johnson in 2015, she indicated that she sought to build a biracial coalition like the one described by Browning et al. (1984). To get the support from progressive whites, she sought the endorsement from People's Alliance. Johnson also sought to gain support from Black voters. She noted, "We still needed a couple thousand votes, and we needed to get those votes primarily from Black voters and the easiest way to do that would have been to get the endorsement of the Durham Committee on the Affairs of Black People" (Johnson, 2015). However, she did not gain that endorsement, nor did she receive the support from the Blacks in this sample. But this did not prevent her from winning a seat on the council. These results suggest that Black voters in this sample were not successful at gaining electoral incorporation in this election. They preferred Hart and/or Stephens to Johnson. However, Johnson was elected to the council, and so they gained representational incorporation, though not of their own volition.

Other demographics do a good job explaining vote choice as well. In addition to race, partisanship explained vote choice for Reece and Shiftlett. Democrats were more likely to support Reece and less likely to support Shiftlett. Ideology also explained vote choice for three candidates. Liberals were more likely to support Schewel and Johnson, but less likely to support Hart. Younger voters were more likely to support Johnson and Stephens, while older voters were more likely to support Hart. Women were more likely to support Hart. Finally, those with more educational attainment were more likely to support Johnson and less likely to support Shiftlett and Hart.

While several political and demographic factors explained vote choice for a few candidates, the race of the voters explained vote choice for five out of six candidates. Again, by examining only one dimension of political incorporation, or relying solely on the BMT political incorporation scale, we could conclude that Blacks in Durham have achieved full/the highest levels of political incorporation. However, the aforementioned analysis reveals that their candidate preferences did not translate into electoral outcomes in this election. Perhaps more concerning, Black voters in the sample were *less likely to support each of the candidates that won the election*. Browning et al. (1984) assumed that electing Black and Latinx councilmembers and mayors came with the unified Black and Latinx vote. Then once elected, these Black and Latinx representatives assured policies that would benefit Black and Latinx residents in the city. However, this case shows that voters in Durham did elect a new Black city councilmember, but this occurred without support from Black voters.

Despite the lack of support for Johnson among Blacks, her election returned the city council to a majority Black status, which provides them representational incorporation in the city. For Browning et al. (1984), political incorporation was about more than just electing minority bodies on the council. They were interested in having significant minority participation in the dominant governing coalition. At a certain level, electoral and representational incorporation guaranteed some amount of policy incorporation. The case of Johnson is perhaps the most interesting. While she set out to build a biracial coalition, she was elected with less support from Blacks in this sample. There might be several reasons Blacks did not support Johnson in this election, but one *potential* reason might be that she didn't campaign on issues that were important to Blacks in Durham. In the next section, I assess levels of policy incorporation among Blacks in Durham.

Black Issues in the Election

Based on the previous analysis, it is clear that Blacks voted distinctively in the city council election; they overwhelmingly supported two Black candidates, but neither candidate won a seat on the council. But the race of the voter and the race of the candidate are not the only factors that explain vote choice. There is plenty of research suggesting that voters use issue positions to make their decisions about candidates (Abrajano, Nagler, & Alvarez, 2005; Boudreau, Elmendorf, & MacKenzie, 2015). In this case, Black voters might have been more interested in the policy incorporation promised by the candidates running for city council. I turn to the issues candidates highlighted in their campaigns. The exit poll asked voters, "Which issue was the most important in the election?" Response options were affordable housing; economic development/job creation; Durham Police Department; crime and gangs; public programs (e.g., parks, libraries); the proposed light rail; education; transportation; sidewalk repair; and Other. Table 4.4 shows the top issues facing the city according to Blacks: crime/police, economic development, and affordable housing (see Table 4.4).

While many of the candidates included crime/police, economic development, and affordable housing in their platforms, two candidates ran on all three

TABLE 4.4 Top Issues Among Blacks

Issue	Percent Blacks Listing Issue
Crime/Police	30
Economic development	25
Affordable housing	23
Parks	5
The light rail	3
Other issues (Education, transportation, sidewalk repair, other)	14

Source: Data from Durham Votes 2015 Exit Polls.

of these specific issues—Johnson and Reece. The other four candidates mentioned one or two of these issues in their campaigns but did not include all three as outlined in Table 4.1. Given that Johnson and Reece won the election, Blacks' policy preferences were translated into political outcomes and this brought them closer to achieving policy incorporation. That is, Blacks in Durham could still expect to have two new councilmembers working on the issues that mattered to them. The original conception of political incorporation placed a value on the ability for representatives to be a part of the governing coalition—this would allow them to generate policies that had the potential to make life in the city better for Blacks and Latinxs. Despite not having the support of Black voters in this sample, Johnson and Reece have the potential to promote policies that benefit Blacks in Durham (policy incorporation).

Issues are just one way that voters evaluate candidates. Many voters rely on cues or heuristics when casting ballots (Campbell, Converse, Miller, & Stokes, 1960; Gerber & Phillips, 2003; Krebs, 1998; Lieske, 1989; Lupia, 1994). While partisanship is the most common cue, the elections in Durham are nonpartisan, so voters may be looking for an alternative shortcut. Previous research on endorsements shows that Blacks are both receptive to and rely on co-ethnic endorsements (Benjamin, 2016, 2017; Keech, 1968). In particular, the endorsements may help Blacks achieve both electoral, representational, and policy incorporation by unifying the Black vote behind candidates that will represent Blacks' interests well. Johnson hoped to get the endorsement from the DCABP, as she believed it would help her gain support from Blacks in the city (Johnson, 2015). Though she did not receive the endorsement, three candidates did. It is possible that Blacks in Durham used the endorsement from the DCABP when casting their ballots. In the next section, I determine the extent to which an organization that is concerned with Black citizens continues to unite and influence the Black vote.

The Durham Committee on the Affairs of Black People

The DCABP continues to be very active in politics in the city of Durham. Through their Political Action Committee, they interview candidates running for mayor and city council and endorse the candidates that they feel will represent Blacks well. They are not the only organization to offer such endorsements; most notably, there is also a progressive organization, the People's Alliance, a socially liberal, but fiscally conservative organization the Friends of Durham; and a local newspaper, the INDY Week (better known as The Indy).

In order to provide some additional context to the 2015 election, let's consider endorsements and winners for recent elections. Between 2009 and 2015, 59 candidates ran for city council in Durham.[6] Of those, 29 made it to the general election. In 2009 and 2013, the ward seats were contested. In 2011 and 2015, the at-large seats were contested. The People's Alliance endorsed 20 winning candidates and endorsed no losing candidates. The DCABP endorsed eight winning candidates and six losing candidates. The Friends of Durham endorsed seven winning candidates and five losing candidates. The Indy endorsed 12 winning candidates and no losing candidates, confirming previous research showing that endorsements from newspapers help candidates (Erickson, 1976; Liu, 2003).

In terms of the racial identity of the candidates, endorsements, and getting into office, the People's Alliance endorsed five Black candidates, all of whom were elected. The Indy went three for three. The DCABP endorsed four Black candidates and only one was elected. The Friends of Durham endorsed four Black candidates and two of them were elected.

Taken together, these results suggest that in recent elections, the People's Alliance endorsement is quite powerful, as they have been successful quite often, while the DCABP and the Friends of Durham have not been as successful at electing Black candidates. The People's Alliance has been more successful at electing Black candidates than the other two PACs. This was the case for Jillian Johnson in 2015, as whites in the city elected her to office.

Despite this mixed record of success, the endorsement from the DCABP may still be important to Black *voters* in the city. Given that Blacks did not support the candidates running on a slate of issues Blacks listed as the most important in the election, I explore the relationship between awareness of the endorsement from the DCABP and vote choice among Blacks. During the 2015 election, three candidates received the endorsement from the DCABP (Schewel, Shiftlett, and Hart). If Black voters are using this cue, then awareness of the endorsement will be positively associated with vote choice.

In order to explore the relationship between endorsements and electoral and representational incorporation, I estimate a logistic regression model of overall support for each candidate, similar to the model in the previous analysis, but restrict the analysis to Black respondents only. In this case, each model includes demographic factors such as partisanship, ideology, income, education, age, and gender, but also includes the DCABP endorsement.[7] To assess whether voters knew about which organizations had endorsed each candidate, voters were asked, "Do you happen to know if any of the following individuals or organizations endorsed [insert candidate name] for City Council, or didn't you pay attention to that?" For this analysis, I am interested in those voters who correctly identified the endorsement from the DCABP. These logistic regression results are presented in Table 4.5 (see Table 4.5). Figures 4.7–4.9 illustrate the predicted probabilities of support for the endorsed candidate.

Figures 4.7 and 4.8 show that for Schewel and Shiftlett, awareness of the DCABP endorsement is not associated with voting for either among Blacks (see Figures 4.7 and 4.8). However, in Figure 4.9, support for Hart is positively associated with the endorsement (see Figure 4.9). That is, correctly identifying Hart's endorsement from the DCABP is associated with greater support for Hart. Only Hart enjoyed a boost in support because of his DCABP

TABLE 4.5 Support for City Council Candidates with DCABP Endorsement among Blacks

Variable	Schewel (SE)	Shiftlett (SE)	Hart (SE)
Constant	−1.52 (0.89)	0.43 (0.90)	−0.94 (0.98)
Political			
Party	0.98+ (0.56)	0.23 (0.58)	0.77 (0.60)
Liberal	0.75★ (0.36)	0.38 (0.37)	−0.26 (0.390)
Demographics			
Female	−0.21 (0.38)	0.14 (0.38)	0.94★ (0.41)
Age	0.73 (0.67)	−0.41 (1.08)	2.05+ (1.13)
Education	0.97+ (1.06)	−1.98★★ (0.70)	−1.37+ (0.77)
Income	−0.05 (0.70)	0.36 (0.70)	0.20 (0.77)
Endorsements			
DCABP	0.31 (0.39)	0.67 (0.45)	1.55★★ (0.51)
Log likelihood	−91.42	−89.41	−81.74
N	142	142	142

Source: Data from Durham Votes 2015 Exit Poll.

Note. SE = standard errors.
★★★ $p < 0.001+$; ★★ $p < 0.01$; ★ $p < 0.05$; $p < 0.10$ for a two-tailed test.

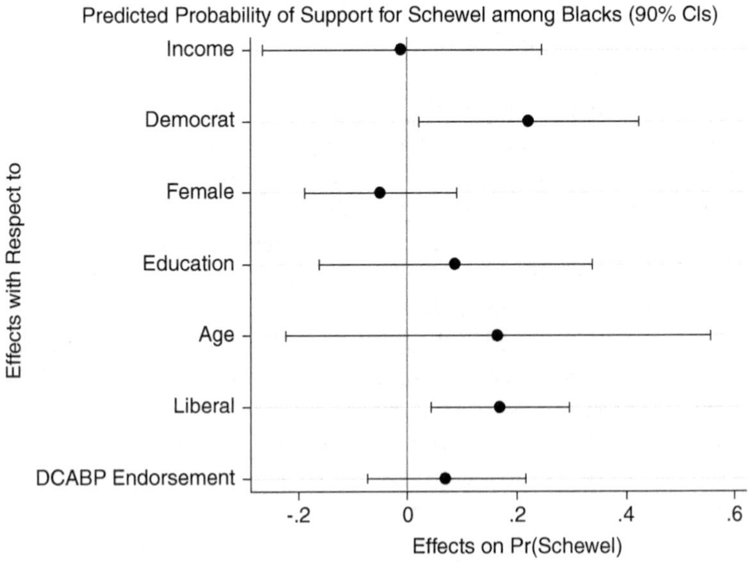

FIGURE 4.7 Predicted Probability of Support for Schewel Among Blacks

Source: Data from Durham Votes 2015 Exit Poll.

Note. See Table 4.5, Column 1.

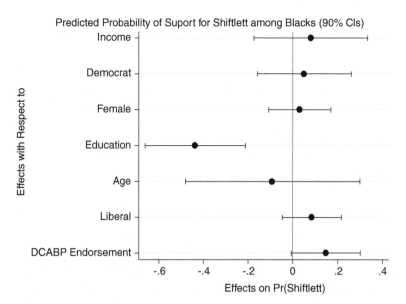

FIGURE 4.8 Predicted Probability of Support for Shiftlett Among Blacks

Source: Data from Durham Votes 2015 Exit Poll.

Note. See Table 4.5, Column 2.

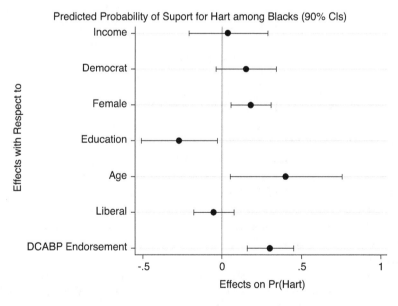

FIGURE 4.9 Predicted Probability of Support for Hart Among Blacks

Source: Data from Durham Votes 2015 Exit Poll.

Note. See Table 4.5, Column 3.

endorsement among Blacks. If these endorsements are supposed to serve as cues about which candidate will represent them well, then the DCABP endorsement is only working for some candidates. There was no relationship between the white candidates that received the DCABP endorsement and Black support in this sample. Further, the endorsement did not help Blacks achieve electoral or representational incorporation in this election, as the DCABP-endorsed Black candidate did not win. Before I turn to the conclusions, I return to the broader notion of political incorporation and consider what it means for Blacks in Durham.

The Impact of Incorporation in Durham, NC

In this last section, I want to consider the impact of policy incorporation for Blacks in the city of Durham. Indeed, Blacks have achieved representational incorporation in the local governing body, but the 2015 election shows that while Blacks voted distinctly, they did not achieve electoral incorporation, as the candidates they preferred did not get elected. Yet, they might still be represented well by the council in terms of policy. According to Browning et al. (1997), Blacks who lived in cities where they achieved incorporation did better on minority appointments to city commissions, but one area that still needed work was police misconduct. Considering both above findings as well recent events in the US that highlight systemic and troubling interactions between the police and Black and Latinx communities, I want to consider police and community relations in the city of Durham as an illustrative case of the link between electoral, representational, and policy incorporation. There are three points of focus that may help us to discern the policy outcomes in a city with a Black mayor and a majority Black council.

First, Baumgartner, Epp, and Love (2014) show that Blacks in the city of Durham are 105% more likely to be searched than whites if they are stopped by the police. The Durham Fostering Alternative Drug Enforcement (FADE) Coalition and the Southern Coalition for Social Justice used the reports generated by Baumgartner, Epp, and Love to advocate for written consent for traffic stops. By the fall of 2014, the city manager in conjunction with the city council implemented a policy requiring that officers get written consent for searches (Wise, 2014). Initially, research showed that in the aftermath of the change in the policy, initially there was an increase in probable cause searches (Bridges, 2015).

Second, members of the FADE Coalition complained about racial profiling in the department and called for the police chief to step down (Bridges, 2017). In 2013, Mayor Bell called on the Human Relations Commission to investigate the situation, and they found that there was a racial bias in the police department (Bridges, 2017). Subsequently, the city manager hired the city's first Black female police chief in 2016 and searches have been down.

Third, there is a Police Review Board in the city of Durham. According to the city's website, "The board's mandate is to determine whether or not the investigation was conducted in an appropriate manner, specifically, whether the Police Department abused its discretion in the conduct of the investigation" (Civilian Police Review Board, n.d.). In essence, the board is only allowed to review the investigation of the complaint. Despite the potential for this board to address police misconduct, it actually has "no power to discipline, reprimand, or fire any officer or employee... the board can make recommendations whether or not a hearing is held" (Civilian Police Review Board, n.d.). This leaves citizens with very little recourse if they are dissatisfied with an interaction with the police department.

The extent to which Blacks' policy preferences around matters of policing are translated into new policies is just one manifestation of policy incorporation, but I believe it is a valuable measure of whether electoral and representational incorporation matters in local government. While representational incorporation has been achieved (even without Black support), there is still much to be done on the dimension of policy incorporation. This disconnect highlights the main limitation of the government structure in cities like Durham that use the manager–council system. Under this system, the council hires the city manager, who handles the day-to-day tasks of the city. It is the city manager's job to hire and fire the police chief. This makes the accountability mechanism much less direct: voter to council to city manager to police chief.

This indirect relationship might help explain why police and community interactions are representative of the challenges of translating preferences into policy at the local level. This is also the case on issues of poverty, affordable housing, and economic development in the city. There are structural constraints that prevent the council from acting. What this means for Blacks is that electoral and representational incorporation do not always translate into the policy outcomes they hoped for.

Are Electoral Politics Enough?

My research also leads me to conclude that residents of the city have to work hard to hold elected officials accountable because the structure does not make it easy. While organizations like the DCABP attempt to help Blacks get their needs met, moving forward, voters have to use the power of the franchise to pull the accountability mechanism. Voter turnout has been low in the last four election cycles, ranging from 8% in 2009 to 17% in 2011. However, the last time the DCABP elected a Black candidate without support from the People's Alliance was 2007, when Farad Ali won an at-large seat. In that election, Durham saw the highest number of voters ever turn out for the election (36,318). The DCABP has to mobilize voters sympathetic to their vision of the city if they want to see the changes they desire in Durham.

My previous work shows that Blacks rely on endorsements from Black organizations when casting their ballots for mayor (Benjamin, 2017) and, to some extent, this is true in Durham at the city council level. Blacks were aware of one candidate's endorsement from the DCABP (Hart), but this did not lead to electoral incorporation in this contest, in part, because Hart did not win. For the other two candidates endorsed by the DCABP, awareness of the endorsements was not associated with support for those candidates among Blacks. As residents of Durham continue to face rising housing costs, being priced out of their homes, seeking more access to public transportation, the need for a living wage, and poverty, Blacks in the city may look to other sources to help them make good decisions in the voting booth. If the DCABP wants to remain relevant, they need to support candidates that fight for Blacks on these issues and the organization needs to get their endorsed candidates into office with Black support.[8]

Latinx Political Incorporation in Durham

Scholars have been asking whether electoral politics is the most efficient and effective tool for political change for some time now. Keech (1968), Browning et al. (1984, 1997), and Mollenkopf (2003) seem to come to the same conclusion, perhaps reluctantly, that the answer is no. Burns (2006) suggests that minorities use extra-electoral channels, such as civic and neighborhood organization, in order to translate their preferences into political outcomes. These organizations help residents overcome the hurdles and fears of interacting with the government, and they also help unify the preferences of those residents.

As the city of Durham changes and the population includes more and more transplants, the organizations must adapt if they want to remain relevant. Further, while Browning et al. (1984) found that Latinx incorporation came *after* Black incorporation in northern California, Latinx people were not represented on the Durham city council until January 2018 when Javiera Caballero was appointed to fill Schewel's seat, but it is still unclear whether they will forge political coalitions with Blacks or whites. While Latinx residents achieved representational incorporation via appointment, they have yet to achieve full policy incorporation.[9]

There has been some progress in response to issues facing the Latinx community, none of which utilized electoral incorporation. The Latino Community Credit Union opened in Durham in response to the rise in crimes perpetrated against Latinx residents. Many Latinx residents lacked the necessary documents to open bank accounts and were seen as easy targets because they had to keep their cash on them. The creation of this financial institution comes as a result of a community coalition.

Additionally, there was a Black–Latinx coalition that formed in response to attempts to privatize Old North Durham Park, which was used by Black and Latinx community members. The coalition demanded that the city council uphold a 2005 resolution to renovate the park. These nonelectoral coalitions emerged to ask the majority Black city council to address specific needs in the community, and policy incorporation was achieved.

While Browning et al. (1984) argue that the electoral route was the most successful way to gain political incorporation, these examples of nonelectoral coalitions in Durham provide some suggestive evidence that groups can successfully make demands outside of the electoral context and that coalitions are viable between Blacks and Latinx. While the DCABP was historically instrumental in aiding Black incorporation, Latinxs do not have a dedicated Political Action Committee at this time. This is something that might make the route to electoral and increased representational incorporation easier if Latinxs decide to enter the political arena in the coming years.

Conclusion

Blacks in this sample had a clear set of candidate preferences, but those candidates did not win seats on the council. From a normative perspective, the prescription is increased voter turnout. They will need to outvote whites in the city. In the last 30 years, voter turnout has only exceeded 30% two times: once in 1989 when the city elected the first Black mayor (42%) and once in 1991 (36%). In 2007, the city saw the highest number of voters show up to vote (37,198 voters), but even that was only 24% turnout. These low levels of turnout suggest that if communities want to see the candidates they support win the election, they need to turn out for those candidates at a higher rate than whites.

Black voters may have experienced a sense of *déjà vu* after the 2017 mayoral election. Exit poll data reveal that across council elections, Black and White voters had a completely different set of preferences (Durham Votes, 2017). Though turnout overall was significantly higher than 2 years prior, Durham's changing electorate elected city councilmember Steve Schewel to become the mayor of Durham. Schewel is the first white candidate to make it to the general election in Durham since 2001, and he defeated Farad Ali, who not only is Black but was also the preferred candidate of Durham's African American constituents. Additionally, even though only Black candidates vied for ward seats, Black and White voters still had very different preferences. Unlike the 2015 contest, Blacks were able to successfully elect one of their preferred candidates, Mark Anthony Middleton, to the council for Ward 2. The new city council has four Black councilmembers and two white councilmembers, and the council will appoint someone to finish Schewel's term on the council. Many people in the community have been vocal in advocating for the appointment of a Latinx community member, thus allowing Latinx residents to achieve representational incorporation in Durham.

The lessons learned from these elections illuminate the idea that electoral incorporation (even accidental) *may* lead to policy incorporation, but it is not guaranteed. In cities all over the country, new groups are arriving, and they have choices about if and how they want to make demands on the political system. The case of Durham shows that policy incorporation is essential to improving the lives of Black and Latinx constituents, but demographics are not destiny. To the extent that these two groups have a shared set of interests in the city (e.g., affordable housing, poverty, and policing), there is the potential for a Black–Latinx coalition. This will require Latinx residents to improve their perceptions of Blacks (McClain et al., 2006). This is more likely to happen when there is an opportunity for meaningful interactions (Valentine, 2008). Although previous research in Durham suggests that even in the most diverse neighborhoods in the city, groups are not engaged in these meaningful interactions (see Mayorga-Gallo, 2014 and in this volume). Perhaps the DCABP can work with the organizations in the city that serve the Latinx community to help encourage these types of interactions. Together with candidates that seek to address the issues affecting both groups, there is the potential for a Black–Latinx coalition and full political incorporation in Durham.

Notes

1 Keech does not provide data on the percentage of eligible Blacks registered in 1928 or 1935. The data are not available.
2 In the primary election, Steve Schewel received 24.95% of the vote, Jillian Johnson received 21.83% of the vote, Charlie Reece received 16.03% of the vote, Mike Shiftlett received 10.26% of the vote, Ricky Hart received 6.84% of the vote, Robert Stephens received 6.69% of the vote, Sandra Davis received 6.07% of the vote, Philip Azar received 3.55% of the vote, Juan Alva received 2.03% of the vote, and John Tarantino received 1.74% of the vote. Voter turnout was 7.64% (Durham County Board of Elections). Juan Alva, a Latinx candidate, planned to run for mayor with a central focus on "advocating for Durham's most marginalized citizens, including Hispanics and African Americans, equal education and improving the city" (Bridges, 2015). However, he had to drop out due to health reasons.
3 Progressive can be distinguished from Liberals in that Liberals want to use tax money to ensure equitable outcomes, while Progressives want to implement a set of rules that businesses must abide by to ensure equitable outcomes.
4 Polling stations were selected for the diversity of registered voters and the number of ballots cast in the primary election. In all, students worked at ten polling stations in the city (there are 58 polling stations in total). Some voters declined taking the poll, but the students were a diverse set (race and gender) and did not report a bias in who declined to take the exit poll.
5 The final 6% come from Native Americans, multirace, other, and undesignated registered voters. Citizenship issues, a common issue amongst Latinx and Asian communities, may explain the lack of parity between population demographics and percent registered voters for Latinx and Asians, though there has been a recent increase in Latinx registering to vote in 2016 (Bump, 2016).
6 We used the Indy's coverage of the PAC endorsements, which were announced online and in the paper.

7 Blacks in the sample overwhelmingly identified as Democrats (108) compared to 16 Republicans and 33 that said other. They also said liberal (84), somewhat liberal (42), moderate (13), somewhat conservative (9) and conservative (8). DCABP is a dichotomous variable where 1 indicates that the respondent correctly identified the DCABP endorsement and 0 indicates that the respondent did not correctly identify that endorsement.

8 While Schewel was endorsed by the DCABP, Blacks in the sample were less likely to vote for him.

9 It is hard to measure whether Latinx have achieved electoral incorporation in the city. In our sample, we did not have enough Latinx respondents to analyze the data.

References

Abrajano, M., Nagler, J., & Alvarez, R. M. (2005). A natural experiment of race-based and issue voting: The 2001 city of Los Angeles elections. *American Politics Quarterly*, *58*, 203–218.

Anderson, J. B. (2011). *Durham County. A history of Durham County, North Carolina*. Durham, NC: Duke University Press.

Baumgartner, F. R., Epp, D. A., & Love, B. (2014). Police searches of black and white motorists. *Presented to North Carolina Advocates for Justice*. Retrieved from https://www.unc. edu/~fbaum/TrafficStops/DrivingWhileBlack-BaumgartnerLoveEpp-August2014.pdf

Benjamin, Andrea. (2015). Durham votes 2015 exit poll.sss

Benjamin, A. (2016). Co-ethnic endorsements and candidate preferences in local elections. *Urban Affairs Review*. doi:10.1177/1078087416644840

Benjamin, A. (2017). *Racial coalition building in local elections: Elite cues and cross-ethnic voting*. New York, NY: Cambridge University Press.

Benjamin, Reed. (2015a). Ricky Hart. *INDY Week* https://www.indyweek.com/ indyweek/ricky-l-hart/Content?oid=4756990

Benjamin, Reed. (2015b). Jillian Johnson.*INDY Week* https://www.indyweek.com/ indyweek/jillian-johnson/Content?oid=4756628

Benjamin, Reed. (2015c). Charlie Reece. *INDY Week* https://www.indyweek.com/ indyweek/charley-reece/Content?oid=4756575

Benjamin, Reed. (2015d). Steve Schewel. *INDY Week* https://www.indyweek.com/ indyweek/steve-schewel/Content?oid=4756621

Benjamin, Reed. (2015e). Michael Shiftlett. *INDY Week* https://www.indyweek.com/ indyweek/michael-mike-shiflett/Content?oid=4756985

Benjamin, Reed. (2015f). Robert T. Stephens. *INDY Week* https://www.indyweek.com/indyweek/robert-t-stephens/Content?oid=4756998

Boudreau, C., Elmendorf, C. S., & MacKenzie, S. A. (2015). Lost in space? Information shortcuts, spatial voting, and local government representation. *Political Research Quarterly, 68*(4), 843–855.

Bridges, V. (2015). Durham's probable-cause searches rise after consent policy is implemented. *The Herald-Sun*. Retrieved from http://www.newsobserver.com/news/ local/community/durham-news/article28025146.html#storylink=cpy

Bridges, V. (2017). Durham traffic stops, searches down; concerns about disparities continue. *The Herald-Sun*. Retrieved from http://www.heraldsun.com/news/local/ counties/durham-county/article149576884.html

Brown, Leslie. (2008). *Upbuilding Black Durham: Gender, class, and black community development in the Jim Crow south*. Chapel Hill, NC: University of North Carolina Press.

Browning, R. P., Marshall, D. R., & Tabb, D. (1984). *Protest is not enough: The struggle of blacks and Hispanics for equality in Urban politics*. Berkeley, CA: University of California Press.

Browning, R. P., Marshall, D. R., & Tabb, D. (Eds.). (1997). *Racial politics in American cities* (2d ed.). New York, NY: Longman.

Bullock, C. S. III, & Campbell, B. A. (1984). Racist or racial voting in the 1981 Atlanta municipal elections. *Urban Affairs Quarterly, 20*(2), 149–164.

Burns, P. F. (2006). *Electoral politics is not enough: Racial and ethnic minorities and Urban politics*. Albany, NY: State University of New York Press.

Campbell, A., Converse, P., Miller, W., & Stokes, D. (1960). *The American voter*. New York, NY: Wiley.

"City Quickfacts: Durham, N.C." (n.d.) *U.S. Census Bureau*. Retrieved from https://www.census.gov/quickfacts/fact/table/durhamcitynorthcarolina/PST045216

"Civilian Police Review Board" (n.d.) *City of Durham*. Retrieved from https://durhamnc.gov/277/Civilian-Police-Review-Board

DuBois, W. E. B. (1912). The upbuilding of Black Durham. The success of the negroes and their value to a tolerant and helpful Southern City. *World's Work, 23*, 334-338.

"Durham, NC. City Profile." (n.d.) *diversitydata.org*. Retrieved from http://www.diversitydata.org/Data/Profiles/Show.aspx?loc=440

"Durham, North Carolina (NC) Poverty rate Data Information about Poor and Low Income Residents." *City-Data.com*, City of Durham, 2015. Retrieved from http://www.city-data.com/poverty/poverty-Durham-North-Carolina.html.

Erikson, Robert S. (1976). The influence of newspaper endorsements in presidential elections:

The case of 1964. American Journal of Political Science 20(2), 207-33.

Flanigan, P. (1998, December 9). Durham voters say yes-62% usher in cut of council in 2001 to seven members. *Herald-Sun*, he (Durham, NC). Front Page: A1.

Florida, R. (2002, May). The rise of the creative class: Why cities without gays and rock bands are losing the economic development race. *Washington Monthly*.

Fraga, L. R., & Ramírez, R. (2003). Latino political incorporation in California, 1990–2000. In D. López & A. Jiménez (Eds.), *Latinos and public policy in California: An agenda for opportunity* (pp. 301–335). Berkeley, CA: Institute for Governmental Studies, University of California at Berkeley.

Frazier, E. F. (1992). Durham: The capital of the black middle class. In A. Locke (Ed.), *The new Negro: An interpretation* (pp. 331–341). New York, NY: Albert and Charles Boni, 1925. Reprint, New York, NY: Antheneneum/McMillan, 1992.

Gerber, E. R., & Phillips, J. H. (2003). Development ballot measures, interest group endorsements, and the political geography of growth preferences. *American Journal of Political Science, 47*, 625–639.

Hajnal, Z., & Trounstine, J. (2005). Why turnout does matter. *Journal of Politics, 67*(2), 515–535.

Hero, R. E. (1992). *Latinos and the U.S. political system. Two-tiered pluralism*. Philadelphia, PA: Temple University Press.

Johnson, J. (2015, September 31). Interview with Andrea Benjamin.

Keech, B. (1968). *The impact of Negro voting: The role of the vote in the quest for equality*. Chicago, IL: Rand McNally.

Krebs, T. B. (1998). The determinants of candidates' vote share and advantages of incumbency in city council elections. *American Journal of Political Science, 42(3)*, 921–935.

Lieske, J. (1989). The political dynamics of urban voting behavior. *American Journal of Political Science, 33*, 150–174.

Liu, Baodong. (2003). Deracialization and urban racial contexts. *Urban Affairs Review,* 38(4), 572-91.

Lupia, A. (1994). Shortcuts versus encyclopedias: Information and voting behavior in California Insurance reform elections. *American Political Science Review, 88(1),* 63–76.

Mayorga-Gallo, S. (2014). *Behind the white picket fence: Power and privilege in a multiethnic neighborhood.* Chapel Hill, NC: University of North Carolina Press.

McClain, P., Carter, N. M., DeFrancesco Soto, V. M., Grynaviski, J. D., Nunnally, S. C., Scotto, … Cotton, K. D. (2006). Racial distancing in a southern city: Latino immigrants' views of Black Americans. *Journal of Politics, 68*, 571–584.

Mollenkopf, J. H. (2003). New York: Still the great anomaly. In R. P. Browning, D. R. Marshall, & D. Tabb (Eds.). *Racial politics in American cities* (3rd ed., pp. 115–141). New York, NY: Longman Publications.

Pattillo, M. (2017, February 1). The future of black metropolis. The Race Workshop at Duke University. Lecture.

People's Alliance. (2015). People's Alliance PAC 2015 Endorsements. https://www. peoplesalliancepac.org/2015_endorsements

Valentine, G. (2008). Living with difference: Reflections on geographies of encounter. *Progress in Human Geography, 32,* 321–335.

Walton, H., Jr. (1972). *Black politics. A theoretical and structural analysis.* Philadelphia, PA: Lippencott Press.

Washington, B. T. (1911). Durham, North Carolina: A City of Negro enterprise. *Independent, 70,* 644–648.

Willets, S. (2017a). Durham county has an Eviction Crisis. Can a new diversion program help? *The Independent Weekly Online.* Retrieved from https://www.indyweek.com/indy week/durham-county-has-an-eviction-crisis-can-a-new-diversion-program-help/ Content?oid=7102818

Willets, S. (2017b). Mayor bill bell has overseen a bull city renaissance. So why has Durham's poverty rate gone up on his watch? *The Independent Weekly Online.* Retrieved from https://www.indyweek.com/indyweek/mayor-bill-bell-has-overseen-a-bull-city-renaissance-so-why-has-durhams-poverty-rate-gone-up-on-his-watch/ Content?oid=6711289

Wise, J. (2014). Police will need written consent for most searches come Oct. 1. *The Herald-Sun.* Retrieved from http://www.newsobserver.com/news/local/community/ durham-news/article10064414.html#storylink=cpy

PART III

Keeping Up with the Joneses

The Politics of Black Suburbanites

5

THE NEEDLES IN THE HAYSTACK

Assessing the Effects of Time, Place, and Class on Blacks in Majority-White Suburbs

Ernest B. McGowen III

Following the removal of *de jure* race-based discriminatory barriers in the Civil Rights Act of 1964, scholars began to examine and speculate on the prospects for Black progress. It soon became apparent that two tracks were emerging. One group—that scholars generally labeled the Black middle class—capitalized on this newfound access to educational and occupational opportunities and began to improve their socioeconomic situation. The other, larger segment of the group did not see the same progress, and scholars began to describe this group as an underclass, a label to denote a situation worse than even the working lower class.[1] One of the clearest delineators between the groups was the neighborhood where they resided. Once constrained to substandard neighborhoods by law and custom, middle-class African Americans in large metropolitan cities were increasingly able to move out of the substandard inner-city neighborhoods into more prestigious areas characterized by single-family homes. These neighborhoods, still in the city, were being vacated by the white ethnics who now had the chance to move into the newly built suburbs. The places where the Black middle class resided were termed "Black belt" suburbs since they surrounded the poorer Black neighborhoods. For the African Americans that remained in inner-city neighborhoods, federal, state, and local governments' solution to their subpar conditions was to construct multifamily public housing, built not for aesthetics or community development but for efficiency—effectively ensuring that racial residential segregation would continue.

Though the Black middle class was often believed to be more respectable (see Frazier, 1957), and there was a large diversity of opinions that was delineated on class, ideological, and gender lines, scholars speculated that this geographic and socioeconomic separation, and the different life circumstances they produced, would exacerbate divergent racial opinions and political behaviors among Blacks. That is to say, scholars, the most prominent being William

Julius Wilson (1978), predicted that class would take a predominant role in dictating the life chances, opportunity structure, and tastes of those who were now afforded the opportunity to increase their occupational and educational prestige, thereby lessening their commitment to a racial agenda in favor of more self-interested class interests.

Contemporary data suggests this divergence has not yet happened, and more specifically, the *prima facie* evidence of the 1980s and 1990s was just that—*prima facie*. Using a theory rooted in the power of place, this chapter seeks to answer why. In short, research proposing said shift in opinion given the ostensible declining significance in race misses one key element that separates early Black-belt suburbanites from those in majority-white suburbs today: the effect of finding oneself most often in majority-white social networks, such as the neighborhood and workplace.

This chapter will examine whether the proposed separation based on class (that appears not to have materialized contemporarily) failed to account for the fact that as the Black middle class continued to thrive, and barriers to their residential mobility lessened, they would begin to live, work, and therefore socialize in majority-white settings. These settings heighten the salience of racial identity and may make African Americans in them more racially radical (McGowen, 2017). Luckily, the National Black Election Studies for 1984, 1988, and 1996 will allow us to test the racial makeup proposition on the very African Americans that Wilson, and later Michael Dawson (1994), were examining.

I find that while African Americans in white neighborhoods are more affluent and educated, in most cases they are just as liberal and appear more group-conscious than those in majority-Black neighborhoods. On the vast majority of issues—from race relations to policy preferences—there is no statistical difference between them and African Americans in majority-Black areas. However, on certain key issues, such as whether Blacks should shop in Black stores or support for affirmative action, there are differences, but not in the direction Wilson (1978) predicted. From opinions on group-conscious norms to group-based political behavior and policy preferences, African Americans who lived in white neighborhoods during the 1980s and 1990s are actually more racially radical than their majority-Black neighborhood counterparts.

As stated earlier, living and working in majority-white areas means the majority of one's interactions, save for the immediate household, are majority-white. The neighbors with whom you share a fence, the coworkers with whom you share lunch, the small talk before the PTA meeting or in the line at the grocery store, are likely to be in settings where an African American, Latinx, or Asian American is in the racial/ethnic minority. When discussions in these networks turn to political (or more acutely racial) issues, the differences in opinion and ideology will likely appear.

A long lineage of research shows that one's social networks—the people with whom an individual interacts—will influence opinions and behaviors.

The literature suggests the basic human desire for inclusion and to avoid conflict will make network participants adjust their opinions to conform to the group norm (Berelson, Lazarsfeld & McPhee, 1954; Huckfeldt, Plutzer & Sprague, 1993; Huckfeldt & Sprague, 1995; McClurg, 2006; Scott, 2012; Scheufele et al., 2004). As Gay (2004) and others make plain, the racial makeup of one's social context is important because it determines one's social interactions (see also Eveland & Hively, 2009; Huckfeldt & Sprague, 1995; Huckfeldt & Mendez, 2008; Ibarra, 1995; Kossinets & Watts, 2009). Those who hold divergent opinions feel uncomfortable, as the network is most often based on (some) commonality, if not affinity (Huckfeldt et al., 2004; McClurg, 2006). One's neighbors all live in the same place, coworkers all work for the same organization, the members of a recreational basketball team all play the same sport. However, even when the nature of association categorizes people into the same group on one dimension, there are other dimensions where they differ. The basketball team may have tall and short members, the coworkers may be male and female, etc. This is also the case with race. The literature shows that most networks are racially homogeneous (McPherson, Smith-Lovin, & Cook, 2001). As such, the newly affluent African American who is moving into an all-white neighborhood or gaining employment in a newly integrated workplace may share some characteristics with others, but on perhaps the most salient one, race, they will always be seen as different. One way to gain acceptance in the group may be to show that while one's race is different, one's opinions on politics, and especially racial issues, are not.

While minority status has been studied in terms of familial ties and religion (Huckfeldt & Sprague, 1995) and party affiliation (Eveland & Hively, 2009), as McPherson et al. (2001) assert, race is by far the most salient demographic. To the best of my knowledge, scholars have not yet studied the political effect of the racial makeup of Blacks' social networks. My research finds that the racially conservative norms presented in majority-white neighborhood and workplace networks—for example, the illegitimacy of NFL protests or the culpability of Black males in their encounters with police—are rejected by group-conscious African Americans in white networks in the twenty-first century. Not only do they express opinions closer to urban Blacks, they will engage in participatory behaviors like working specifically for African American campaigns or volunteering through Black churches or civil rights organizations to aid majority-Black areas (McGowen, 2017). Looking retrospectively, it will be fascinating to see if this same mechanism was at work more than 35 years ago when Blacks first took the opportunity to integrate predominately and historically white suburbs.

The State of Black America in the 1980s and 1990s

William Julius Wilson published his famous book *The Declining Significance of Race* in 1978. It that book, its 1987 follow-up, *The Truly Disadvantaged*, and the recent 2011 revisit of the thesis, he postulates as to how Black class separation may occur. He argues that as African Americans are afforded opportunities in employment sectors from which they were previously excluded, there will be an economic separation from other African Americans in the urban poor who are not able to acquire the skills necessary for those jobs. Wilson's contention was that government policies designed for Black uplift that are only focused on social ills will not address the unique economic concerns of the Black underclass and, therefore, not improve their life situations (Wilson, 1987). An underlying concern of his work was to ascertain whether affluent, middle-class Blacks would lose concern for their poorest group members, as they faced fewer race-based barriers. Predicting that their policy preferences would shift from race-based to economic, Wilson (1987) suggested that upwardly mobile Blacks would have less support for the redistributive policies that their less well-off African American counterparts would need.

Such a postulation was understandable at the time. Many of the components that might lead Blacks to take on a similar line of assimilation into the mainstream as European immigrants existed. The country was only a decade removed from the Civil Rights Act and Voting Rights Act, and African Americans continued to migrate north to situations that, while imperfect, were better than life in the Jim Crow South. According to the Pew Research Center, between 1964 and Wilson's 1978 publication, the proportion of all African Americans who had graduated high school jumped 21 points, from just 27% to 49% (Pew Research Center, 2013). In the same time period, the African American median income rose by more than a third ($8,252) from $23,940 (1967) to $32,192 (1978). For reference, in the same timeframe, white high school graduation rose by 18%–69% and income rose by $12,207 to $55,507. However, this rising tide did not lift all boats. In 1978, the African American poverty rate was still 30.6% (compared to only 7.9% for whites). More than 15 years later, in the post-Reagan 1990s, racial inequality was still a concern for those invested in Black uplift, particularly as African Americans of different classes seemed headed down a splintered path, both economically and geographically.

Even the casual observer could see the different portrayals of the groups in popular culture and academic research. Colloquially referred to as the *Cosby effect*, the increasing educational and occupational success of some African Americans like the fictional Cosby family (in combination with major policy changes, such as the Voting Rights Act, Civil Rights Act, and affirmative action), allowed whites to view racism as a thing of the past, or a small barrier that could be overcome with hard work (Larson, 2006). Unfortunately, this begets the logic that those who did not succeed were not working hard. At the same time, the face of criminality and welfare dependence was becoming increasingly Black with African Americans shown as (violent) criminals more so than other races (Dixon, 2015; Dixon & Linz, 2000) and most often shown in media depictions as the nonworking poor (Gilens, 1996).

Language usage even evolved to show two Black Americas. A 2015 piece titled "A Rose by any other Name? The Consequences of Subtyping 'African Americans' from 'Blacks'" (Hall, Phillips, & Townsend, 2015) found that the media uses different terms for group members depending on the subject matter. Newspaper paragraphs that employed the term "Black" were associated with negative emotions compared to those that used "African American." Furthermore, the primary association with the word Black was anger as opposed to emotions like anxiety or sadness. Possibly more impactful—or maybe a consequence of the newspaper content—is the fact that experiment participants associated people referred to as Black with less warmth, perceived them to be of a lower status, and projected them as having a lower salary, lower education level, and a less prestigious job. Taken together, the Black middle class was seeing their economic fortunes move them further away from other less fortunate African Americans, and the (white) American imagination reinscribed that shift and separation.

A central question of Black Politics research in the 1980s and 1990s was "Would the split between the 'two Black Americans' continue to grow?" The four major underlying assumptions guided some people's thinking at that time were multifaceted and cumulatively adverse for the Black urban poor. First, it was presumed that increasing socioeconomic status for the Black middle class would lead to full social/political/economic integration of Blacks into the white mainstream and white social networks. Second, some presumed that class matters would trump the Black middle class' racial anxieties, or at least adjust the relative salience of each. A third assumption was that attitudes of Blacks were shaped by ghetto living or living among too many poor Black people (see The 1965 "Moynihan Report"), rather than by reactions to the reality of a larger racialized social system/structural racism. Finally, it was assumed that Blacks would follow the assimilation path of white ethnic groups.

Michael Dawson attempted to answer that question using the same 1984 and 1988 National Black Election Studies analyzed in this chapter. In *Behind the Mule* (1994), he found that there was ideological and opinion cohesion between the different classes of African Americans because there was a strong sense of racial group consciousness among African Americans at all class levels. This sense of linked fate caused them to evaluate policies from a racial (as opposed to an economic self-interest) lens. However, he suggested that we may see a lessening of racial identity among the Black middle class if they no longer have information about the state of Black society, particularly as they move away from the Black communities and, therefore, have less access to the historical institutions that "reinforce the political salience of racial interests" (Dawson, 1994, p. 11).

One year later, writing in an edited volume titled *The Black Public Sphere*, Dawson (1995) delved further into his postulation about historic counterpublic institutions. The Black counterpublic is the broad term scholars use to describe parallel institutions African Americans set up because they were not welcomed into those of the mainstream. White society created (segregated) churches, volunteer organizations, fraternal organizations, newspapers, etc., and so African Americans set up their own forms of these institutions due to their exclusion. Many of these Black institutions espoused a norm of Black uplift and cohesion, a norm so strong that in the half century following Emancipation, it muted class differences in policy preferences among Blacks. Dawson (1995) writes that systematic attempts in the 1990s by the white political establishment to delegitimize Black-specific grievances as well as a declining sense of urgency for racial problems felt by the Black middle class served to erode these institutions; the sharpness of these institutions' rhetoric and goals dulled, and financial resources and proportion of affluent participants declined. He goes on to suggest that if the deterioration of Black counterpublics continued, the effect may manifest in class differences, as the norm of muting one's (material) self-interest will no longer direct Black middle-class behaviors.

In the same volume, Steven Gregory (1995) gives a slightly different reason for a presumed divergence, one that deals with place. Gregory notes that as increased socioeconomic gains by some Blacks allowed them to move into more prestigious neighborhoods, society imposed a simultaneous change in acceptable political discourse and the proper avenues for Blacks to exert their racial preferences. Specifically, acceptable avenues to express political opposition were shifting from "unconventional" behaviors like protests, marches, or social disruptions (which were increasingly scaring white Americans following the urban riots of previous decades) to more bureaucratic institutions and procedures with entities set up at the hyper-local level. Meanwhile, as America moved further from the Civil Rights Movement, whites on the left and right of the political spectrum were less likely to embrace racial discussions of disparate treatment. Gregory (1995) explains that the confluence of these dynamics shifted the issues that Black suburban residents contested at the local level to things like low property taxes and zoning controls. This was because the largely white bureaucracy no longer deemed racial issues as urgent or important; or, they felt they had effectively solved these concerns with the Civil and Voting Rights Acts. Additionally, since competition for government resources was now superficially based on economics rather than race, this meant that not only were Black middle-class suburbanites' issues of importance different from poor Black people (who were largely renters in public housing) but also political contestation occurred in places where the Black urban poor neither had standing nor where governments would design policies to address their unique economic needs.

The rifts that both Dawson (1994, 1995) and Gregory (1995) noted were so prominent that Dawson (2001) believed that they constituted a reawakened strand of African American ideology: Black conservatism. He writes that the ideology had come back to prominence following the election of Ronald

Reagan. Its focus is on economic rather than political or social solutions to Black uplift, usually with market—not government—based policies. A key crux of this ideology is the belief Blacks have not "suffered *special* oppression and deserve special consideration" (Dawson, 2001, p. 20, emphasis added). Clearly, these are the African Americans that Wilson predicted would come to the forefront. If there is a correlation between such an ideology and higher socioeconomic status then the divergent paths seem more than plausible.

Dawson's (1994) did, indeed, find that more affluent Blacks in the National Black Election Study (NBES) surveys were less likely to support policies like welfare and economic redistribution.

Both camps based their predictions on the underlying assumption that fewer race-based barriers would mean increased white acceptance of middle-class Blacks, particularly by embracing them in their neighborhoods, social networks, and institutions. However, this does not appear to have been the case. It soon became apparent that while overt comments about Black inferiority or state-sanctioned discrimination were out of bounds (thereby showing racial "progress"), whites still held a strong "resentment" toward African American claims for further state-sponsored redress of their situation beyond simple removal of barriers. Donald Kinder and Lynn Sanders's *Divided by Color* (1996) centers on the idea and theory of racial resentment.[2] They find that whites are more likely to frame their opinions about Blacks based on a supposed lack of individualism and work ethic (e.g., "It's really a matter of some people not trying hard enough; if Blacks would only try harder they could be just as well-off as whites") (Kinder & Sanders, 1996, p. 106). While these sentiments could be legitimate expressions of individualism or principled conservative opposition to redistribution (as argued by Sniderman & Carmines, 1997), Kinder and Sanders (1996) suggest that these not simply race-neutral, policy-based opinions for a number of reasons. First, people who have high levels of racial resentment are less receptive to redistributive policies when the subjects of those policies are described as Black (as opposed to unspecified racial groups). Second, racially resentful people also oppose policies directed at Blacks on seemingly conflicting issue dimensions. For example, there is no reason to think an individual who believes African Americans could advance in society through hard work would also think Blacks have gotten more than they deserve from America *and* that discrimination is not an impediment to Blacks' life chances. Yet those high on the racial resentment scale do just that. Third, they find that the expression of racial resentment is lower when the survey interviewer is African American. Finally, those high on the scale are more likely to say African Americans are lazy, less intelligent, and more violent, while those on the lower end of the resentment scale do not hold these sentiments.

Writing about the history of race opinion in the US, Bobo, Charles, Krysan, and Simmons (2012) describe a study taken a decade after the NBES surveys (in 2000); there, whites still expressed negative feelings about African Americans who may even be their neighbors. In the study, one in five whites preferred a neighborhood that was all white and one in four created a fictional one with no Blacks (see Charles, 2003). Whites continue to believe Blacks' concerns to be illegitimate; sizable numbers of whites think their group is more intelligent than Blacks, and many believe a "lack of motivation or willpower" to be a larger explanation of the Black plight than racial discrimination.

The African Americans in white neighborhoods who I studied for this chapter were likely to have daily interactions with whites who hold these well-documented attitudes, as a nontrivial portion of one's neighbors and coworkers clearly held these views. It would not be a stretch to imagine that whites expressed such sentiments in social conversations, especially if one subscribes to the idea that a small segment of Blacks are in their situation because they did all the "right" things while most have not. As Bobo et al. assert, "Contemporary negative views of Blacks have a gradational or qualified, rather than categorical, character," and further explain that their data show "both significant progressive changes regarding race, as well as substantial enduring frictions and conflicts that continue to make race such fraught terrain" (2012, p. 75, p41).

Indeed, in the face of contemporary race relations, Dawson—and even Wilson—have reexamined and even slightly revised their predictions. In 2012, Dawson wrote that "although economic polarization among African Americans has indeed increased over the past thirty years, such class conflicts have not undermined many aspects of African American political unity … racial affiliation continues to be a decisive political identification" (p. 1). In a revision to his earlier work, Wilson (2011) asserts that evaluations of his previous research as having a naive belief that race will no longer matter or that the declining significance of race will have opinion and voting (as opposed to policy) consequences is a misreading. Instead, Wilson (2011) emphasizes that his argument, at the time, asserted that race was declining in significance in the economic sector and moving to the sociopolitical sector; therefore, economic policies directed at poorer African Americans may not have support among the Black middle class.

The Power of Place

The previous discussion is not to suggest Wilson was the only scholar predicting a class split in the African American community, and to be fair, Wilson's and Dawson's evidence was solid, but perhaps only temporally relevant. Scholars like Allen, Dawson, and Brown (1989) showed that African Americans of higher socioeconomic status were less supportive of Black political autonomy and felt more distant from the Black masses. Others found that higher socioeconomic status (SES) African Americans had lower levels group attachment (Demo & Hughes, 1990), were less likely to identify strongly with the race (Tate, 1994), and had lower support for policies like affirmative action (Dawson, 1994). Class differences were clear, as was (preliminary) evidence of division on opinion and policy preferences.

Yet, as economic differences between Blacks have grown (see Wilson, 2011), their contemporary feelings on these issues, and others dealing more generally with race look very similar. This chapter questions whether focusing primarily on class differences overlooked the necessity of an analysis on an important mechanism that has great potential to drive a wedge between Blacks: place.

Place is important for multiple reasons—some tangential to class.[3] First, place matters because it structures municipal boundaries and resource allocation. Oliver (2001) explains that one of the primary reasons for the intentional creation of the suburbs is that more affluent (white) residents did not want their tax dollars going to political machines and therefore white ethnics.[4] Second, these neighborhoods also structure available political behavior opportunities. If one's political jurisdiction is predominately white and economically affluent, political competitors neither need to address race nor consider ways to improve the poor Blacks' well-being. There is even evidence that suburban African Americans do not vote in their local congressional elections as much as suburban whites or urban African Americans likely because the issues that are most relevant to them are not addressed (McGowen, 2017).

Third, the racial makeup of a neighborhood can have particular effects on racial identity, dependent upon minority or majority status. Integrated neighborhoods seem to have a particularly negative effect on whites, leading them to not treat their Black neighbors well or make them feel particularly comfortable (see also Mayorga-Gallo in this volume). Research has shown having African American neighbors promotes racial animosity among whites already living there (Brief et al., 2005; Oliver, 2010) and increases the perceived threat of Blacks (Dixon 2006) (though Oliver and Mendelburg, 2000, find that this threat can be lessened if the SES of both groups is equal – which numerous scholars like Alba, Logan, and Stults, 2000, show is rarely the case).

The effects on the African Americans who live in integrated neighborhoods are also impactful. African Americans in white neighborhoods have been found to have heightened perceptions of discrimination (Gay, 2004), increased racial consciousness (Oliver, 2001), stronger feelings of racial alienation (Bobo & Hutchings, 1996), and they will, depending on the level of group consciousness, reject the norms of the neighborhood and work toward more group-based solutions (McGowen, 2017).

Fourth, place—particularly suburban residence—is important because it structures the people you encounter most often, which, in turn, determines the social and political norms to which you are exposed, and ultimately your calculations of salient behaviors. Living in the suburbs means you are more likely to encounter social networks where the racial makeup—and therefore one's minority status—is predetermined. This was not always the case for African Americans. In short, there was little reason to study the *network* effects of Black suburban residence in the 1980s and early 1990s because the Black-belt "suburbs" weren't actually that far from the inner city.

Geographic proximity between inner-city and Black-belt African Americans meant both groups were still in majority-Black social networks, institutions, and political jurisdictions, but work on these Black-belt suburbs does highlight some minor class differences. Pattillo-McCoy (2000), for example, finds that Black suburban residence led to different social circles based on class and produced a unique hybrid culture with old customs like Black church participation and new, more expensive, customs like cotillions. There was also conflict over the location of community institutions, such as the YMCA, and the sites of new public housing units because they would attract lower class Blacks to the area. Middle-class Black suburbanites believed both would place a stigma on the suburb and its residents (Haynes, 2001). In some cases, suburban African Americans even sided with the white political establishment over less affluent inner-city Blacks in effort to get the government to allocate resources to more property-based issues (Johnson, 2002).

However, in each instance, the inner-city and Black-belt suburb neighborhoods were geographically contiguous. As such, even Black suburbanites would likely have majority-Black social networks. They would also be in close proximity to, and therefore likely frequent, Black counterpublic institutions. Both suggest that the prevailing norms and subsequent behaviors of those Black suburbanites would be pro-Black. The extant research largely studies Black-belters, not the small population of Blacks who lived in predominately white neighborhoods in the 1980s and 1990s. I will examine them in this chapter because they are the group that scholars theorized about—Blacks who are significantly removed from predominately Black communities and the Black counterpublic—but did not necessarily study, in part due to their small size and the difficulty (and expense) of attaining data on them in high-quality, nationally representative surveys.

Theory and Hypotheses

In social networks, political, economic, and socially dominant groups shape norms and expectation for acceptable behaviors. In a majority-white environment, be it now or three decades ago, we would expect the prevailing norm to be conservative on racial issues with expressions rooted in resentment (Bobo et al., 2012; Bonilla-Silva, Goar & Embrick, 2006). This could make affluent suburban African Americans with high levels of racial identity uncomfortable with the proffered norms in their most encountered social network situations (as one spends most of their time in the neighborhood or workplace). Imagine being the only African American in a majority-white lunchroom or block party setting and the topic of Black grievance comes up. The choice is either to adhere to the prevailing norm and appear to conform—as one's race is already conspicuous—or (as my research in the contemporary context finds) reject those norms and seek out more racially reinforcing places (McGowen, 2017). We know that contemporary African Americans in majority-white suburban neighborhoods reject those norms on racial issues—as evidenced by their quite divergent opinions from their white neighbors and coworkers. The question is whether our 1980s and 1990s respondents behaved in similar ways.

Again, while the extant literature provides a great deal of knowledge about the political outcomes that arose from increased socioeconomic diversity among Blacks, scholars were neither focused on the unique role of place nor, more specifically, the effect of living in a majority-white area. I return to the question of whether upward mobility *as well as* social and physical distance increased these folks' predilection toward conservatism. I argue that African Americans who primarily navigate white spaces have always acutely felt their racial minority status and, therefore, are likely to reject white (political) norms. We just did not know we should be looking at them.

I hypothesize that African Americans in white neighborhoods in the 1980s and 1990s will not show an opinion separation from those in majority-Black neighborhoods on racial questions, and in some cases, it is likely that Blacks who live in predominately white neighborhoods will reveal more racially radical attitudes. I also predict that on some questions that reinforce the respondent's geographic separation from majority-Black areas, such as the ability to shop in Black stores, Black come-outers (a term borrowed from Rogers in this volume) will have more racially radical opinions than Blacks who reside in predominately Black neighborhoods.

However, support for those actions is different from actually engaging in them. On questions gauging participation, I expect the participation of Blacks who live in predominately white neighborhoods to be lower precisely due to geographic distance, particularly participation in behaviors that are constrained to the inner city or will come with a stronger (majority-white social network) sanction (i.e., unconventional political activities).

I examine data that was collected over the course of a dozen years. In that short amount of time, the Black community went from rising SES gains and the galvanizing presidential campaign of Jesse Jackson to the rise of the Republican Right, the Clinton crackdown on crime and welfare, and data showing that early economic gains had stagnated for middle-class Blacks (but not middle-class whites). The historical contexts are likely to have a particular effect on racial identity and, therefore, the potential rift between Blacks who live in predominately white neighborhoods and those who do not, but I hypothesize that by 1996, the idea of full integration in white society would appear less likely for Blacks in all neighborhoods, and, therefore, we will continue to see the same unity between both groups.

Data and Design

One reason why we may see Wilson's predicted divergence of opinion is methodological. When securing survey respondents of a certain demographic, the most efficient use of resources is to sample in the places where they are concentrated. Scholars refer to this as cluster sampling. With the historic *de jure* and *de facto* segregation of African Americans and whites in separate neighborhoods, researchers can easily identify those areas of concentration. The NBESs use this cluster sampling technique. Before the days of cellular phones and number portability, telephone numbers indicated geographical location. In addition to the area code, the first three numbers of a phone number—called an exchange— roughly indicated the neighborhood where the telephone was located. The potential problem with this technique is that African American respondents in majority-Black neighborhoods may have different opinions and behaviors than African Americans in other types of neighborhoods.

While suboptimal, the overrepresentation of African Americans from majority-Black neighborhoods may be one of practical necessity. As Tate (2004) describes in the introduction to the 1996 NBES, interviews in majority-white areas cost four times as much as in majority-Black areas. Think of knocking on four doors or calling four telephone numbers but only being able to interview one respondent—the costs of the first three contacts are wasted. These disparities by neighborhood mean there are fewer African American respondents from these neighborhoods than are represented in society. The solution: let the opinions of every African American in a white area count three times more. While this type of sample weighing is an uncontroversial convention in all surveys, it means that the 25 African Americans they contacted in 1996 may be particularly conservative and have their opinions overrepresented.

Contemporarily, there has been a more concerted effort to oversample African American and other racial/ethnic minority populations, as was undertaken in the 2008 American National Election Study. Given the increasing geographic diversity of African Americans, particularly in the suburbs of major urban areas, studies are showing better balance geographically. Unfortunately, most of these studies are not specific to African Americans, so their share of the total respondent pool is still low. Evolving contacting methods may help solve these problems, especially as disparities in internet access based on race, income, or education lessen. For example, the online 2016 Collaborative Multiracial Post-Election Survey boasts 3,102 African American respondents and geographic coding to pinpoint neighborhood type without the subjectivity of self-reporting.

To test whether these differences in opinion exist and if they get larger or smaller over time, I will examine common questions in each of the three NBES surveys and compare respondents in two areas (see Table 5.1). For 1984 and 1988, respondents in high Black areas (Strata 1) are compared with respondents in low Black density areas (Strata 3). For the 1996 NBES, which added a fourth stratum, respondents in standard metropolitan statistical areas (SMSAs) with populations of 1 million or more and Black populations of 15% or more (Strata 1) are compared with respondents in areas with Black populations less than 5% (Strata 4).

TABLE 5.1 Stratum by Survey

Strata	1984 & 1988	1996
1	High Black density – telephone exchanges in all SMSAs with Black population density of 15% or more	MSAs with population of 1 million or more and Black populations of 15% or more
2	Medium Black density – telephone exchanges in small SMSAs and non-SMSAs in AL, FL, GA, LA, MS, SC, and VA	The southern states (AL, FL, GA, LA, MS, SC, and VA), excluding the MSAs that fall into Strata 1
3	Low Black density – all remaining telephone exchanges	Telephone exchanges serving the remaining continental US with 5% or greater Black population
4		All remaining telephone exchanges in the continental United States with Black populations less than 5% ⋆Strata 3 and 4 are essentially the 1984s NBES's third stratum split into two

Note. SMSA = standard metropolitan statistical areas; AL = Alabama; FL = Florida; GA = Georgia; LA = Los Angeles; MS = Massachusetts; SC = South Carolina; VA = Virginia.

The analysis was restricted to questions that directly pertain to racial ideology. Table 5.2 outlines the questions I analyzed (see Table 5.2). In order to gain a global sense of the differences that arose between Blacks who live in predominately white neighborhoods and those who live in high-density Black neighborhoods, I do a series of T-tests of mean differences. I then further investigate those that show statistically significant differences by using ordinal or logistic regressions, which include statistical controls for income, education, ideology, group consciousness, and age.

In 1984 and 1988, the survey measures income in increments of $10,000 and $5,000 respectively between "less than $9,999" and "more than $40,000"; the average income is in the $10,000–$20,000 range in 1984. In 1988, the average range is $20,000–$30,000. The surveys measure education on a five-point scale, ranging from "8 grades or less" to "University/College degree." The averages for 1984 and 1988 were between "High school diploma or equivalency" and "some college." I used the seven-point scale for ideology ranging from strong liberal to strong conservative, and in both years, the averages were between "moderate" and "moderate slightly liberal."[5]

The survey measured group consciousness with the question, "Do you think what happens generally to Black people in this country will have something to do with what happens in your life (Yes or No)?" All respondents register well over the midpoint of the question. Particularly in terms of ideology and group consciousness, it appears place may have a liberalizing effect on the Black respondents that live there.

TABLE 5.2 Variable List by Survey

1984 & 1988 NBES	Black people who have "made it" are doing a lot to improve the social and economic position of poor Blacks.
	(Strongly agree, somewhat agree, somewhat disagree, strongly disagree, not sure/don't know)
	Blacks should always vote for Black candidates when they run.
	(Strongly agree, agree, disagree, strongly disagree, don't care/don't know)
	Do you think Blacks should form their own political party?
	(Yes, no, don't know)
	Do you think that the movement for Black rights has affected you personally?
	(Yes, no, don't know)
	Black people should shop in Black-owned stores whenever possible.
	(Strongly agree, somewhat agree, somewhat disagree, strongly disagree, not sure/don't know)
	In the last 5 years have you ever... Attended a protest meeting or a demonstration?
	(Yes, no, don't know)
	Because of past discrimination, minorities should be given special consideration when decisions are made about hiring applicants for jobs.
	(Strongly agree, somewhat agree, somewhat disagree, strongly disagree, not sure/don't know)
	Should federal spending on food stamps be increased, decreased, or kept about the same?
	(Increased, kept about the same, decreased, don't know)
1996 NBES	Blacks should always vote for Black candidates when they run.
	(Strongly agree, agree, disagree, strongly disagree, don't care/don't know)
	Should federal spending on food stamps be increased, decreased, or kept about the same?
	(Increased, same, decreased, don't know)

The control variables are the same in 1996; however, some of the measurements differ. Income ranges between "up to $10,000" to "$105,000 and more" in increasingly larger increments at higher income levels. The average for the majority-Black stratum is between $25,000–$30,000 and $30,000–$40,000 for the majority-white stratum. The instrument measures education on a nine-point scale between "grade school (grades 1–8)" and "doctorate/law degree," the average of which is between "some college, no degree" and "associates/2 year degree." Group consciousness is now a four-point scale (strongly agree, somewhat agree, somewhat disagree, strongly disagree), and respondents maintain their high levels of agreement.

For simplicity, I standardized these measurements to a scale between 0 and 1. Much like their opinions and behaviors, the demographics between the two groups are similar, with those in white neighborhoods being slightly more affluent and generally more group-conscious, as shown in Table 5.3 (see Table 5.3).

TABLE 5.3 Relevant Demographics by Strata

	1984		1988		1996	
	Majority White	*Majority Black*	*Majority White*	*Majority Black*	*Majority White*	*Majority Black*
Income	0.275	0.272	0.607	0.458★	0.500	0.430+
	(0.258)	(0.241)	(0.399)	(0.403)	(0.385)	(0.272)
	348	515	186	221	42	480
Education	0.512	0.509	0.577	0.558	0.550	0.460★★
	(0.327)	(0.305)	(0.338)	(0.325)	(0.184)	(0.185)
	390	574	207	250	62	518
Ideology	0.506	0.559★	0.589	0.556	0.562	0.549
	(0.325)	(0.358)	(0.314)	(0.354)	(0.419)	(0.378)
	309	482	165	195	60	430
Group consciousness	0.769	0.753	0.811	0.754	0.637	0.666
	(0.421)	(0.431)	(0.391)	(0.431)	(0.354)	(0.352)
	378	552	207	240	62	507

Source: Data from 1984, 1988, & 1996 National Black Election Studies.

Note. Each entry includes the mean, the standard errors in parentheses, and the sample size. All variables were scaled between 1 and 0. Significant differences are between each stratum using an independent sample T-test. Higher means for ideology (seven-point scale in 1984 and 1988; three-point scale in 1996) indicate more liberal. Income in 1984 was measured in increments of $10,000, with the highest category being "$40,000 or more." The 1984 mean roughly corresponds to $10,000–$20,000. In 1988, it was measured in increments of $5000. The 1988 means for both strata roughly correspond to $20,000–$30,000.
$+ p > 0.10$; $★ p > 0.05$; $★★ p > 0.001$.

In addition to the regression outputs, I have also included predicted probabilities to summarize the results more clearly. A predicted probability takes the regression coefficient and the respondent values and calculates the probability of a particular respondent (in this case African Americans in majority-white or Black neighborhoods) choosing a particular category. In cases where there were four categories in the ordinal regression analysis (e.g., strongly agree, somewhat agree, somewhat disagree, strongly disagree), the predicted probabilities were collapsed into "agree" and "disagree" for the sake of simplicity.

Results

The results appear to confirm the hypotheses. As stated previously, on the vast majority of the means tests and the regressions, there is no statistical difference between African Americans in each type of neighborhood. While a null result does not preclude the fact that either group could have higher or lower values, it does mean that we cannot definitively rule out the idea that there is no difference between the two groups and, therefore, was no major separation on racial issues based on neighborhood racial makeup.

More importantly, on those questions that did show statistical differences, they were in the expected directions: African Americans in majority-white neighborhoods had more racially radical opinions than African Americans in majority-Black areas. The differences were also more consistent in the 1984 and 1988 panel study, as ten variables reached significance compared to only two in 1996. I will discuss whether this is a result of actual movement or the different methodologies in the subsequent section.

Full regressions with controls are available in Tables 5.4 and 5.5, and the corresponding predicted probabilities (see Figures 5.1 and 5.2) are quite prescriptive (see Tables 5.4 and 5.5). African Americans in white neighborhoods show an adherence to group-conscious norms, at times more than those in majority-Black neighborhoods. On the question of whether African Americans should vote for Black candidates whenever possible (1984), African Americans in white neighborhoods were 5% more likely to say yes (19.4%–14.7%). In 1988, this gap increases slightly (29.3%–23.9%). While these numbers may not seem terribly far apart, remember that the statistical controls mean the racial makeup of the neighborhood has an *independent* effect on the answer without regard to any other demographic variables. In other words, imagine two African Americans of the same age, with the same income, education, ideology, and group

TABLE 5.4 Neighborhood Residence Effects on Black Political Attitudes (1984 & 1988)

	Blacks Vote Black Candidates (1984)	Blacks Vote Black Candidates (1988)	Blacks Shop Black Stores (1988)	Blacks form Own Party (1984)	Black Movement Affect R (1988)
Black in white	0.479★	0.357	0.446	0.644★★	0.651★
neighborhood	(0.153)	(0.211)	(0.212)	(0.192)	(0.279)
Income	0.476★★	−0.559	1.420	−1.511★★	0.527
	(0.153)	(0.448)	(0.451)	(0.312)	(0.571)
Group	0.326	0.132	1.134	0.165	1.716★★
consciousness	(0.181)	(0.246)	(0.253)	(0.222)	(0.307)
Education	−0.285	−0.006	−0.415	−1.451★★	2.123★★
	(0.280)	(0.401)	(0.403)	(0.380)	(0.554)
Age	0.017★★	0.025★★	0.014	−0.030★★	0.004
	(0.005)	(0.007)	(0.007)	(0.006)	(0.009)
Ideology	−0.067	0.065	0.356	0.113★★	1.179★
	(0.215)	(0.320)	(0.321)	(0.192)	(0.408)
N	702	328	327	691	329
−2 Log likelihood	1469.891	779.907	762.092	708.857	328.652

Source: Data from 1984 and 1988 National Black Election Studies.

Note. ★ $p > 0.05$; ★★ $p > 0.001$.

TABLE 5.5 Neighborhood Residence Effects on Black Political Attitudes
(1984 & 1988)

	Increase Food Stamps (1984)	Participate in Protest (1988)	Support Affirmative Action (1984)	Blacks Help Other Blacks (1984)	Blacks Help Other Blacks (1988)
Black in white neighborhood	0.309*	−0.818*	0.291*	0.249	0.700**
	(0.155)	(0.362)	(0.143)	(0.144)	(0.220)
Income	−0.741*	0.143	−0.348	−0.381	−1.755**
	(0.242)	(0.751)	(0.223)	(0.229)	(0.475)
Group consciousness	0.792**	0.334	0.481*	−0.397*	0.234
	(0.182)	(0.450)	(0.169)	(0.170)	(0.252)
Education	−0.448	2.783**	0.093	−0.653*	0.316
	(0.282)	(0.665)	(0.261)	(0.269)	(0.413)
Age	−0.006	0.012	0.006	−0.001	−0.014*
	(0.005)	(0.012)	(0.004)	(0.004)	(0.007)
Ideology	0.667*	2.545	0.379	−0.009	0.491
	(0.218)	(0.665)	(0.201)	(0.201)	(0.329)
N	701	328	703	692	329
−2 Log likelihood	1275.723	221.249	1875.485	1842.082	730.240

Source: Data from 1984 and 1988 National Black Election Studies.

Note. $* p > 0.05$; $** p > 0.001$.

consciousness. The only thing that differs is the racial makeup of their neighborhood. In such a situation, the African American in the white neighborhood would be more likely to support Black candidates.

The trend continues when asked if Blacks should form their own party (1984); those in white neighborhoods had a probability of agreeing at 31% compared to 23.4% as well as on whether Blacks should shop in Black stores when possible (80.1% of Blacks in white neighborhood versus 67.3% for their counterparts). The same goes for whether the "Black movement" has affected the respondent; 71.7% of Blacks in white neighborhoods agreed compared to 58.8% of Blacks in predominately Black neighborhoods.

The data shows a similar relationship on policy and behavior questions. When asked whether food stamp funding (1984) should be increased, the probability of agreement for an African American in a white neighborhood was 49.7% compared to 45.2% for an African American in a Black neighborhood. The same goes for support for affirmative action (1984); African Americans in white neighborhoods had a 65% probability of support compared to 59.8% of African Americans in Black neighborhoods.

The question of whether "Black people who have 'made it' are doing a lot to improve the social and economic position of poor Blacks" produces an interesting result. In 1984, African Americans in white neighborhoods had a 52%

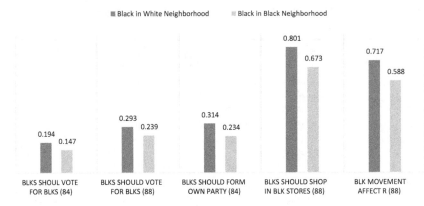

FIGURE 5.1   1984–1988 NBES Racial Opinion (1)
Source: Data from 1984 and 1988 National Black Election Panel Survey.

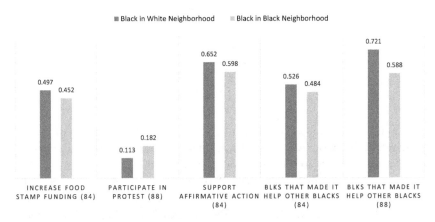

FIGURE 5.2   1984–1988 NBES Racial Opinion (2)
Source: Data from 1984 and 1988 National Black Election Panel Survey.

chance of agreeing compared to 48.4% for African Americans in Black neighborhoods. In 1988, this number jumped to 72.1% in white neighborhoods compared to 58.8% in Black neighborhoods. However, one can read this result in multiple ways. Were those in white neighborhoods just oblivious to the plight of those less fortunate and naively believe they had done enough or were they actually doing more than others and were therefore confident others were doing the same? The answer to this question is beyond the scope of the data, but it speaks to a debate that continues in Black communities across the country.

The only significant difference where Blacks in white neighborhoods were not more racially radical was when the respondent had attended a protest. Blacks in white neighborhoods were predicted to answer affirmatively at 11%

compared to 18.2% for Blacks in Black neighborhoods. One of the major logistical hurdles for a protest is having enough participants for it to seem impactful (and garner media attention) (McAdam, 1999). Protests are also likely more effective in proximity to the problem. As such, an African American in a white neighborhood may have a higher behavioral cost to attend a protest and the organizing institutions may not be mobilizing them to attend the event.

As stated earlier, there were only two significant differences—voting for Black candidates and attitudes about food stamps—in the 1996 survey, and both went in unexpected directions. When asked whether Blacks should vote for Blacks, the probability of an African American in a white neighborhood agreeing was only 6% compared to 10% for African Americans in Black neighborhoods. The data show the same relationship with food stamp funding, as the probability of Blacks in white neighborhoods agreeing was 7.6% compared to a full 20% for Blacks in Black neighborhoods (see Table 5.6).

The lack of significant differences could be for a variety of reasons, but the different methodologies may hold the answer. As stated earlier (see Table 5.1), the majority-white stratum in 1996 was much more restricted and therefore much smaller. This introduces the compounding problem: survey weights. To get a representative population, some groups have their scores "weighted up"—their response counts as more than one person. When there are too many of a certain demographic that one wants to make representative, those respondents' scores are "weighted down." The 25 Blacks in white neighborhoods in 1996 have their responses weighted up by 2.48 to get to 62 "people." While the weight of 3.0 is slightly higher in the 1984 and 1988 studies, they started with 131 people to get to 393. Both methods were important and necessary; however, at its core, we are examining 25 people versus 131.

Relatedly, while it may be tempting to compare the 1988 finding directly with the results from 1996 in order to suggest that there have been

TABLE 5.6 Neighborhood Residence Effects on Black Political Attitudes (1996)

	Blacks Vote Black Candidates	*Fund Food Stamps*
Black in white neighborhood	−0.621+ (0.337)	−1.033★ (0.342)
Income	−0.240 (0.460)	−0.534 (0.473)
Group consciousness	−0.006 (0.326)	0.888★ (0.341)
Education	0.450 (0.657)	−0.489 (0.680)
Age	0.004 (0.008)	0.005 (0.008)
Ideology	−0.188 (0.294)	0.498★ (0.303)
N	308	309
−2 Log likelihood	617.209	570.080

Source: Data from 1996 National Black Election Study.

Note. $+ p > 0.10$; $\star p > 0.05$; $\star\star p > 0.001$.

significant important changes in attitudes, we should resist. Due to the use of different methodologies, sampling methods, and numbers of respondents, we should constrain our conclusions to comparisons within surveys rather than across them.

Conclusion

It has been quite interesting and gratifying to peer back in time at this particular group of African Americans. Given the high prevalence of contemporary Blacks in the suburbs (some estimates place the figure above 50%), it is difficult for those of us in later generations to understand the social and racial environment of African Americans living in areas that are less than 5% Black fewer than 20 years from the height of the Civil Rights Movement and the assassination of Martin Luther King. It does not appear that such an environment and the new racial makeup of some social networks that these watershed moments helped to produce muted the salience of race on Black Americans' opinion and behavior—instead, it heightened it. The norms of group consciousness and, therefore, expressions of linked fate appear to have been working on these respondents and caused a rejection of the (likely) prevailing norms of their immediate surroundings.

Again, on the vast majority of issues tested, there was no statistical division between African Americans in each type of stratum. However, on certain dimensions, the data confirmed the hypothesis that African Americans in white neighborhoods would be more racially radical. We see the expected differences on racial opinions that pique group consciousness, like supporting Black candidates and businesses, on some behaviors like whether Blacks who are upwardly mobile are doing enough to help Blacks who are not (exactly the opposite of Wilson's dire premonition) and also on opinions about policies that should help the poor Black communities, like affirmative action or increasing food stamp funding. In each of these cases, our target African Americans appear to be more eager to help. This relationship does not appear to hold in 1996, but it is difficult to unpack whether this result is substantive or methodological.

None of this is to say Wilson and his contemporaries were incorrect in their assessment of the time. Had African Americans stayed in contiguous neighborhoods, or if race relations had taken a different turn—say, the subtle race-baiting of the late 1980s and early 1990s had been rejected, and whites became more comfortable with African Americans taking affirmative steps to achieve full equality—it is possible that the Black middle class would have deracialized their identity and behaviors. Yet, if the latter were necessary to produce the former, then it is understandable why we did not see that divergence then nor do we see it now for Blacks in suburban neighborhoods.

Moving forward, it will be interesting to see whether the particular dimensions of difference continue to hold. It is possible that the particular aspects of thought and behavior where differences arose—such as increased social spending, participation in Black counterpublic institutions, or privileging race-based participation like campaigning for a Black candidate— were temporally bound. This is especially true given the novelty (and resultant empowerment) of candidacies like Jesse Jackson and the increasing number of African Americans running for office in large municipalities. Further research would do well to test this idea on larger datasets with questions specifically designed to measure each of these disparate yet related dimensions.

One thing is clear: place matters; and solely viewing differences among Blacks of different classes may have missed an interesting driver of opinion cohesion that we continue to see, as more middle-class Blacks live and work in majority-white settings.

Notes

1 I should note that usage of this term was beyond a simple description of socioeconomic status. Scholars like William Julius Wilson more pointedly direct the term at the urban African American population in inner-city neighborhoods plagued by poor educational and occupational opportunities.

2 Racial resentment is an offshoot of Kinder and others' previous work on symbolic racism (see Kinder & Sears, 1981).

3 It is important to note that the concept of a "neighborhood" varies in the literature. It can range from explicit and exclusive geographical boundaries (that separate one neighborhood area from another and may determine things like separate neighborhood associations or school zoning) to more subjective concepts like living on the "Northside" or the "hipster" area that loosely denote a specific location. While these are not official designations, they still imply some group membership. Lastly, there are intangible individual level ideas of neighborhood where residents of a particular area feel a commonality and kinship to the point of planning social gatherings, like block parties or neighborhood garage sales, on that basis. While all three concepts are slightly different, for this project, the idea that all of these designations structure those with whom one is in social proximity, which in turn affects the salience of identities and influences behavior, is paramount.

4 While most of the history of the suburbs is about exclusion (first of white ethnics, then of racial and ethnic minorities) contemporarily, the racial homogeneity of certain "suburban" locales comes from whites moving even farther from the inner city (Frey, 2011). Defined as exurbs, these are areas lie within the 100 largest metropolitan areas, but have less than 25% of their population living in what the Census Bureau defines as urbanized areas. Relatedly, Fischer (2008) finds that the increasing suburban diversity is based less on black–white integration as it is the neighborhoods becoming more multiethnic.

5 It should be noted that there is often a disconnect between a respondent's stated ideology and their actual policy preferences (see Zaller, 1992 among others). The "moderate" label may not correspond to the respondents' actual policy preferences, especially on racial issues.

References

Alba, R., Logan, J., & Stults, B. J. (2000). How segregated are middle-class African Americans? *Social Problems, 47*(4), 543–558.

Allen, R. L., Dawson, M. C., & Brown, R. E. (1989). A schema-based approach to modeling an African-American racial belief system. *The American Political Science Review, 83*(2), 412–441.

Berelson, B. R., Lazarsfeld, P. F., & McPhee, W. N. (1954). *Voting.* Chicago, IL: University of Chicago Press.

Bobo, L., Charles, C. Z., Krysan, M., & Simmons, A. D. (2012). The real record on racial attitudes. In P. V. Marsden (Ed.), *Social trends in American life: Findings from the general social survey since 1972* (pp. 38–83). Princeton, NJ: Princeton University Press.

Bobo, L., & Hutchings, V. L. (1996). Perceptions of racial group competition: Extending Blumer's theory of group position to a multiracial social context. *American Sociological Review, 61*(6), 951–972.

Bonilla-Silva, E., Goar, C., & Embrick, D. G. (2006). When whites flock together: The social psychology of white habitus. *Critical Sociology, 32*(3–2), 229–253.

Brief, A. P., Umphress, E. E., Dietz, J., Burrows, J. W., Butz, R. M., & Scholten, L. (2005). Community matters: Realistic group conflict theory and the impact of diversity. *The Academy of Management Journal, 48*(5), 830–844.

Charles, C. Z. (2003). The dynamics of racial segregation. *Annual Review of Sociology, 29*, 167–207.

Dawson, M. C. (1994). *Behind the mule: Race and class in African-American politics.* Princeton, NJ: Princeton University Press.

Dawson, M. C. (1995). A black counterpublic? Economic earthquakes, racial agenda(s), and black politics. In The Black Public Sphere Collective (Ed.), *The Black Public Sphere* (pp. 199–227). Chicago, IL: University of Chicago Press.

Dawson, M. C. (2001). *Black visions.* Chicago, IL: University of Chicago Press.

Dawson, M. C. (2012). The black public sphere and black civil society. In L. D. Bobo, L. Crooms-Robinson, L. Darling-Hammond, M. C. Dawson, H. L. Gates, G. Jaynes, & C. Steele (Eds.), *The Oxford handbook of African American citizenship, 1865–present* (pp. 1–19). Oxford, England: Oxford University Press.

Demo, D. H., & Hughes, M. (1990). Socialization and racial identity among black Americans. *Social Psychology Quarterly, 53*(4), 364–374.

Dixon, J. C. (2006). The ties that bind and those that don't: Toward reconciling group threat and contact theories of prejudice. *Social Forces, 84*(4), 2179–2204.

Dixon, T. L. (2015). Good guys are still always in white? Positive change and continued misrepresentation of race and crime on local television news. *Communication Research, 44*(6), 1–18.

Dixon, T. L., & Linz, D. (2000). Overrepresentation and underrepresentation of African Americans and Latinos as lawbreakers on television news. *Journal of Communication, 50*(2), 131–154.

Eveland, W. P., & Hively, M. H. (2009). Political discussion frequency, network size, and heterogeneity of discussion as predictors of political knowledge and participation. *Journal of Communication, 59*(2), 205–224.

Fischer, M. J. (2008). Shifting geographies: Examining the role of segregation in blacks' declining suburbanization. *Urban Affairs Review, 43*(4), 475–496.

Frazier, F. (1957). *Black bourgeoisie.* New York, NY: Simon and Schuster.

Frey, W. (2011). *Melting pot cities and suburbs: Racial and ethnic change in metro America in the 2000s.* Brookings Institute Metropolitan Policy Program (pp. 1–16).

Gay, C. (2004). Putting race in context: Identifying the environmental determinants of black racial attitudes. *The American Political Science Review, 98*(4), 547–562.

Gilens, M. (1996). Race and poverty in America: Public misperceptions and the American news media. *Public Opinion Quarterly, 60*(4), 515–541.

Gregory, S. (1995). Race, identity and political activism: The shifting contours of the African American public sphere. In The Black Public Sphere Collective (Ed.), *The Black Public Sphere* (pp. 151–168). Chicago, IL: University of Chicago Press.

Hall, E. V., Phillips, K. W., & Townsend, S. M. (2015). A rose by any other name? The consequences of subtyping "African Americans" from "blacks." *Journal of Experimental Social Psychology, 56*, 183–190.

Haynes, B. (2001). *Red lines, black spaces*. New Haven, CT: Yale University Press.

Huckfeldt, R., & Mendez, J. M. (2008). Moths, flames, and political engagement: Managing disagreement within communication networks. *The Journal of Politics, 70*(1), 83–96.

Huckfeldt, R., Plutzer, E., & Sprague, J. (1993). Alternative Contexts of Political Behavior: Churches, Neighborhoods, and Individuals. *The Journal of Politics 55*(2), 365–381.

Huckfeldt, R., & Sprague, J. (1995). *Citizens, politics, and social communication: Information and influence in an election campaign*. New York, NY: Cambridge University Press.

Ibarra, H. (1995). Race, opportunity, and diversity of social circles in managerial networks. *The Academy of Management Journal, 38*(3), 673–703.

Johnson, V. C. (2002). *Black power in the suburbs: The myth or reality of African American suburban political incorporation*. New York, NY: State University of New York Press.

Kinder, D. R., & Sanders, L. M. (1996). *Divided by color: Racial politics and democratic ideals*. Chicago, IL: University of Chicago Press.

Kinder, D. R., & Sears, D. O. (1981). Prejudice and politics: Symbolic racism versus racial threats to the good life. *Journal of Personality and Social Psychology, 40*(3), 414–431.

Kossinets, G., & Watts, D. J. (2009). Origins of homophily in an evolving social network. *American Journal of Sociology, 115*(2), 405–450.

Larson, S. G. (2006). *Media and minorities: The politics of race in news and entertainment*. Lanham, MD: Rowman & Littlefield.

McAdam, D. (1999). *Political process and the development of Black insurgency, 1930–1970*. Chicago, IL: University of Chicago Press.

McClurg, S. D. (2006). "Political disagreement in context: The conditional effect of neighborhood context, disagreement and political talk on electoral participation. *Political Behavior 28*(4), 349–366.

McGowen, E. B. (2017). *African Americans in white suburbia: Social networks and political behaviors*. Lawrence, KS: University Press of Kansas.

McPherson, M., Smith-Lovin, L., & Cook, J. M. (2001). Birds of a feather: Homophily in social networks. *Annual Review of Sociology, 27*, 415–444.

Oliver, J. E. (2001). *Democracy in suburbia*. Princeton, NJ: Princeton University Press.

Oliver, J. E. (2010). *Paradoxes of integration: Race, neighborhood, and civic life in multiethnic America*. Chicago, IL: University of Chicago Press.

Oliver, J. E., & Mendelberg, T. (2000). Reconsidering the environmental determinants of white racial attitudes. *American Journal of Political Science, 44*(3), 574–589.

Pattillo-McCoy, M. (2000). *Black picket fences*. Chicago, IL: University of Chicago Press.

Pew Research Center. (2013). Race in America: Tracking 50 years of demographic trends. Washington, DC. The URL is http://www.pewsocialtrends.org/2013/08/22/race-demographics/

Scheufele, D. A., Nisbet M. C., Brossard, B., & Nisbet, E. C., (2004). Social structure and citizenship: Examining the impacts of social setting, network heterogeneity, and informational variables on political participation. *Political Communication 21*(3), 315–338.

Scott, J. (2012). *What is social network analysis?* New York, NY: Bloomsbury Publishing.

Sniderman, P. M., & Carmines, E. G. (1997). *Reaching beyond race.* Cambridge, MA: Harvard University Press.

Tate, K. (1994). *From protest to politics.* Cambridge, MA: Harvard University Press.

Tate, K. (2004). *National black election study.* 1996 [Computer File]. ICPSR Version. Columbus, OH: Ohio State University [Producer], 1997. Ann Arbor, MI: Inter-University Consortium for Political and Social Research [Distributor], 2004.

Wilson, W. J. (1978). *The declining significance of race: Blacks and changing American institutions.* Chicago, IL: University of Chicago Press.

Wilson, W. J. (1987). *The truly disadvantaged.* Chicago, IL: University of Chicago Press.

Wilson, W. J. (2011). The declining significance of race: Revisited and revised. *Daedalus, 140*(2), 55–69.

Zaller, J. R. (1992). *The nature and origins of mass opinion.* New York, NY: Cambridge Univeristy Press

6

BLACK COME-OUTERS AND THE COUNTERPUBLIC

How Suburbanization Is Diversifying Black Attitudes

Reuel R. Rogers

It has not been accurate for some time now to think of African Americans as a mostly urban population, confined to central cities or distressed inner-city neighborhoods.[1] This fact, however, had drawn little notice in American politics until the 2016 presidential election. During the course of his wildly unorthodox yet startlingly successful bid for the presidency, Donald Trump let loose a litany of outlandish racially tinged statements. His incendiary rhetoric fired up supporters, enraged detractors, and made careful fact-checking a staple of mainstream news coverage on the man who would become the forty-fifth president of the United States. Most of his racial provocations, early in the campaign, centered on Latinx immigrants. But Trump also turned his invective on the other minority population that has long triggered racial anxiety among whites: African Americans. In both cases, he resorted to familiar code words to stereotype the two groups. His standard stump speech included his infamous vow to build a wall along the country's southern border to keep out undocumented Mexican immigrants, casting the whole lot as a threatening criminal horde of rapists and murderers. His characterization of Blacks was no less racially charged. Recalling the race card rhetoric of Ronald Reagan, he repeatedly referred to the group using the term "inner city," with all of its negative connotations of social disorder, crime, and persistent poverty. Trump's coded comments brought swift condemnation and complaints about their racially corrosive impact on the campaign. Scores of political science studies have confirmed that these code words tend to prime racial resentment and conjure feelings of racial threat among whites (e.g., Abrajano & Hajnal, 2015; Hurwitz & Peffley, 2005).[2]

The media fact-checking that followed Trump's racially charged references also brought crucial correctives. It turns out that unauthorized immigrants from Mexico and other countries are actually less prone to commit crimes than citizens (Perez-Pena, 2017; Yee, Davis, & Patel, 2017). His "inner city" label for Blacks prompted a revealing racial geography lesson that exposed the fallacy of that characterization too. As several media outlets noted, most Blacks do not live in inner-city neighborhoods (e.g., Sebastian, 2016; Semuels, 2016). The numbers declare the truth. US Census figures reveal that African Americans have been exiting not just inner-city areas, but central cities as a whole, at accelerated rates over the last four decades. Cities that have long been major Black population centers have been losing substantial shares of their Black residents to the suburbs in what demographers describe as a widespread pattern of "Black flight." The teeming trail of Blacks leaving central cities has led to a sharp, unprecedented rise in Black suburbanization (Frazier & Anderson, 2006; Frey, 2015). By 2010, the number of Blacks living in the suburbs of the country's largest metropolitan areas began to rival the proportion in city centers for the first time in history. Roughly 51% of all Blacks in these areas now call the suburbs home (Frey, 2015).

This mass exodus to the suburbs is one of the most significant shifts in the racial geography of the African American population in the last half-century. Although this fact was lost on Donald Trump, it has not escaped the notice of researchers. Demographers, for instance, have documented the rise in Black suburbanization from the slow, halting rates of the middle and late twentieth century to the more accelerated pace of the new millennium (e.g., Frazier & Tettey-Fio, 2006, Frey, 2015). Historians too have chronicled African Americans' long, winding pursuit of the suburban dream over the course of the twentieth century (e.g., Wiese, 2004). Sociologists, along with economists and demographers, have analyzed how these suburbanization trends bear on a range of social and economic status indicators for Blacks, from residential segregation rates to employment and education levels (e.g., Alba & Logan, 1991; Fischer, 2008; Glaster, 1991; Timberlake, Howell, & Staight, 2011). Yet the academic literature is relatively silent on the political ramifications of this unprecedented Black flight to the suburbs.[3] This oversight is especially striking at a time when political scientists are keen to explore the link between people's political views and where they live (e.g., Cramer, 2016; Gainsborough, 2001; Oliver, 2001).

It is also curious because recent generations of scholarship on Black politics have been quite closely attuned to the political consequences of emerging demographic changes and divisions within the population, from class to generational to nativity differences (e.g., Cohen, 2010; Dawson, 1994a; Greer, 2013; Simpson, 1998; Smith, 2014). Michael Dawson's seminal study, for instance, revealed that deepening income inequality among Blacks in the closing decades of the twentieth century did not translate to significant class-based cleavages in Black political views. High-income African Americans are predictably less supportive of redistributive policies than their lower-income counterparts; yet, on the whole, class differences in Black political attitudes have been largely muted due to widespread perceptions of linked racial fate within the population (1994a). Few have considered, however, whether the recent suburban shift in where Blacks live is transforming Black politics. At the turn of the new millennium, historian Andrew Wiese (2004) lamented that Black suburbanites were still a "people without a history." He corrected the record by writing one. It remains an open question whether they are a people with politics. Researchers have yet to explore whether these new Black suburban arrivals have distinct political views setting them apart from other Blacks or to examine how the suburban context is affecting the trajectory of Black political incorporation.

A thoroughgoing analysis of the political contours of Black suburbanization is beyond the scope of this single chapter. What it offers instead is a theoretical roadmap that charts one pathway through which suburbanization might be reshaping African American political attitudes. The recent suburban wave is not just an unprecedented shift in the migration and residential patterns of Blacks in this country. It also represents perhaps the most substantial spatial restructuring of the "Black counterpublic" since the Great Migration. The Black counterpublic is the network of all-Black institutions that historically has served as a staging ground for collective action and a site for opinion formation, debate, and consensus-building among African Americans. Several researchers have noted that this Black public sphere has undergone massive transformation over the last four decades due to a number of structural and technological developments (e.g., Dawson, 1994b, 2011; Harris-Lacewell, 2004). This chapter argues that the Black exodus to the suburbs is another factor that has had a transformative impact on the Black counterpublic. With African Americans beating a path to the suburbs, central cities are no longer the geographic epicenter of the Black counterpublic that they were for much of the twentieth century. As Blacks have become suburban-bound "come-outers," the Black counterpublic has decentralized.[4] At a minimum, this spatial restructuring has led to greater differentiation in the institutional bases that comprise the Black public sphere. But Black suburbanization also may be contributing to the recent degeneration in the Black counterpublic that Dawson and others have diagnosed and lamented (Dawson, 1994b, 2011).

The key theoretical claim I advance in this chapter is that the spatial splintering of the Black counterpublic precipitated by suburbanization has heightened the potential for diversification and moderation in African American public opinion. For much of the post-Civil Rights era, Blacks have stood apart from the rest of the American electorate for the striking homogeneity and liberal cast of their political attitudes, as reflected in public opinion surveys and voting patterns (Kinder & Winters, 2001; Tate, 1993). It is practically axiomatic that they are the most uniformly liberal group in the population, particularly on racial and economic issues. As Gay, Hochschild, and White have put it, "African Americans' consistent policy liberalism [has helped] to maintain whatever progressive politics survives in the United States" (2016, 118). But liberal consensus within the group may be on the wane. Recent survey data indicate growing diversity and even creeping moderation in African Americans' political attitudes (e.g., Pew Research Center, 2007; Tate, 2010). Researchers have pointed to a handful of factors to account for these new public opinion trends, most notably class and generational cleavages within the Black mass public and institutional incorporation at the elite level (Cohen, 2010; Dawson, 1994a, 2011; Tate, 2010). Suburbanization may well be another—albeit largely unexamined—source of the increasing variation in African American political attitudes. Insofar as the Black counterpublic has been a site for structuring Blacks' opinions, the geographic decentralization of this network through suburbanization may be driving predictable divisions in political attitudes within the population.

The chapter offers a set of empirical predictions about the potential effects of suburban migration on Blacks' political views. I deduce hypotheses based on how this suburban trend is producing shifts in the Black public sphere, and how these dynamics, in turn, might be generating new fault lines and moderate turns in African Americans' attitudes. I then present analyses of Pew Research Center survey data that find support for some of the hypothesized relationships. I also rely on a handful of interviews with Black suburbanites to interpret and add to the findings. Admittedly, these are all observational data. The results, then, do not allow for precise inferences about causation. But the patterns uncovered by the analyses suggest that the increasing geographic sorting of Blacks between urban and suburban places is associated with cleavages in racial attitudes within the population. African Americans suburbanites view some issues that have been at the forefront of the Black political agenda differently than their central city counterparts. I begin with an overview of recent Black suburbanization trends, followed by a discussion of how these shifts in the racial geography of the population have reverberated in the Black counterpublic to significant political effect. I then turn to the analysis of the data on the views of Black suburban and urban dwellers.

Historical Trends in Black Suburbanization

Students of urban history characterize the last one hundred years of metropolitan development in the United States as the century of the suburb for good reason. Americans have been leaving central cities for the suburbs since the 1920s, but at an especially rapid clip since the end of World War II (Jackson, 1985). The trend has been steady and relentless. By 1970, the nation's suburban population exceeded the number of Americans living in central cities for the first time in history (Timberlake et al., 2011). The pattern continued unabated into the new millennium. Yet African Americans barely figured in this postwar suburban boom. For much of the twentieth century, the suburbs were practically the exclusive province of whites. By 1980, well over two-thirds of all whites resided in the suburbs compared to less than a third of Blacks (Timberlake et al., 2011).[5] It was this conspicuously color-coded pattern of residential settlement that gave rise to the description "chocolate cities and vanilla suburbs" (Farley, Schuman, Bianchi, Colasanto, & Hatchett, 1978). It betrayed the host of racial factors, economic handicaps, and exclusionary zoning policies working against Blacks in suburban housing markets. Redlining and other discriminatory practices by mortgage lenders, the Veterans Administration, and the Federal Housing Administration discouraged Blacks' entry into the suburbs, while at the same time underwriting whites' pursuit of suburban residence and its privileges (Coates, 2014; Jackson, 1985; Sugrue, 1996). Even as the suburban idyll beckoned and became home to the majority of whites in the country, Blacks, by and large, remained stranded in central cities.

But this highly racialized metropolitan geography has shifted in recent decades. The complexion of American suburbanization patterns began to change at the close of the twentieth century, when increasing numbers of Blacks, Latinxs, and Asians started moving to areas outside of central cities. These three racial minority groups are now suburbanizing at faster rates than whites, upending the white-dominated trends that held for so much of the twentieth century (Frey, 2015). As a proportion of their respective populations, more Latinxs and Asians reside in the suburbs than African Americans. These two other groups seem to encounter fewer obstacles to suburbanization than Blacks do. But it is not clear whether the relatively lower rates of suburban residence among Blacks are due strictly to ongoing discrimination in suburban housing markets or also stem from Blacks' greater preference for central city addresses (Timberlake et al., 2011).

Still, the increase in Black migration to the suburbs has been pronounced. Slow and stuttering for much of the twentieth century, it has gone from a trickle to a rising tide over the last three decades. With the elimination of some of the most flagrant racial barriers in the housing market and the growth of the Black middle class in the period following the Civil Rights Movement, the suburbs are no longer off limits or out of reach for many African Americans. While these developments made suburbanization possible for Blacks, a combination of push and pull factors, such as the rising costs of high-quality central city housing, growing employment opportunities beyond city boundaries, and grim inner-city conditions, also whetted Blacks' appetite for suburban living.[6] Black suburbanization started to increase appreciably in 1970. The acceleration reached exponential rates by the 1980s. During the last two decades of the twentieth century, the Black suburban population doubled from 6.1 million to roughly 12 million (Wiese, 2004). One estimate puts the number of Blacks that moved to suburban zip codes between 1960 and 2000 at 9 million—a figure that actually exceeds by a considerable margin the total that participated in the Great Migration when Blacks transformed from a mostly rural to a predominantly urban population (Frazier & Anderson, 2006). It is no wonder then that some observers call this historic Black exodus to the suburbs a second Great Migration.

As this Black suburban tide has swelled and spread across the country, its relationship to the overall racial geography of the Black population has come into sharper relief. It has dramatically altered the residential patterns of Blacks in metropolitan areas. Black suburbanization has been driven at least in part by Black flight, the departure of hundreds of thousands of African Americans from central cities. Demographer William Frey (2015, p. 154) notes that cities with substantial, long settled Black populations actually have been experiencing Black flight since the 1970s; but the volume and reach of this trend hit unprecedented proportions in the first decade of the new millennium. Over half of the country's twenty cities with the largest Black populations saw steep declines in their share of Black residents between 2000 and 2010.[7] Three of them—Detroit, Chicago, and New York—were among the primary destinations for Blacks during the Great Migration (Frey, 2015, p. 154). Cities all over the country, in northern, midwestern, southern, and western metropolitan areas, registered losses (Frey, 2015, pp. 154–155).

Six of the fifteen cities that experienced the largest Black population decreases were in metropolitan areas that also logged some of the biggest Black suburban gains in the same period. Times series maps of the last two decades of Black population changes in metropolitan Chicago, Detroit, and Atlanta illustrate this inverse relationship between trends in the central cities and their suburbs (see Figures 6.1–6.3). As all three cities were hemorrhaging Black residents, their surrounding inner- and middle-ring suburbs were experiencing Black population increases. The countervailing population dynamics captured in the maps typify patterns across the country: Black presence is diminishing in the big cities where the population has long been concentrated and surging in the suburbs. This metropolitan-wide inversion in Black residential patterns amounts to a remarkable reshuffling of the racial geography of the population.

This massive shift in African American residential dynamics is likely to have far-reaching ramifications for the population. Contrary to the familiar aphorism, demography is not destiny—at least not with any scientific reliability. But an established body of research confirms that Black migration patterns have been associated with major changes in African Americans' socioeconomic fortunes (e.g., Massey & Denton, 1993). For instance, researchers attribute the mid- to late twentieth century expansion in the Black middle class partly to the population's almost wholesale move from rural areas to cities during the Great Migration. Of course, the timing of their urban arrival also coincided with deindustrialization, which augured more ominous economic outcomes for low-income Blacks (e.g., Wilson, 1987). But urbanization initially improved the economic lot of many Blacks. Likewise, the earliest Black suburbanites often experienced at least a modest upgrade in neighborhood quality with the move out of central cities (Schneider & Phelan, 1993). Suburbanization today,

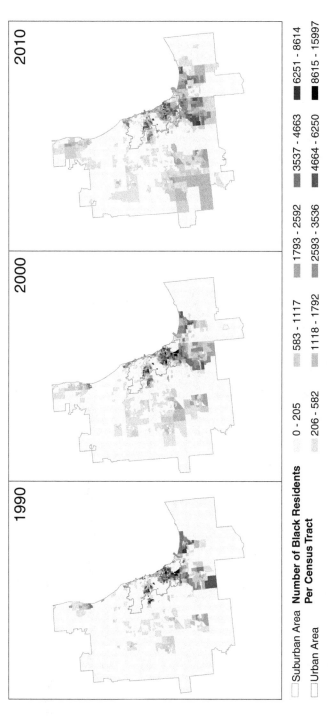

1990	2000	2010

Suburban Area	**Number of Black Residents**	0 - 205	583 - 1117	1793 - 2592	3537 - 4663	6251 - 8614
Urban Area	**Per Census Tract**	206 - 582	1118 - 1792	2593 - 3536	4664 - 6250	8615 - 15997

FIGURE 6.1 Metro Chicago: Black Population Change in Central City and Suburban Areas, 1990–2010

Source: US Census Bureau.

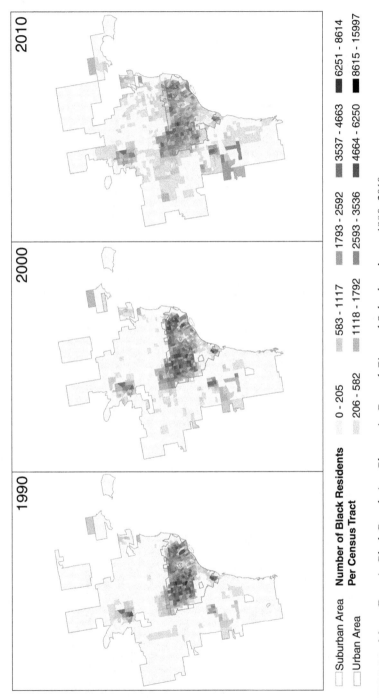

FIGURE 6.2 Metro Detroit: Black Population Change in Central City and Suburban Areas, 1990–2010

Source: US Census Bureau.

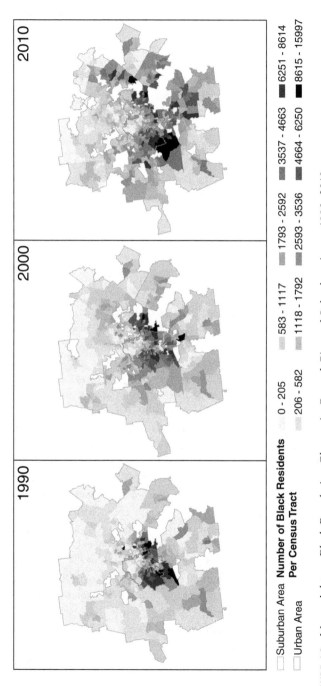

FIGURE 6.3 Metro Atlanta: Black Population Change in Central City and Suburban Areas, 1990–2010

Source: US Census Bureau.

however, is not the surefire pass to mobility or signal of middle- and upper-class status it once was. Blacks in the suburbs tend to live in poorer neighborhoods than whites. Still, Black suburbanites typically live in less economically distressed neighborhoods than their central city counterparts (Timberlake, 2002). Black suburbanization also may be contributing to recent modest declines in Black–white segregation rates (Fischer, 2008; Frey, 2015).[8] All in all, the trends in where Blacks migrate and reside have shaped their socioeconomic horizons for better and for worse, sometimes hastening economic progress and other times generating distress.

The political consequences of Black migration patterns have not been studied as extensively as the social and economic outcomes. But even a casual historical glance suggests that major Black population flows have had far-reaching political reverberations in this country. The political entailments of Black migration trends are not always post hoc or incidental either. Some researchers insist that the decision to migrate is not simply a socioeconomic calculation to secure access to better housing, employment, or schools. Moving from one place to another, they argue, is often also an expression of political agency (e.g., Hunter, 2013). As Albert Hirschman famously noted, exit is a "direct way of expressing one's unfavorable views" of the institutions or practices of a government—or even the norms and habits of a place and the people who live there (1970, 17). For example, many scholars insist that the White urban exodus of the mid-twentieth century was an explicitly political act. Whites chose exit to the suburbs to escape Blacks, the poor, and big-city governments prone to catering to the redistributive needs of these groups (e.g., Jackson, 1985; Kruse, 2005). Their movement to the suburbs was in part an expression of race and class politics. Likewise, some Blacks today might be beating a path to the suburbs to establish physical and social distance from undesirable conditions and groups in central cities. This distance, in turn, could produce a new fault line in Black politics between these new suburban arrivals and central city dwellers.

Migration also might be a move to elevate civic or political standing. African Americans certainly have turned to migration to improve their political fortunes. The Great Migration again proves the point. Most historians agree that this enormous Black exodus from the rural South to cities in the region and beyond was a heroic act of political agency (e.g., Wilkerson, 2010). Rejecting the racial repression, terror, and disenfranchisement of the Jim Crow South, African Americans voted with their feet, fled the region by the millions, and thereby altered their political destiny. The political consequences of this mid-century mass exodus by Blacks have been considerable. Not only did the Great Migration announce Blacks' refusal to accept a second-class, counterfeit brand of citizenship, the move to cities also generated many of the opportunities and conditions that gave rise to the Civil Rights Movement. As research has shown, these included resource and strategic benefits, such as the electoral and collective action potential associated with the concentration of millions of

African Americans living in big cities. Blacks capitalized on these urban assets to support the activities of the movement (e.g., McAdam, 1982). Even after the movement ended, Blacks continued to leverage some of the same advantages that came with urbanization to muster grassroots mobilization, elect leaders to office, and pursue other political gains. For example, cheek-by-jowl urban living conditions have been pivotal to getting out the Black vote during fiercely competitive biracial mayoral contests in cities such as Chicago and New York. When Harold Washington became Chicago's first African American mayor, high population density in Black neighborhoods facilitated the massive Black voter turnout campaign that ensured his victory.

The Geography of the Black Counterpublic

One of the most politically consequential developments fueled by Black migration to cities was the emergence of the consolidated network of all-Black institutions dubbed the Black counterpublic by scholars of Black politics. As Dawson explains, African Americans created many of the early institutions of this counterpublic as a response to their exclusion from the mainstream civil society and as an assertion of their group autonomy (2001). The institutional bases of this network, which historically has included Black churches, colleges, trade unions, social clubs, and civil rights organizations, first developed in the wake of the Civil War and crystallized during the segregationist Jim Crow era. Although Black organizations traditionally have constituted the counterpublic's main institutional infrastructure, information networks and informal public spaces, such as barbershops and beauty salons, also have been integral to its operation (Harris-Lacewell, 2004). Whether serving as a site for key episodes of collective action like the Civil Rights Movement or functioning as a forum for aggregating and shaping Black political opinions, the network has occupied a central place in Black political life for much of American history. But it assumed its modern form in the middle of the twentieth century when Blacks became a largely urban population in the wake of the Great Migration. Prior to this period, the poverty and spatial separation that characterized life for the mass of Blacks residing in the rural South limited the growth of the Black counterpublic. Without a steady supply of financial resources and the logistical benefits of spatial proximity, the incipient counterpublic remained in a state of arrested development. Black urbanization, however, brought a watershed period of expansion.

Researchers have documented the dizzying proliferation in Black counterpublic organizations triggered by African American urbanization (e.g., Biondi, 2006; McAdam, 1982; Morris, 1984). As the Black population swelled in cities such as Chicago, New York, Detroit, and Atlanta, the numbers of Black churches, social clubs, literary circles, and fledgling civil rights groups multiplied, fueled by unprecedented increases in membership. The occupational, income, and educational gains of middle- and working-class Blacks in the middle of the twentieth century gave the population new financial resources and skills to invest in Black organizations. McAdam (1982) provides a detailed inventory of the astonishing rise in urban Black church membership and National Association for the Advancement of Colored People (NAACP) chapters in the South during this period. As one contemporary observer put it, "In the urban [B]lack belts, Negro institutions... flourished" (Burgess, 1965, p. 344). Similar patterns of Black organizational growth registered in the primary destination cities of the Great Migration in the North and Midwest (Dawson, 2001). These trends in the institutional development of the Black counterpublic reached an apex during the Civil Rights Movement, when even ostensibly nonpolitical organizations became hotbeds of political dialogue and activism. When the movement crested in the late 1960s, African Americans had established almost 40 national Black organizations, most of them headquartered in cities (Yearwood, 1978). Driven by the population shifts of the Great Migration, the spatial architecture of Black institutional life had restructured and consolidated. Cities had become the demographic center of gravity for the Black counterpublic.

Much of the established political science literature on the counterpublic has glossed over or ignored the significance of urban dynamics in accounting for its emergence and its political effects. But cities should figure prominently in any analysis of why the Black counterpublic flourished and how it influences African American political attitudes and behavior. Cities have spatial and demographic features that make them uniquely fertile terrain for the development of public spheres. The two that are most relevant are density and a public realm (Conn, 2014). Demographers and others who study cities point to density—the ratio of a place's population to its size—as a key criterion that distinguishes urban areas from rural and suburban geographic units. As Jane Jacobs (1961) observed more than a half-century ago, cities are dense places. They put diverse groups of people into close, sometimes complicated, contact, forcing them to interact. The logistics of living in these dense urban conditions often give rise to what philosophers call a public sphere. These are public spaces that "[enable] private individuals to come together to identify, discuss, debate, and act on areas of shared concern" (Conn, 2014, p. 4).

In the language of political science and economics, positive and negative externalities pile up quickly in densely populated cities. Consider, for instance, the pros and cons of gentrification. The wave of pedestrian traffic that might come with the opening of a new restaurant in a city neighborhood often brings collateral economic benefits, but also inconveniences or the threat of displacement to those residing or trying to make a living in the same area. Even more quotidian and ostensibly private concerns can become public issues in cities. A leak in one apartment can be a public nuisance for an entire building or even a city block. One neighbor's private distress easily can become another's concern either by virtue of spatial proximity or mutual recognition. In short, the externalities register as shared preoccupations for city residents. They draw private individuals toward recognition of a public, or any number of potential issue publics. As Conn notes, "the creation of a public sphere makes it possible for individuals to conceive of themselves as a public with... [a] collective set of interests" (2014, p. 4).

In light of these distinctive features of urban life, it is no wonder that cities became the hub of the Black counterpublic in the mid-twentieth century. The high rates of residential segregation that Blacks tend to experience in cities actually intensified these spatial and public dimensions of the urban environment for the group. To be sure, segregation and the spatial conditions that go with it have exacerbated poverty and economic disinvestment in many urban Black neighborhoods. Segregation has isolated African Americans by drawing a perverse racial cordon around the places where they live in cities. It has stymied socioeconomic mobility for generations of Black families and left them literally "stuck in place" in distressed neighborhoods in areas like Chicago's Black Belt (Massey & Denton, 1993; Sampson, 2012; Sharkey, 2013). But segregation in the mid-twentieth century also kept middle-income Blacks spatially tethered to their low-income counterparts. The close urban quarters imposed by segregation enabled African Americans from these distinct economic strata to not only interact but also coordinate and husband their resources for institution-building (Dawson, 1994a; Tate, 1993). In sum, the geographic ties binding urban Blacks at the neighborhood level created the conditions for the consolidation of the Black counterpublic.

How the Black Counterpublic Structures Black Attitudes

The pivotal role that the counterpublic has played in structuring a Black political agenda and shaping Black political attitudes and behavior is well established in the research literature (e.g., Cohen, 1999; Dawson, 1994a, 2011; Harris-Lacewell, 2004; Tate, 1993). The counterpublic historically has served myriad political functions. It has been a site for information-sharing and consciousness-raising; a crucible for fostering perceptions of linked fate; a place for fashioning strategies to combat racism; a forum for building policy consensus; and a network for identifying leaders, activating campaigns, and promoting political engagement in the population. For instance, the dense spatial dimensions of the network have afforded logistical advantages for Black mobilization. One recent study found that Black political participation rates rise in tandem with the size and density of the Black population at the city level (Spence & McClerking, 2010; also, Oliver, 2001). As their share of the population increases, Blacks in cities are more likely to attend community meetings, assist with voter drives, donate to campaigns, and so on. The demographic density and spatial proximity that come with increasing numbers facilitate Blacks' participation in these political activities, presumably by making them more accessible to each other.

But it is the social dynamics of the Black counterpublic that are particularly relevant for understanding how Black political attitudes take shape. A long line of research has demonstrated that African Americans rely on their racial identity as a heuristic for making political decisions (e.g., Dawson, 1994a; Gay, 2004; Gay & Hochschild, 2010). It turns out that group identities hold considerable sway and intuitive force over individual political judgments, not just among African Americans, but across the broad gamut of American social groups— even those that are ostensibly nonpolitical (e.g., Achen & Bartels, 2016; Conover, 1984; Cramer, 2016; Huddy, 2001). For instance, whites living in rural places have developed what Katherine Cramer calls a "rural consciousness" that informs their political preferences and often puts them at odds with people living in cities and policies that seem to benefit city dwellers (2016). Among African Americans, racial identity is an especially salient heuristic because race—or racial discrimination, to be more exact—has had such a determinative impact on their life outcomes and experiences. Their individual life chances still rise and fall as Blacks as a group gain or lose economic, political, and social standing (Gay & Hochschild, 2010). Consequently, African Americans often calculate their personal utility, and thus make political decisions, on the basis of what is good for the entire racial group rather than on strictly individualistic considerations (Dawson, 1994a).[9] Despite the pervasive influence of race in the lives of African Americans, however, whether and how they apply their racial identity to political judgments is contingent on social factors.

First, social interactions are integral to how identities, including those based on racial group membership, develop and acquire meanings that can be applied to political situations. Cramer Walsh has described these fundamentally social dynamics. Social identities, she explains, "are psychological connections achieved through the active process of linking oneself to other people, partly through interpersonal interaction" (2004, p. 53). People develop their social identities not simply because they notice shared characteristics with in-group members. Rather, individuals rely on others in their social networks for cues on what it means to belong to a particular group and how members of the group should think and act (Rothschild, 2017). In fact, researchers have found that the political commitments and policy preferences that people associate with their social identities or perceive as integral to their group interest depend to a great degree on the social networks in which they are embedded (e.g., Berelson, Larzarsfeld, & McPhee, 1954). The political beliefs and preferences that people associate with their identities, then, are not constructed in a social vacuum (Huckfeldt & Kohlfeld, 1989). They are inculcated via interactions with in-group members within the context of social networks. These social interactions supply the information that makes identities useful political heuristics.

The interactions also function as a source of social pressure that prods individuals to conform to the norms of their in-group. People tend to be acutely aware of their standing within social groups and eager to maintain comity with in-group peers. Consequently, when individuals are immersed in social networks where other in-group members can observe or inquire about their positions or actions to see if they comport with group expectations, they typically conform to dominant group norms—they go along to get along with the other group members. Otherwise, they risk incurring a steep social cost: exclusion or rejection by the group, which in turn calls into question their commitment to their group identity.[10] Recent studies have demonstrated that even heterogeneous networks that commingle people of different backgrounds can exert pressures on individual political actions and attitudes, including voting behavior and partisanship (e.g., Sinclair, 2012). Existing research also indicates that conformity to in-group political norms appears to deliver emotional payoffs that reinforce the salience of group identity (Suhay, 2015). The relationship between social pressure and group identity is fundamentally reciprocal. Strong group identifiers are especially susceptible to in-group social pressure, but social pressure also heightens individual identification with an in-group. These dynamics ultimately generate consensus and uniformity in political attitudes within a social group.

Among African Americans, these social processes historically have unfolded in the formal and informal networks of the Black counterpublic. When African Americans are embedded in these networks, they learn lessons about what it means to be Black and how Blacks should think and act politically. A number of studies have shown that participation in these networks tends to heighten racial identity and its political salience among African Americans (e.g., Herring, Janowski, & Brown, 1999). Social interaction in these Black dialogic spaces also helps to explain why African Americans rely on their perceptions of racial group interests to formulate their individual political preferences (e.g., Cohen, 1999; Dawson, 1994a; Harris-Lacewell, 2004). The informational cues that circulate in these social settings drive this well-documented political effect. Following the logic outlined by Dawson (1994a), African Americans immersed in these networks learn crucial information about the interests of their racial group. With this group-centric information at hand, they are inclined to substitute racial group interests as a proxy for their individual interests when making political decisions, especially under low information conditions. The information-sharing and deliberation that transpire within these settings, then, ultimately contribute to "linked fate politics" among Blacks.

Recent research indicates that the social pressure at work in these networks is also a key catalyst for these effects, particularly the high degree of political homogeneity typically observed among African Americans. White, Laird, and Allen (2014) find that social monitoring by racial in-group peers accounts for why Blacks often act against their individual self-interests and favor positions thought to advance racial group interests when making political choices. The presence of racial peers increases the likelihood that Blacks will follow the proverbial crowd in their political decisions. On the other hand, the study shows that defection from in-group political norms or perceived racial group interests is more common when individual Blacks are free from social monitoring by their peers, as in predominantly White settings or geographic locations at a distance from large numbers of Blacks. These findings indicate that "racialized social pressure" has the capacity to "rein in such defection," incentivize conformity with in-group norms, and enforce political homogeneity among Blacks.

Presumably, these interactive social dynamics were quite robust within the Black counterpublic in the middle of the twentieth century when the network was at its peak in central cities with large Black populations. In places such as Chicago, Detroit, and New York, the dense spatial conditions that characterized the Black public sphere helped to structure political attitudes among African Americans. The geographic centralization of the network facilitated the circulation of information about perceived racial group interests in politics and public policy across different segments of the population, including middle- and low-income Blacks. It also crystallized in-group political norms by making them plainly observable and easy to convey in the close urban quarters of the period. Finally, these conditions allowed for active peer monitoring, which intensified the social pressure on individual Blacks to follow the herd and conform to in-group political norms. Taken together, these distinctly urban counterpublic dynamics contributed to the high levels of homogeneity in African American political attitudes and behavior that prevailed for much of the mid- and late twentieth century.

Although this pattern of Black political uniformity stems from what appear to be democratic deliberative and interactive social dynamics within the Black counterpublic, these processes carry clear biases. For instance, it is not surprising that middle-class Blacks have had greater influence than their less well-off counterparts in defining the collective racial interests of the population and shaping the Black political agenda (Cohen, 1999; Reed, 1999). Middle-class African Americans tend to have informational and communicative advantages that enhance their standing and impact on deliberation in Black associational spaces.[11] The consolidated urban dynamics of the Black counterpublic network in the middle and late twentieth century helped to generate high levels of racial consensus and uniformity around positions advocated by middle-class Blacks and other influential segments of the population.

As Dawson has described, however, the counterpublic started to atrophy in the last quarter of the century due to a number of factors, such as economic restructuring in cities, government repression of many Black organizations, and internal dissension within these same groups (Dawson, 1994b, 2001; Harris-Lacewell, 2004). The counterpublic lost its robust multiclass character as some middle-income Blacks exited cities, low-income Blacks fell on hard times in extreme poverty neighborhoods, and economic segregation within the Black population increased. As many middle- and working-class Blacks left for the suburbs, the geography of the counterpublic also reconfigured. Along with the well-studied economic changes, the geographic decentralization of the counterpublic precipitated by suburbanization paved the way for new shifts in Black political attitudes.[12] Relative to cities, suburbs typically have lower levels of population density and civic capacity (Oliver, 2001). Black suburbanites, then, are likely to encounter very different social dynamics in the counterpublic beyond central city boundaries. Not only are these suburban Blacks geographically separated and perhaps socially detached from their central city counterparts, some of them may have only limited contact with each other in their suburban environs. The thick social density that encouraged in-group conformity and ultimately heightened political homogeneity in the city-centered Black counterpublic of the mid- to late twentieth century may be missing or hard to reproduce in the places where Black suburbanites live today.[13]

Black Suburbanization and the Growing Diversity in Black Attitudes

Since the closing decades of the twentieth century, there have been signs that the long-standing pattern of political homogeneity and policy liberalism among African Americans is receding and giving way to incipient political diversity and moderation in the population (e.g., Pew Research Center, 2007; Tate, 2010). When it comes to their policy stances and voting behavior, Blacks remain more cohesive and farther to the left of the ideological spectrum than most groups in the American electorate, to be sure. They still overwhelmingly back the Democratic party, view unequal treatment and discrimination as bedeviling barriers to their success, and support affirmative measures to combat racial inequality (e.g., Chong & Kim, 2006; Pew Research Center, 2007, 2016; Tate, 2010; Teixeira & Halpin, 2012). But even as far back as the 1980s, Dawson noticed modest evidence of diversity in Blacks' attitudes, specifically toward redistributive policies and the advisability of Black autonomy. These nascent trends were held in abeyance by perceptions of linked fate (1994a). Tate's more recent analysis confirms growing demographic variation in Blacks' policy opinions, and even more notably, finds that Blacks' views on welfare and government assistance policies have moderated over the last quarter century (2010). Even African Americans' unusually intense feelings of linked fate appear to be waning (Gay et al., 2016; McClain & Stewart, 2013; Pew Research Center, 2007).

The leading scholarly explanations for this increasing diversity and creeping moderation in Black political attitudes have focused on socioeconomic, generational, and elite-level factors. The economic variables have drawn the most attention. Socioeconomic trends, such as increases in wealth, deepening poverty, and the concomitant rise in inequality, are among the most significant demographic changes in the Black population in recent decades. Sure enough, studies show that variations in factors such as neighborhood quality and individual-level economic status influence racial and policy attitudes among African Americans (Chong & Kim, 2006; Gay, 2004). In contrast, very few studies have investigated the effects of suburbanization on Blacks' racial or policy outlooks, despite the fact that this residential trend also surely ranks as one of the most sweeping changes in the demography of the Black population in the last quarter century.[14] Just as the emerging economic cleavages among Blacks have prompted questions about their diversifying and moderating impact on Black political attitudes, it is reasonable to wonder whether the residential and spatial divisions in the population precipitated by mass suburbanization are producing similar effects.

Theory and Hypotheses

There are certainly theoretical and empirical grounds for predicting that the recent wave of Black come-outers to the suburbs might have political views that are distinct from those of central city Blacks. I hypothesize that these differences in political attitudes are mediated through the restructuring of the Black counterpublic precipitated by suburbanization. First, the empirical record on suburbanization in this country is a well-worn pattern of upwardly mobile Americans exiting cities, not only to find better opportunities, but also to escape the huddled undesirable masses of the urban core: the poor, the foreign-born, and non-whites. Suburban residence long has implied that moving up and "making it" in America required moving out of cities and away from city dwellers and their problems, in line with Stilgoe's White ethnic "come-outer ideology" (Rae, 2003, p. 20). Although African Americans are relative latecomers to suburbanization, they too have been eager to distance themselves from undesirable inner-city groups and conditions. As Wiese explains, early "middle class suburbanites [had] concerns about class and distance from poorer [B]lacks... [They]drew implicit contrasts between the types of neighborhoods to which they aspired and those in which they had been 'bottled up' with other African Americans" (2006, pp. 116–117). When Trump wrongly conflated Black people and inner cities, he ignited outrage from Black suburbanites who were quick to take to social media to underscore the status distinctions between themselves and Blacks living in the urban core.

Suburbanization enables upwardly mobile African Americans to translate these status distinctions into greater spatial distance and differentiation from their poorer inner-city counterparts. Black suburbanites can signal Black respectability from their zip codes beyond the urban core and attempt to ward off the stigma of association with inner-city residents. The perverse irony of drawing these distinctions is that they impose what Cohen (1999) calls secondary marginalization on the poorest segments of the Black population, adding weight to the negative stereotypes already saddling them. When the Black counterpublic network was at its peak in cities, it was riven by class and status differences among African Americans, to be sure (Dawson, 1994b, 2001). These divisions were telegraphed geographically then too, as Black middle-class strivers sorted themselves from their less well-off counterparts by neighborhood (Drake & Cayton, 1945; Patillo-McCoy, 1999). But as Dawson has noted, these distinctions were often negotiated and even papered over in the urban-centered counterpublic by unifying perceptions of a linked fate. Class-based tensions among Blacks often could be overcome with the mutual recognition that they faced common challenges in the urban places where they resided. The shared predicaments of place reinforced Blacks' awareness of the shared struggles of the race, all within the context of the urban-centered counterpublic. But with the recent wave of Black suburbanization, place and residence have become spatial and status distinctions that fragment and decentralize the Black counterpublic. These shifts—and the geographic and social distance they entail—ultimately may diminish perceptions of linked fate between suburban and central city African Americans.

Second, Black suburban neighborhoods are typically far less dense than central city areas. The low-density development that characterizes much of suburbia in this country contributes to the problem of vanishing social capital and weak civic capacity that many researchers have lamented (e.g., Oliver, 2001; Putnam, 2000). Contrary to the idealized mid-twentieth century picture of suburban life, suburbanites today are hardly embedded in rich social networks in their neighborhoods and rarely engage in the public square. The prevalence of large lots, high fences, low social density, socioeconomic homogeneity, and exclusionary policies in the suburbs makes for a rather anemic public sphere. Citizens rarely come together to debate contentious issues or pursue common purposes—aside from keeping out the undesirables (e.g., Macedo, 2011; Oliver, 2012). These not-too-close suburban quarters presumably make it much more difficult to reconstitute the robust Black counterpublic networks that flourished in central cities in the middle of the twentieth century. Cohen and Dawson (1993) have pointed out that the same low-density spatial arrangements have hollowed out and weakened the bonds of the counterpublic in blighted inner-city Black neighborhoods as well. They hypothesize that the social isolation of these neighborhoods might "break down feelings of racial solidarity" (1993, p. 290). Similar dynamics of isolation might be at work even in the more well-to-do Black suburbs. The low-density residential patterns that typify suburban municipalities make it hard to impose the usual racialized social pressure that compels consensus and uniformity in Black political attitudes. Suburban Blacks are also at a distance and thus free from the social monitoring of their racial confederates in central cities and vice versa. With geographic distance separating the two groups and the likelihood of social contact diminished, Black city dwellers and suburbanites are less likely to worry about their standing with each other. Consequently, they may be less inclined to take the other group's preferences or situation into account when formulating their own opinions. Out of sight could mean out of mind. These dynamics portend greater diversity in Blacks' racial and political views across metropolitan areas.

Finally, with access to more neighborhood amenities, better schools, and so on, Black suburbanites simply may enjoy a better quality of life than their central city counterparts. They also may have more contact with whites to the extent that some Blacks live in suburbs with only modest rates of Black–White segregation. Both of these factors—the superior socioeconomic character of suburban neighborhoods and the greater potential for interracial contact—likely have moderating effects on the racial and political views of Black suburbanites vis-à-vis Black central city dwellers. Researchers have noticed that Blacks tend to express more moderate views in the presence of whites (Gurin et al., 1989; Sanders, 1995). Likewise, Gay finds that Blacks living in neighborhoods rich in resources are less likely to endorse linked fate beliefs and pessimistic views about anti-Black discrimination (2004). It follows that the informational cues about Black life circulating in suburban Black social and institutional spaces are probably much more optimistic than the lessons Blacks in central city counterpublic networks absorb.

This last assumption is harder to justify, at first blush. Although Black suburban residents tend to be upwardly mobile and better educated than their urban counterparts, they live in neighborhoods that vary greatly in their economics and racial demographics. Recall that most Black suburbanites live in predominantly or overwhelmingly Black neighborhoods, whereas a much smaller fraction resides in majority-White or evenly mixed areas. In their economic profile, Black suburbs range from solidly middle-class areas well removed from central cities to fiscally starved inner-ring neighborhoods that border their urban cores. The economics of inner- and middle-ring Black suburbs are not always markedly better than those of distressed inner-city neighborhoods. Blacks in suburban Ferguson, Missouri, for example, struggle with many of the same challenges that Blacks in inner-city St. Louis face, from meager tax revenues to the miseries of concentrated poverty to problems with police brutality. Black suburbs, in general, are saddled with more economic disadvantages than White suburbs.[15]

Black suburban residence is simply not a reliable proxy for a better quality of life or residential exposure to whites. To the extent that migration to the suburbs is hardly a sure ticket to economic stability, social mobility, or racial integration, Black suburbanites might continue to believe that their fate is linked to the fortunes of Blacks as a whole, including those living in cities. Consequently, they also might have the same racial views and assessments of ongoing discrimination as their central city counterparts. But recall that suburban Blacks on average live in less poor neighborhoods than their central city counterparts

(Timberlake, 2002). Further, anecdotal and survey evidence suggests that many middle- and low-income Blacks move to the suburbs to escape the grim social conditions and economic hardships of central city neighborhoods, including gun violence and skyrocketing housing prices. If Black suburbanites consider their neighborhoods an upgrade from central city areas, a shared perspective on Blacks' racial fortunes across metropolitan areas may be elusive.

All in all, if Black suburbanization has restructured the Black counterpublic and, in turn, diversified Blacks' racial views, then the following hypotheses should be verifiable with Black public opinion data:

H_1: Place of residence (i.e., urban or suburban) is likely to be a significant source of variation in Blacks' racial attitudes.

H_2: Suburban Blacks will be less likely to express perceptions of racial-linked fate than urban Blacks, particularly vis-à-vis each other.

H_3: Suburban Blacks will have more optimistic assessments of anti-Black discrimination trends and the level of racial equality in the country than urban Blacks.

Data and Methods

As scholars of Black politics frequently point out, surveys with large representative samples of African Americans and wide-ranging questions are hard to find. Geocoded survey data that sort Blacks by place of residence are an even scarcer commodity. I rely here on the 2013 Pew Research Center Martin Luther King, Jr. Race Survey. This nationally representative survey of 2,231 adult Americans of White, Black, and Hispanic backgrounds features a series of questions inviting respondents to share their perceptions of racial equality and experiences with discrimination. The data are linked to US Census data files to designate regional and residential geographic codes for the respondents. The survey includes an oversample of 376 African Americans, the basis for this analysis.

The key independent variable in the analysis is place of residence (i.e., suburban vs. urban). The dependent variables are based on respondents' answers to the questions probing their assessments of racial equality in specific arenas and their personal exposure to discrimination (see Table 6.1). The questions tap survey participants' views on institutional racism. They ask whether Blacks are treated fairly by police, the courts, public schools, and so on. The survey's focus on racial issues makes it well-suited for investigating the potential for variation by place in Blacks' opinion. Questions about racial inequality are a stiff test because they typically yield considerable consensus among African Americans. Blacks historically have been in strong agreement that America has not lived up to its creedal promise to afford equal treatment to all citizens regardless of race.

TABLE 6.1 Description of Variables in Pew Research Martin Luther King, Jr. Race Survey

Independent Variable	
Suburban or urban residence	
Dependent Variables	
Perceptions of economic inequality	Now thinking about the financial situation of Blacks compared with whites today, would you say the average Black person is better off, worse off, or just as well-off as the average White person in terms of income and overall financial situation? (Pew Q12) 1 Better off 2 Worse off 3 About as well-off 9 Don't know/refused
Equality at work Equal treatment by police Equality in court Equality in local public schools	Just your impression, are Blacks in your community treated less fairly than whites in the following situations? (Pew Q13, A-G)
Equality in restaurants Equality in health care Equality in voting	1 Yes, treated less fairly 2 No, not treated less fairly 9 Don't know/refused

Source: Pew Research Martin Luther King, Jr. Race Survey, August 1–11, 2013.

Some caveats about the limitations of the survey are in order. First, the list of items on the survey do not provide leverage for testing all the hypotheses about the effects of suburbanization on Blacks' racial or political views. Specifically, there are no questions tapping linked racial fate perceptions, so I cannot validate H_2 with the survey data. But I turn to interview data to explore this hypothesis. These data are from an ongoing project that included 45 interviews with Blacks in the suburbs of Chicago conducted over the last 3 years. Second, Pew conducted two rounds of data collection for the African American sample and elected to account for the oversampling by weighting the data based on the Census Bureau's 2011 American Community Survey population parameters for gender, age, and education. Those adjustments make the survey ill-suited for drawing inferences about the socioeconomic composition of the neighborhoods where the Black suburban and urban respondents reside. Still, this limitation is more of a wrinkle than a knot. The theoretical assumptions underlying the hypotheses are based as much on African Americans' subjective perceptions of their suburban and urban neighborhoods as they are on the objective socioeconomic composition of these places. Add to that the fact that the areas where Black suburbanites live vary considerably in their economic profiles and the adjustments seem less consequential for this first-cut analysis. A more fine-grained dataset with details on the socioeconomic profile of Black suburban and urban neighborhoods seems in order for future research.

Finally, the data do not allow for direct causal inferences about the relative dynamics of Black institutional and social networks in suburbs and central cities. The survey does not include questions on Black associational activities. The analysis takes as a matter of inferential faith then the causal significance of the changing Black counterpublic, based on recent suburban trends. The a priori assumption is that Black suburbanization has led to greater spatial fragmentation and decentralization in the Black counterpublic. The counterpublic that shapes and informs Blacks' opinions today is no longer centered and consolidated in cities. It is now more spatially differentiated. Whereas the Black counterpublic of the mid- to late twentieth century had an urban nucleus, today it has multiple nodes located across urban and suburban areas—some with stronger institutional moorings than others. This marks a significant geographic shift in the networks that historically have influenced African Americans' racial attitudes. The main motivation for the analysis is to determine whether urban and suburban African Americans hold distinct racial views that might be due to this restructuring of the counterpublic. Taking the limitations of the survey into account, the data provide a foundation for investigating the ramifications of suburbanization for Black political attitudes.

Findings

The descriptive statistics from the survey reported by the Pew Research Center reveal familiar racial divisions in Americans' perceptions of racial inequality and discrimination (Pew Research Center, 2013). For example, the perceptual chasm between Blacks and Whites on the degree of colorblindness in the criminal justice system is quite wide. Seventy percent of Blacks report that their racial group is treated less fairly than whites by the police. Only 37% of whites agree that Blacks encounter such color-coded unfairness. Likewise, less than a third (32%) of Blacks compared to almost two-thirds of whites (63%) say that Blacks can expect fair treatment in the courts. Although Black–White gaps in public opinion on matters involving race are not new, these particular differences are striking at a time of heightened media attention to the issue of police abuse against African Americans and calls to address racial disparities in criminal sentencing.

But interracial disagreement does not imply intraracial uniformity in opinions on racial inequality. I relied on a series of comparison of means tests to analyze Blacks' responses to the eight survey items on racial inequality in various institutions and areas of community life. The overall results confirm my first hypothesis that place of residence is a significant source of variation in Blacks' opinions. Suburban and urban Blacks evince notably different views on several of the questions. As Table 6.2 shows, the differences tilt in the direction predicted in the third hypothesis for five of the eight items and are significant for four of them (see Table 6.2). Suburban Blacks are more likely than their urban counterparts to perceive racial equality in major institutions and key areas of community life.

TABLE 6.2 Comparison of Means

Variable Name	Urban Mean	Suburban Mean	Difference in Means	Lower Bound	Upper Bound	p-value
Economic inequality	2.516	2.486	0.030	−0.121	0.182	0.700
Equality at work	1.706	2.434	−0.728	−1.224	−0.232	0.004★★★
Treatment by police	1.406	1.814	−0.408	−0.793	−0.023	0.04★★
Equality in court	1.600	1.972	−0.372	−0.821	0.077	0.10★
Equality in schools	1.944	2.379	−0.436	−0.962	0.090	0.10★

Source: Data from Pew Research Martin Luther King, Jr. Race Survey.

Note. ★ $p < 0.1$; ★★ $p < 0.05$; ★★★ $p < 0.01$

Figures 6.4–6.8 illustrate the perceptual differences between the two groups. Suburban Blacks are more likely than urban Blacks to report that Blacks enjoy economic parity with whites (see Figure 6.4). Although the difference in perspective captured in the survey is not statistically significant ($p = 0.69$), it indicates that more Blacks living in the suburbs than those residing in cities believe that Blacks as a whole are on equal financial footing with whites (i.e., urban Blacks perceive greater economic inequality but not by much). I include it here because previous research has shown that Blacks often gauge their group's status via economic comparisons with whites. This finding suggests that suburban Blacks may be more satisfied than their city-dwelling counterparts with the group's standing in the country. Significant differences show in other areas. Most striking is the gap between the two groups on the question of fair treatment in the workplace (see Figure 6.5). Suburban Blacks are significantly more likely to perceive racial equality on the job when compared to their urban Black counterparts ($p = 0.004$). If Black suburbanites' perceptions of racial fairness at the workplace extend to wages and salaries, it is no wonder that many of them believe that Blacks are as financially well-off as whites.

The comparison of means tests also uncovered surprising differences in the views of suburban and urban Blacks on how African Americans are treated by the police (see Figure 6.6). As recent news headlines have announced, interactions with police are among the most vexing encounters that Blacks across the country, particularly those living in cities, have with government authority. They are also a salient part of the ordeal of adjustment to life in the suburbs for many Black come-outers (e.g., Samaha, 2017). Yet, the data indicate that suburban Blacks are significantly more likely ($p = 0.038$) than urban Blacks to report fair treatment by police. Blacks in both places have decidedly gloomy perceptions of how they are treated by police, to be sure, particularly in comparison

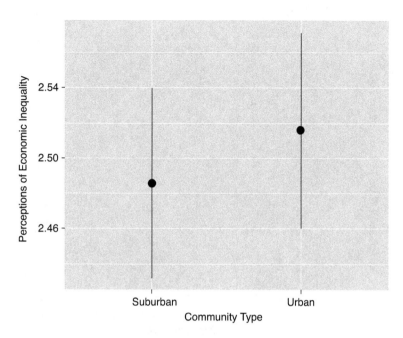

FIGURE 6.4 Economic Inequality
Source: Data from Pew Research Martin Luther King, Jr. Race Survey, August 1–11, 2013.

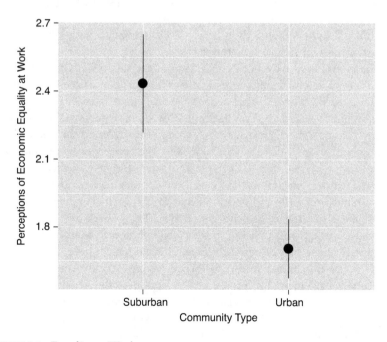

FIGURE 6.5 Equality at Work
Source: Data from Pew Research Martin Luther King, Jr. Race Survey, August 1–11, 2013.

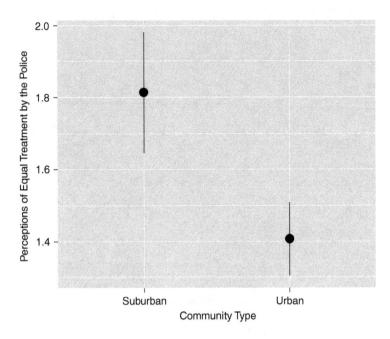

FIGURE 6.6 Equal Treatment by the Police
Source: Data from Pew Research Martin Luther King, Jr. Race Survey, August 1–11, 2013.

to whites. But the impressions of urban Blacks are significantly more negative than those of their suburban counterparts.

The interviews I have been conducting in the suburbs of Chicago illuminate these place-based differences in Blacks' perceptions. One respondent, a middle-aged Black man, explained, "One challenge Blacks [in my suburban neighborhood] don't face that Blacks in Chicago do is supposedly harassment by the Chicago Police Department." A young African American woman in the same suburb insisted that she can count on "the police to respond quickly if [she and her son] need them." On their face, these sentiments are hard to square with the familiar anecdotes about racially fraught interactions and distrust between suburban Blacks and police officers. But the first respondent's observation suggests that the assessments are relative. These Black suburbanites seem relatively satisfied with policing in their neighborhoods, compared to nearby Chicago, where scores of news stories and official reports have exposed widespread police misconduct and racial bias targeting African Americans. Black Chicagoans have massed in protest against episodes of police brutality in the city with almost seasonal regularity in recent years. Judging from this example, it is no wonder that Blacks in cities have a bleaker view of the police. Likewise, although the differences just barely pass the threshold of statistical significance, urban Blacks perceive less-than-equal treatment for Blacks in the courts and public schools, compared to suburban Blacks (see Figures 6.7 and 6.8). No

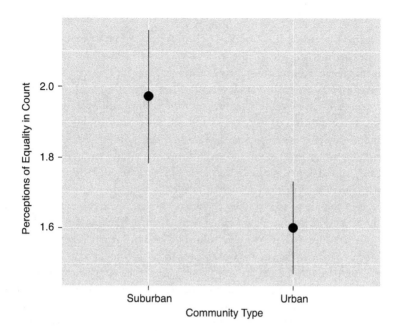

FIGURE 6.7 Equality in Court

Source: Data from Pew Research Martin Luther King, Jr. Race Survey, August 1–11, 2013.

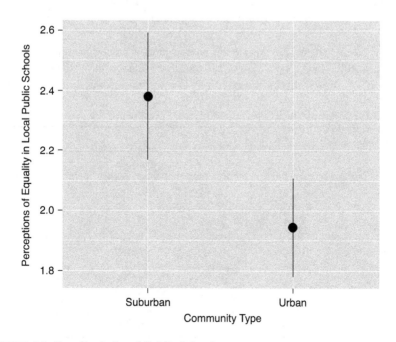

FIGURE 6.8 Equality in Local Public Schools

Source: Data from Pew Research Martin Luther King, Jr. Race Survey, August 1–11, 2013.

significant differences between the two groups were uncovered for the items on the relative treatment of Blacks and Whites in stores and restaurants, the healthcare industry, and the voting booth.

For the areas where I found variation between the two groups, the data also were analyzed in multivariate regressions with controls for individual-level income and education to provide an additional degree of robustness. Previous research shows that heterogeneity in racial attitudes among African Americans often tracks along lines of education and income.[16] Sure enough, the analyses, presented in Table 6.3, confirm that outlooks vary by education, although less so by income (see Table 6.3). Place of residence remains a significant source of cleavage in the views reported by Blacks in this survey. Even when individual income and education levels are taken into account, Black urban dwellers offer more dismal appraisals than their suburban counterparts on how Blacks are treated relative to whites in the workplace and by public institutions such as the courts. Better-educated Blacks also provide grimmer assessments than the less educated. Although this particular finding might seem counterintuitive, it is in keeping with a familiar, long-standing pattern in Black public opinion on issues of race. Among Blacks, the educated tend to be the most race-conscious and the bleakest in their perceptions of how Blacks are faring in the country (e.g., Dawson, 1994b; Hochschild, 1995). Several underlying factors likely account for this pattern, but it is probably due in part to the fact that educated Blacks are more attached to the institutions of the Black counterpublic than the less educated.

Income levels, on the other hand, were not associated with statistically significant differences in the views of Blacks that participated in the survey. The lack of significant effects for income in the models actually underscores how

TABLE 6.3 Determinants of Perceptions of Equal Treatment

	Equal Treatment			
	At Work	By Police	By Courts	By Schools
Urban	−0.772★★★	−0.446★★	−0.395★	−0.439★
	(0.245)	(0.188)	(0.224)	(0.265)
Income	−0.094	−0.045	0.001	0.048
	(0.059)	(0.046)	(0.054)	(0.064)
Education	−0.088	−0.142★★	−0.130★	−0.105
	(0.076)	(0.059)	(0.070)	(0.082)
Constant	3.231★★★	2.634★★★	2.538★★★	2.629★★★
	(0.346)	(0.267)	(0.317)	(0.375)
Observations	305	305	305	305
R2	0.053	0.055	0.024	0.014

Source: Data from Pew Research Martin Luther King, Jr. Race Survey.

Note. ★$p < 0.1$; ★★$p < 0.05$; ★★★$p < 0.01$.

much urban vis-à-vis suburban residence impacts Blacks' attitudes. Suburbanization in earlier decades used to be a symbol of success, commensurate with attaining higher levels of economic and social status (e.g., Alba & Logan, 1991). Recent research, however, suggests that this is no longer the case, particularly for whites. With a supermajority of whites living in the suburbs today, White households of all economic backgrounds are more likely to reside in suburbs than cities. But the suburbanization trend among Blacks remains relatively selective (Frey, 2015). The most upwardly mobile Blacks tend to opt for homes in suburban zip codes. As Frey explains, "among [B]lacks, suburban residence is likely only for those who achieve some post-high school education" (2015, p. 164). Almost 60% of Blacks with college degrees live in the suburbs of the country's 100 largest metropolitan areas (Frey, 2015). To the extent that better-educated, higher-earning Blacks reside in the suburbs, it would be reasonable to assume that any effects for residence on Blacks' attitudes might be due to income differences between Black suburbanites and their central city counterparts. But the regression analyses show that whether Blacks live in a city or suburb has a bigger impact on their racial views than how much they earn.[17] In fact, for the key items analyzed, residence exceeds or rivals both education and income in the significance of its impact on Blacks' opinions.

Although the survey did not include items about racial-linked fate, I have been exploring perceptions of racial solidarity in my ongoing interviews with Black suburbanites around the country, starting with the Chicago metropolitan area. The interviews in Chicagoland to date reveal considerable nuance in Black suburbanites' perceptions of linked fate with central city Blacks. Although many of the respondents report that they relate to urban Blacks as targets for discrimination, they believe that the challenges are more severe for Blacks living in cities and do not feel especially close to Blacks there, except their relatives and friends. One 50-year-old male respondent explained, "I do not feel very close to Blacks in Chicago, except family... [But] life in Chicago has a direct impact on what happens to Blacks in [my suburb] because the two communities are interrelated through family connections." Still, he noted, "I feel life here is much better for Blacks. For one, there is very little crime compared to neighborhoods in Chicago. I know because I work in some of those dangerous neighborhoods on the South Side." A mother in her forties highlighted one conspicuous commonality between Blacks in Chicago and her suburb. "I think one challenge that I face that other mothers in Chicago face is that I worry when my son ventures out of our neighborhood... that he will be targeted because of his race." Yet she drew a critical distinction. "When he's hanging out in our neighborhood I feel more comfortable. I know I couldn't say that if we still lived in Chicago." On the whole, these suburban Black respondents assess their own lives more positively than those of Black city residents and do not think that their fortunes rise and fall in tandem with those of their central city counterparts. Confirming other anecdotal evidence reported in news stories, they express negative stereotypes about inner-city Blacks in particular and bristle at any association with them, including the prospect of them moving to their suburban neighborhoods (e.g., Associated Press, 2011).

Conclusion

These findings suggest that suburbanization is an important, albeit understudied, source of variation in Blacks' racial and political attitudes. On issues of racial equality and fairness, the data show that urban Blacks have a gloomier view than their suburban counterparts of how Blacks are treated relative to whites in several spheres of life. Although Black suburbanites' perceptions of racial dynamics are not exactly sunlit, their perspectives seem considerably brighter from their zip codes outside central city areas. Judging from these results, it is not only that Blacks in suburbs and cities hold distinct racial views, it appears that suburbanization may be associated with moderation in how Blacks perceive racial issues. This contrasting pattern of suburban moderation and urban liberalism in African Americans' views about inequality and discrimination invites further questions about its implications for their policy attitudes and electoral behavior. For instance, are Black suburbanites more likely than their central city counterparts to prefer moderate candidates for local and national office? Likewise, has Black descriptive representation produced different policy outcomes in suburban municipalities than it has in central cities? If moderate or even conservative policy regimes dominate in the places where Black suburbanites live, is it due to their own taste for moderation or the overall racial and socioeconomic demographics of their suburban environs? After all, Blacks' views may be influenced by the racial or economic mix of their neighborhoods. Finally, how much of the moderation that has surfaced recently in Black politics at the national level is driven by the preferences of Black suburbanites? Are they less supportive of welfare and government assistance policies than Blacks living in the urban core?

More research on whether the opinion differences between urban and suburban Blacks extend to national policy questions and debates seems warranted. Although heterogeneity in Black public opinion is often masked by the truncated range of policy options that make it to the national agenda, it is not a new phenomenon. Still, Blacks have exhibited strikingly high levels of homogeneity in their views of policies to combat racial discrimination and inequality. As issues of institutional racism, such as mass incarceration, garner more elite and public attention, the question of whether these differences in Black suburban and urban racial views translate to policy preferences will assume greater political importance. They will be particularly critical when it comes to debating, defining, and framing Blacks' policy priorities and meeting the challenge of mustering collective action to address them. If Blacks in the suburbs and central cities see the political world differently from their respective zip codes, sorting out their distinct views and seeing if they can be reconciled for the sake of fashioning a unified agenda could become a prime preoccupation for Black politics at the national level and across metropolitan areas.

The survey data did not allow for an investigation into political attitudes or policy views. But the underlying theory about the diversifying effects of the spatial restructuring of the Black counterpublic suggests that policy preference differences between urban and suburban Blacks are possible and predictable. Black suburbanites may be distinct from their urban counterparts in their greater taste for moderation and their lesser appetite for government solutions to racial inequality and other challenges that limit opportunities for Blacks. It is not simply that they have a more positive assessment of anti-Black discrimination trends and the level of racial equality, it also may be that they are exposed to different public spheres with emphases and concerns that do not mirror those circulating in what remains of the urban Black counterpublic. Black public spheres in big cities historically have had a long reach and disproportionate influence on African American public opinion. The interests and concerns articulated in these urban spaces often have shaped the Black political agenda writ large. Their impact was particularly evident in the latter half of the twentieth century when the counterpublic was at its political apex.

With the fragmentation and decentralization of the Black counterpublic due to suburbanization, however, Black public spheres have emerged in places outside of cities. These new nodes are located in suburbs where municipal governments are quite different from the big, active governments of the urban centers where the Black counterpublic took root and consolidated in the mid- and late twentieth century. Suburban municipal governments tend to be more limited (Oliver, 2012). Most are not nearly as flush with resources, nor are they as intensively engaged in distributive and redistributive politics, or as involved in arbitrating among as many competing interests as big-city governments typically are. As urban researchers have documented, the governments of large central cities often have locational and tax resource advantages that give them greater latitude to pursue redistributive policies than the small governments of most suburban municipalities (e.g., Oliver, 2012; Peterson, 1981). Central city constituents also tend to be more heterogeneous. The commingling of socioeconomically disadvantaged groups who stand to benefit directly from such policies with more affluent constituents who might be inclined to resist them makes for more contentious politics. But it also encourages deliberation about common problems across groups, and under certain conditions, can produce policy outcomes that promote social equality.

The mid- to late twentieth century Black counterpublic may have been deeply informed by the more active governments of big cities featuring these social and political dynamics. The liberal cast of African American policy views during the period, then, may have been due partly to that geographic coincidence. African American policy liberalism may be a legacy of the mid-twentieth century urban locus of the Black counterpublic. In contrast, the public spheres where Black suburbanites live today may be influenced by the more limited, often managerial governments of those places. That distinction may inform the policy preferences and political attitudes of Black suburban come-outers, particularly their more moderate outlooks on racial issues—but perhaps in other areas too. In short, the political context of suburban municipalities may be moderating the views of Black suburbanites. On the other hand, selection bias may be lurking behind these effects. Black suburbanites may be moderates who are voting with their feet, rejecting the more liberal policies of central cities, and choosing suburban municipalities that suit their political preferences. In light of these questions, future research should take stock of the Black counterpublic in the suburbs and places beyond the urban Black beltway.[18] Researchers may find signs of Black political diversity and transition there too.

Notes

1 My thanks to the three Matthews—Matthew Nelsen, Matthew O'Connor, and Matthew Ryan—for their indispensable research support on this chapter and the ongoing project. Thanks also to Kelsey Rydland for his instruction and guidance on the GIS mapping.

2 See Mendelberg (2001) for a seminal discussion on how implicit racial messages prime racial resentments and influence vote choice.

3 For two notable exceptions, see Haynes (2006) and Johnson (2002). Also, see Gay (2004) for an insightful analysis on how differences in the socioeconomic character of central city and suburban neighborhoods affect blacks' racial attitudes.

4 I borrow the term "come-outers" from John Stilgoe, quoted in Rae 2003.

5 The stark racial disparity in suburbanization patterns that marked the latter half of the twentieth century contrasts with the first quarter of the century, when whites and Blacks resided in the suburbs at roughly equivalent, albeit very low, rates (Timberlake et al., 2011).

6 Recent increases in the suburban housing supply also have facilitated the move to the suburbs for racial minority groups, at least ostensibly. The growing inventory of market rate and affordable housing in the suburbs has been especially pivotal in the last few decades as housing prices in central cities have risen sharply due to unfettered redevelopment and gentrification. But researchers note that Black suburbanization rates have been least responsive to the surge in the suburban housing supply (Timberlake et al., 2011). This suggests that impediments to Black suburban residence remain significant, even if they are not nearly as daunting as they once were.

7 They include Detroit, Chicago, New Orleans, New York, Los Angeles, Washington, DC, Cleveland, Atlanta, Baltimore, Birmingham, St. Louis, and Dallas.

8 Suburban residence is hardly synonymous with Black–White integration. Segregation rates between Blacks and Whites remain quite high even in the suburbs. Most Black suburbanites live in predominantly Black neighborhoods. Suburbanization has been a more effective driver of economic segregation among Blacks than it has been a vehicle for racial integration between Blacks and Whites (Gay, 2004).

9 Dawson (1994a) calls this identity-based shortcut for making political decisions the "Black utility heuristic."

10 See Kennedy (2008) for a revealing historical exploration of the costs of betraying racial group norms in Black politics.

11 See Cramer Walsh (2004) for a detailed discussion of the disproportionate influence that well-established individuals wield in dialogic spaces.

12 Geographic change is not the only driver of reconfiguration in the Black counterpublic. The rise of information technologies, such as the internet, has created new counterpublic hubs. Younger generations of Blacks have migrated to online public realms and social media like Black twitter to foster alternative spaces for deliberation and consensus-building.

13 Following this logic, suburbanization also might depress some forms of political participation among Blacks, specifically activities driven by social contact and pressure.

14 Analyses in Welch, Sigelman, Bledsoe, and Combs (2001) provide a telling exception. The researchers are primarily interested in the effects of neighborhood racial composition on individual attitudes in the Detroit metropolitan area. But their analyses indicate that Black suburbanization is negatively correlated with support for Black autonomy and lockstep Black solidarity in the electoral arena.

15 On average, White suburbs boast more resources and amenities than Black suburbs. Similarly, middle-class status nets far fewer residential benefits for Blacks than it does for Whites. As Gay notes, "the majority of upwardly mobile African Americans reside in communities with more abandoned housing, higher crime rates, fewer local services, less spending on infrastructure and development, lower environmental quality, higher public debt, and poorer prospects for economic growth than the neighborhoods in which Whites of comparable socioeconomic status reside" (2004, pp. 549–550).

16 Studies have found variation in attitudes by generation and nativity status as well (e.g., Cohen, 2010; Greer, 2013; Smith, 2014).

17 If income has an effect on the views on Black suburbanites, it might be at the contextual rather than the individual level. That is, it might operate as a compositional variable that captures the proportion of particular income groups living in a suburban neighborhood (e.g., Gay, 2004). The individual-level political effects of these contextual distinctions among suburbs and cities are an important topic for further research.

18 The views of rural Blacks warrant in-depth exploration as well.

References

Abrajano, M., & Hajnal, Z. (2015). *White backlash: Immigration, race, and American politics.* Princeton, NJ: Princeton University Press.

Achen, C., & Bartels, L. (2016). *Democracy for realists: Why do elections not produce responsive government.* Princeton, NJ: Princeton University Press.

Alba, R. D., & Logan, J. (1991). Variations on two themes: Racial and ethnic patterns in the attainment of suburban residence. *Demography, 28,*431–453.

Associated Press. (2011, February 28). *Foreclosures changing the color of many metro detroit suburbs.* New York, NY: Associated Press.

Berelson, B., Lazarsfeld, P., & McPhee, W. (1954). *Voting: A study of opinion formation in a presidential campaign.* Chicago, IL: University of Chicago Press.

Biondi, M. (2006). *To stand and fight: The struggle for civil rights in postwar New York City.* Cambridge, MA: Harvard University Press.

Burgess, E. (1965). Race relations and social change. In J. C. Thompson & E. T. Thompson (Eds.), *The South in continuity and change.* Durham, NC: Duke University Press, 337–358.

Chong, D., & Kim, D. (2006). The experiences and effects of economic status among racial and ethnic minorities. *American Political Science Review, 100*(3), 335–351.

Coates, T. (2014, June). The case for reparations. *The Atlantic.*

Cohen, C. (1999). *The boundaries of blackness: AIDS and the breakdown of black politics.* Chicago, IL: University of Chicago Press.

Cohen, C. (2010). *Democracy remixed: Black youth and the future of American politics.* New York, NY: Oxford University Press.

Cohen, C., & Dawson, M. (1993). Neighborhood poverty and African American politics. *American Political Science Review, 87*(2), 286–302.

Conn, S. (2014). *Americans against the city: Anti-urbanism in the twentieth century.* New York, NY: Oxford University Press.

Conover, P. (1984). The political influence of group identifications on political perceptions and evaluations. *Journal of Politics, 46*(3), 760–785.

Cramer, K. (2016). *The politics of resentment: Rural consciousness in Wisconsin and the rise of Scott Walker.* Chicago, IL: University of Chicago Press.

Dawson, M. (1994a). *Behind the mule: Race and class in African-American politics.* Princeton, NJ: Princeton University Press.

Dawson, M. (1994b). A black counterpublic? Economic earthquakes, racial agenda(s), and black politics. *Public Culture, 7,* 195–223.

Dawson, M. (2001). *Black visions: The roots of contemporary African-American political ideologies.* Chicago, IL: University of Chicago Press.

Dawson, M. (2011). *Not in our lifetimes: The future of Black Politics.* Chicago, IL: University of Chicago Press.

Drake, S., & Cayton, H. (1945). *Black metropolis: A study of Negro life in a Northern City.* Chicago, IL: University of Chicago Press.

Farley, R., Schuman, H., Bianchi, S., Colasanto, D., & Hatchett, S. (1978). Chocolate city, vanilla suburbs: Will the trend toward racially separate communities continue? *Social Science Research, 7,* 319–344.

Fischer, M. J. (2008). Shifting geographies: Examining the role of suburbanization in blacks' declining segregation. *Urban Affairs Review, 43*(4), 475–496.

Frazier, J. W., & Anderson, R. (2006). People on the move: African Americans since the great migration. In J. W. Frazier & E. L. Tettey-Fio (Eds.), *Race, ethnicity, and place in a changing America* (pp. 83–96). Albany, NY: State University of New York Press.

Frazier, J. W., & Tettey-Fio, E. L. (Eds.). (2006). *Race, ethnicity, and place in a changing America.* Albany, NY: State University of New York Press.

Frey, W. (2015). *Diversity explosion: How new racial demographics are remaking America.* Washington, DC: Brookings Institution.

Gainsborough, J. F. (2001). *Fenced off: The suburbanization of American politics.* Washington, DC: Georgetown University Press.

Gay, C. (2004). Putting race in context: Identifying the environmental determinants of black racial attitudes. *American Political Science Review, 98*(4), 547–562.

Gay, C., & Hochschild, J. (2010, January). Is racial linked fate unique? Comparing race, ethnicity, class, gender, and religion. *ResearchGate.* https://www.researchgate.net/profile/Jennifer_Hochschild/publication/228212272_Is_Racial_Linked_Fate_Unique_Comparing_Race_Ethnicity_Class_Gender_and_Religion/links/0c960537e0f2c5dabb000000.pdf

Gay, C., Hochschild, J., & White, A. (2016). Americans' belief in linked fate: Does the measure capture the concept? *Journal of Race, Ethnicity, and Politics, 1*(1), 117–144.

Glaster, G. C. (1991). Black suburbanization: Has it changed the relative location of the races? *Urban Affairs Quarterly, 26*(4), 621–628.

Greer, C. (2013). *Black ethnics: Race, immigration, and the American dream.* New York, NY: Oxford University Press.

Gurin, P., Hatchett, S., & Jackson, J. (1989). *Hope and independence: Blacks response to electoral and party politics.* New York, NY: Russell Sage Foundation.

Harris-Lacewell, M. (2004). *Barbershops, Bibles, and BET: Everyday talk and black political thought.* Princeton, NJ: Princeton University Press.

Haynes, B. (2006). *Red lines, black spaces: The politics of race and space in a black middle class suburb.* New Haven, CN: Yale University Press.

Herring, M., Janowski, T., & Brown, R. (1999). Pro-black doesn't mean anti-white: The structure of African-American group identity. *The Journal of Politics, 61*(2), 363–386.

Hirschman, A. (1970). *Exit, voice, and loyalty: Response to decline in firms, organizations, and states.* Cambridge, MA: Harvard University Press.

Hochschild, J. (1995). *Facing up to the American dream: Race, class, and the soul of the nation.* Princeton, NJ: Princeton University Press.

Huckfeldt, R., & Kohlfeld, C. W. (1989). *Race and the decline of class in American politics.* Urbana, IL: University of Illinois Press.

Huddy, L. (2001). From social to political identity: A critical examination of social identity theory. *Political Psychology, 22*(1), 127–156.

Hunter, M. (2013). *Black citymakers: How the Philadelphia Negro changed urban America.* Oxford, England: Oxford University Press.

Hurwitz, J., & Peffley, M. (2005). Playing the race card in the post-Willie Horton Era: The impact of racialized code words on support for punitive crime policy. *Public Opinion Quarterly, 69*(1), 99–112.

Jackson, K. (1985). *The crabgrass frontier: The suburbanization of America.* New York, NY: Oxford University Press.

Jacobs, J. (1961). The death and life of great American cities. New York, NY: Random House.

Johnson, V. (2002).Black power in the suburbs: The myth or reality of African-American suburban political incorporation. Albany, NY: State University of New York.

Kennedy, R. (2008). *Sellout: The politics of racial betrayal.* New York, NY: Pantheon Books.

Kinder, D., & Winter, N. (2001). Exploring the racial divide: Blacks, whites, and opinion on national policy. *American Journal of Political Science, 45,* 439–456.

Kruse, K. (2005). *White flight: Atlanta and the making of modern conservatism.* Princeton, NJ: Princeton University Press.

Macedo, S. (2011). Property-owning plutocracy: Inequality and American localism. In C. R. Hayward & T. Swanstrom (Eds.), *Justice and the American metropolis* (pp. 33–58). Minneapolis, MN: University of Minnesota Press.

Massey, D., & Denton, N. (1993). *American apartheid: Segregation and the making of the underclass.* Cambridge, MA: Harvard University Press.

McAdam, D. (1982). *Political process and the development of black insurgency, 1930–1970.* Chicago, IL: University of Chicago Press.

McClain, P., & Stewart, J. (2013). *Can we all get along? Racial and ethnic minorities in American politics* (6th ed.). Boulder, CO: Westview Press.

Mendelberg, T. (2001). *The race card: Campaign strategy, implicit messages, and the norm of racial equality.* Princeton, NJ: Princeton University Press.

Morris, A. (1984). *The origins of the civil rights movement: Black communities organizing for change.* New York, NY: The Free Press.

Oliver, J. E. (2001). *Democracy in suburbia.* Princeton, NJ: Princeton University Press.

Oliver, J. E. (2012). *Local elections and the politics of small scale democracy.* Princeton, NJ: Princeton University Press.

Patillo-McCoy, M. (1999). *Black picket fences: Privilege and peril among the black middle class.* Chicago, IL: University of Chicago Press.

Perez-Pena, R. (2017, January 26). Contrary to Trump's claim, immigrants are less likely to commit crimes. *New York Times.*

Peterson, P. (1981). *City limits.* Chicago, IL: University of Chicago Press.

Pew Research Center. (2007). *Optimism about black progress declines: Blacks see growing values gap between poor and middle class.* http://assets.pewresearch.org/wp-content/uploads/sites/3/2010/10/Race-2007.pdf

Pew Research Center. (2013). *The black-white and urban-rural divides in perceptions of racial fairness.* http://www.pewresearch.org/fact-tank/2013/08/28/the-black-white-and-urban-rural-divides-in-perceptions-of-racial-fairness

Pew Research Center. (2016). *On views of race and inequality, blacks and whites are worlds apart.* http://assets.pewresearch.org/wp-content/uploads/sites/3/2016/06/ST_2016.06.27_Race-Inequality-Final.pdf

Putnam, R. (2000). *Bowling along: The collapse and renewal of American community.* New York, NY: Simon and Schuster.

Rae, D. (2003). *City: Urbanism and its end.* New Haven, CN: Yale University Press.

Reed, A. (1999). *Stirrings in the jug: Black politics in the post-Segregation Era.* Minneapolis, MN: University of Minnesota Press.

Rothschild, J. (2017). *Social groups, networks, and coalitions: The indirect identity effects of political elites.* Evanston, IL: Northwestern University.

Samaha, A. (2017, May 20). Police forces are sending a message to black suburbanites: You're not Wanted. *BuzzFeed.*

Sampson, R. (2012). *Great American city: Chicago and the enduring neighborhood effect.* Chicago, IL: University of Chicago Press.

Schneider, M., & Phelan, T. (1993). Black suburbanization in the 1980s. *Demography, 30,* 269–279.

Sebastian, S. (2016, October 10). Trump gets a basic fact wrong about black Americans. *The Washington Post.*

Semuels, A. (2016, October 12). Trump wrongly conflates black people and inner cities. *The Atlantic.*

Sharkey, P. (2013). *Stuck in place: Urban neighborhoods and the end of progress toward racial equality.* Chicago, IL: University of Chicago Press.

Simpson, A. (1998). *The tie that binds: Identity and political attitudes in the post-civil rights generation.* New York, NY: New York University Press.

Sinclair, B. (2012). *The social citizen: Peer networks and political behavior.* Chicago, IL: University of Chicago Press.

Spence, L. K., & McClerking, H. (2010). Context, black empowerment, and African-American political participation. *American Politics Research, 38,* 909–930.

Sugrue, T. (1996). *The origins of the urban crisis: Race and inequality in Postwar Detroit.* Princeton, NJ: Princeton University Press.

Smith, C. W. (2014). *Black mosaic: The politics of black pan-ethnic diversity*. New York, NY: New York University Press.

Suhay, E. (2015). Explaining group influence: The role of identity and emotion in political conformity and polarization. *Political Behavior, 37*(1), 221–251.

Tate, K. (1993). *From protest to politics*. New York, NY: Russell Sage Foundation.

Tate, K. (2010). *What's going on? Political incorporation and the transformation of black public opinion*. Washington, DC: Georgetown University Press.

Teixeira, R., & Halpin, J. (2012). *The Obama coalition in the 2012 election and beyond*. Washington, DC: Center for American Progress.

Timberlake, J. (2002). Separate, but how unequal? Ethnic residential stratification, 1980–990. *City & Community, 1*, 251–266.

Timberlake, J., Howell, A., & Staight, A. (2011). Trends in the suburbanization of racial/ethnic groups in U.S. metropolitan areas, 1970 to 2000. *Urban Affairs Review, 47*(2), 218–255.

Walsh, K. C. (2004). *Talking about politics: Informal groups and social identity in American life*. Chicago, IL: University of Chicago Press.

Welch, S., Sigelman, L., Bledsoe, T., & Combs, M. (2001). *Race and place*. Cambridge, England: Cambridge University Press.

White, I. K., Laird, C. N., & Allen, T. D. (2014). Selling out? The politics of navigating conflicts between racial group interest and self-interest. *American Political Science Review, 108*(4), 783–800.

Wiese, A. (2004). *Places of their own: African American suburbanization in the twentieth century*. Chicago, IL: University of Chicago Press.

Wiese, A. (2006). The house I live in: Race, class, and African American suburban dreams in the postwar United States. In K. Kruse & T. Sugrue (Eds.), *The new suburban history*. Chicago, IL: University of Chicago Press, 99–119.

Wilkerson, I. (2010). *The warmth of other suns: The epic story of America's great migration*. New York, NY: Random House.

Wilson, W. J. (1987). *The truly disadvantaged: The inner city, the underclass, and public policy*. Chicago, IL: University of Chicago Press.

Yearwood, L. (1978). National Afro-American organizations in urban communities. *Journal of Black Studies, 8*(4), 423–438.

Yee, V., Davis, K., & Patel, J. K. (2017, March 6). Here's the reality about illegal immigrants in the United States. *New York Times*.

PART IV

There Goes the Neighborhood

The Complexities of Racialized Neighborhood Change

7

MOVING UP, OUT, AND ACROSS THE COUNTRY

Regional Differences in the Causes of Neighborhood Change and its Effect on African Americans

Jessica Lynn Stewart

The term gentrification was originally introduced by English sociologist Ruth Glass in 1964. She described a discrete process involving residential movement of the middle class to low-income areas of London (Glass, 2010). Following the revitalization of several US cities in the mid-1970s, American sociologists began noticing the same process of neighborhood change described by Glass, with one predictable caveat: race. It was clear that American gentrification involved the accelerated displacement of African Americans by whites (Gale, 1984; Zukin, 1987).

Over the past 30 years, scholars have debated the dynamics of gentrification, including the extent of its effects on majority-Black communities (Brown-Saracino, 2017), and within that time, four broad theories explaining the causes and effects of gentrification have been developed. First, there are a set of theories explaining the causes of gentrification, which may also be seen as two competing schools of thought. There are those who see individual neighborhood preferences as driving neighborhood change, and they contrast those who highlight the role of political economy forces. Relatedly, there are two competing schools of thought concerning the racialized effects of gentrification. On the one hand, there are those who believe gentrification has minimal racial impact; meanwhile, others believe gentrification tends to increase racial inequality.

However, studies often fail to make two key considerations in their analysis of gentrification. First, scholars tend to narrowly focus on contemporary instances of gentrification without explicitly connecting the concept to other historical processes of neighborhood change, such as legalized/*de facto* segregation, white flight, and urban renewal, all of which are driven by political forces (Lipsitz, 2006; Taeuber & Taeuber, 1969). Each of these processes varies in its underlying causes and effects but together point to a continued American tradition of systemic, spatialized racial discrimination.

Second, rarely is a connection made between interregional Black migration and distinct intragroup experiences of gentrification. Scholars rarely consider how gentrification varies by region, specifically given that the degree of African American homeowning power and displacement differs across the country. Beginning in the 1970s, Blacks began voluntarily leaving the Northeast and Midwest in mass, partially for better housing opportunities in the South (Frey, 2004; Iceland, Sharp, & Timberlake 2013; Tolnay, 2003). Due to significant economic shifts over the past 40 years, access to affordable housing, homeownership rates, and overall Black home-buying power varies by place now more than ever (Moretti, 2012; Parks, 2011; Pendergrass, 2013). Traditional theories of gentrification must evolve to accommodate emerging racial, spatial, and socioeconomic complexities, such as regional economic restructuring and Reverse Great Migration trends.

There is need for an updated, integrated analysis of gentrification that addresses diverging housing opportunities; that is to say, there is a necessity for a regional political economy perspective. Due to fact that scholars have not yet recognized regional differences in race–space demographic profiles, the question remains: To what extent does regional socioeconomic context shape gentrification and its effects on African Americans' well-being and Black politics? In this chapter, I argue that gentrification's effects on African Americans vary by region. Regional socioeconomic context, primarily patterns of urban organization, population concentration, and African American home-buying power shape the effects of neighborhood change. A history of white flight combined with limited space and central city manufacturing decline makes the Midwest and Northeast perfect environments for gentrification to thrive. In contrast, the same conditions are not present in the South. Using quantitative analysis and cartographic techniques, I compare African American communities both regionally and at the metropolitan area level. I find evidence that African Americans residing in Midwestern and Northeastern cities are more vulnerable to the negative effects of gentrification compared with African Americans residing along the Sun Belt. Blacks residing in the South—more specifically Black migrants to South Atlantic metropolitan areas—are more likely to reap the benefits of new housing developments. This regionally centered framework updates our understanding of racialized neighborhood change more broadly, while also challenging contemporary notions of what segregation and residential integration looks like, particularly in Southern cosmopolitan neighborhoods.

Within the remainder of this chapter, I review pertinent literature related to gentrification. Next, I outline a theoretical framework for understanding the nuances of gentrification from a regional political economy perspective and detailed research design. Following a description of the data sample and methodological approach, I present findings from a quantitative and spatial analysis, highlighting interregional differences in Black home-buying power. Lastly, the broader impact of regional effects on racialized neighborhood change is discussed. But first, I provide a brief background on the intersection of race and place.

A Brief History

Great Migration and Land Use

In 1910, 73% of African Americans lived in rural areas, mostly farms and villages in the South. By 1960, 73% of African Americans resided in metropolitan areas across the US. The Great Migration began in 1910 and picked up in the 1930s as millions of African Americans moved away from the South to escape Jim Crow and find better opportunities for economic advancement (Taeuber & Taeuber, 1969). The movement of Blacks from the rural South to industrial centers in the Midwest and Northeast was a massive redistribution of the population.

Upon arrival to Midwestern and Northern industrial centers, Blacks were restricted in their employment and housing opportunities (Hyman & Sheatsley, 1956; Taeuber & Taeuber, 1969). Beginning in 1934, the Federal Housing Administration (FHA) began exclusively backing white Americans' mortgage loans, while explicitly refusing to back loans for Blacks or those who chose to live near Blacks. The FHA institutionalized unequal access to homeownership along racial lines and facilitated the flow of capital investments away from Black communities. Though the policy formally ended in 1968, FHA's racist intervention in the housing market, which developed at the federal level and was implemented at the local level, produced a legacy of private and state-sanctioned housing discrimination. Among the most detrimental processes included redlining by the Home Owners Loan Corporation, restrictive covenants, concentration of public housing in majority-Black neighborhoods, higher loan fees for African Americans, racial steering to particular neighborhoods, and publicly subsidized funding of exclusively white suburbs (Lipsitz, 2006; Taeuber & Taeuber, 1969).

Pre- and post-Civil Rights Movement era housing practices and policies have helped sustain racial segregation by stigmatizing African Americans as irresponsible homeowners and undesirable neighborhood residents, myths used to rationalize disinvestment in majority-Black communities. Furthermore, given the value of homeownership as a middle-class asset, racist policies have also limited African Americans' ability to generate generational wealth and upward group mobility. Two prominent, interconnected, and illuminating examples of government intervention facilitating racialized neighborhood change processes are white flight and gentrification.

White Flight, a Regional Phenomenon

In the 1950s and 1960s, the concept of transitioning neighborhoods commonly referred to as white flight—a process where whites flee their homes and neighborhoods for the suburbs once African American residents begin to move in.

During this time, Blacks experienced complete exclusion from suburban development (Lipsitz, 2006; Taeuber & Taeuber, 1969). Black communities were typically located in the central portion of the city and expanded outward from there. White flight during the suburban boom increased the housing supply in Midwestern and Northeastern industrial centers and expanded African American housing options. Yet, it quickly became apparent that majority-Black communities were plagued by disinvestment, which fostered declining living conditions (Wilson, 1987).

A noteworthy case study for the significant impact of white flight on the housing market is Chicago during the 1950s. In the 1940s, all but three Chicago neighborhoods were majority white, while Blacks were confined to a small portion of the city's South Side called "The Black Belt." During the height of American suburbanization, whole neighborhoods went from being monolithically white to monolithically Black. For example, in Englewood, currently one of Chicago's most dangerous majority-Black neighborhoods, the white population went from 51,583 to 818 between 1960 and 1980 (McClelland, 2013). Drastic declines in the city's white residents led to rampant disinvestment as the Black Belt expanded to cover most of the city's South and West sides. Today, despite gentrification, whites continue to reside mostly downtown and on the North side of the Chicago, strategically ensuring that the Black Belt stays intact and systemic disinvestment continues. Pre-white flight segregation evolved into hypersegregation, even during the most current era of gentrification.

However, Chicago's pattern of land use and white flight was not experienced across cities nationwide. Cities in the Northeast and Midwest have higher levels of African American centralization than Southern cities. During the 1950s and 1960s, many Southern cities also experienced a net loss of whites, but the movement did not significantly impact housing conditions for African Americans to the same degree as white flight did in the Northeast and Midwest (Hyman & Sheatsley, 1956).

What Makes Gentrification So Special?

White Americans' preference for cookie-cutter suburb developments began to fade in the 1980s, and scholars began taking notice of more whites moving into historically majority-Black inner-city neighborhoods (Gale, 1984; Zukin, 1987). Over 30 years after the term has been introduced, debates over what drives gentrification and exactly how consequential it is for American city life continue to linger (Brown-Saracino, 2017).

Gentrification is a particularly noteworthy process of neighborhood change for two reasons. First, gentrification violates principle theories of urban growth where low socioeconomic status individuals, predominantly Blacks, live closer to the central business district (Soja, 2013). This flip in urban organizational structure makes gentrification a highly disruptive process. Second, gentrification begins picking up steam in the midst of other less-discussed spatially transformative trends such as, the "new" or "reverse" Great Migration, suburban urbanization, and regional economic restructuring (Frey, 2004; Parks, 2011, 2012; Soja, 2013). Analysts consider the mass movement of African Americans to the South and to the suburbs as fundamentally altering the geographic social landscape, while regional economic restructuring has altered the geography of opportunity. However, traditionally, scholars have not considered gentrification in relation to other historical processes of neighborhood change, broader regional socioeconomic context, and contemporary inter- and intra-regional African American migration patterns.

Black Flight and the Growth of Southern Metros

Currently, highly visible neighborhood changes include whites return to central cities and Black flight to the suburbs and to the South. According to Forbes Magazine (2015), the American South holds nine out of the top ten cities where African Americans fair best economically. From 2005 to 2010, the South gained on average of 66,000 African Americans each year, solidifying a reversal of the Great Migration (Frey, 2004). Movement of Blacks back to the South is particularly noteworthy because the region is largely regarded in scholarship as having the most tenuous image of racial prejudice (Key, 1949).

Black migrants during the Great Migration and the Reverse Great Migration tended to move between large and midsized metropolitan areas and be of higher socioeconomic status than natives in their new destinations (Hunt, 2013). Currently drawing African Americans to the supposed racially hostile South and away from once-booming Midwest and Northeastern industrial centers are the possibilities of buying a home, finding a decent job, and having access to well-established educational institutions (Pendergrass, 2013; Tolnay, 2003). Blacks' increasing economic gains in the post-Civil Rights era has slightly counteracted forces producing segregation but has certainly not eliminated national patterns of racial segregation and racialized neighborhood change process. Thus, further study in this area is warranted.

Understanding Gentrification: Four Perspectives

Scholars have advanced four explanations to account for the causes and effects of gentrification, three of which downplay the role of race, while the fourth explicitly highlights negative racialized consequences. The first two schools of thought speak to an enduring debate over whether individual preferences or political economy forces drive gentrification. To adherents of the individual neighborhood preference theory, gentrification is caused by individuals' preference to live in specific types of communities which can change over time (Goetz, 2011; Ley, 1978; Lipton, 1977; Zukin, 1987). Meanwhile, those in the political economy forces school focus on the ways governments and private firms facilitate gentrification.

The remaining schools of thought look more to the effects of gentrification. Here, the minimal impact theory argues that the impact of gentrification on African Americans and the country as a whole has been overstated. Finally, the last set of scholars points directly to racial undertones embedded in individual neighborhood preferences and political economy forces while making clear the ways in which gentrification exacerbates racial inequality.

While each of these perspectives makes compelling arguments, the latter is the most convincing because recent examples of gentrification confirm that African Americans continue to be most likely to be displaced during racialized neighborhood change processes. Below, each school of thought is explained in more detail.

Causes: Individual Neighborhood Preference versus Political-Economy Forces

The first school of thought, individual neighborhood preferences, also known as the consumer sovereignty theory, suggests that racial transition in neighborhoods simply reflects a change in neighborhood preference, a general process of urban change. The underlying rationale is that the search for housing and the overall housing market is led by those who can afford homes. In the 1950s, newer homes were being built on the periphery of cities, so those who could afford newer homes moved to the suburbs. The patterns of American suburbanization at that time led to the development of neoclassical residential land use theory, which claimed movement to the suburbs reflected an individual preference for space (Alonso, 1964; Mills, 1972; Muth, 1969).

Beginning in the late 1970s, an increase in central city white-collar employment opportunities, frustration with long commutes, and a declining preference for a cookie-cutter suburban aesthetic led new home buyers away from the suburbs (Ley, 1978). Furthermore, as Lipton (1977) suggests, during this period there was a fundamental change in the characteristics of the typical American home buyer. Due to a younger professional middle class with fewer children, along with higher divorce rates, the demand for large suburban homes began to decline (Lipton, 1977). With this in mind, scholars argued that gentrification is caused by a genuine desire for a city residence. Though not without flaws, these individual neighborhood preference theories are useful for understanding who drives housing searches but provide race-neutral reasons for why people move.

In contrast, other scholars suggest racial transition in neighborhoods is driven by market and political factors. The underlying rationale of this set of theories is that there is a clear economic incentive for local government officials and business elite to support racialized neighborhood change. Smith (1979) was one of the first scholars to argue against a purely individual neighborhood preference explanation for gentrification, and pushed, instead, for recognition of hidden economic characteristics. Political economy forces use new developments to entice potential home buyers and generate an individual preference for inner-city residence (Smith, 1979; Zukin, 1987). When inner-city buildings begin to depreciate, in combination with rising land costs and potential rents, the profitability of gentrification is increased.

This body of literature notes that most gentrifying neighborhoods are in close proximity to downtown central business districts, thus creating an opportunity for businesses and politicians to keep valuable middle- and upper-class workers, consumers, and voters within city limits (Smith, 1979). For example, Goetz (2011) examined the ways in which political decisions facilitate gentrification, claiming demolition of public housing with high levels of African American occupancy is a symbol of state-sanctioned gentrification. He explains how the disinvestment of housing in certain neighborhoods, coupled with high levels of publicly funded reinvestment in others is characteristic of gentrification, with race being the primary explanatory variable.

Local government development strategies vary, which contributes to neighborhood change not being monolithic. A configuration of political and economic considerations influences the pace, scale, and intensity of gentrification efforts. The political economy thesis is useful for understanding why local governments cater inner-city development projects to particular subpopulations, while also continuing to engage in selective community disinvestment.

Effects: Minimal Racial Impact versus Increasing Racial Inequality

Just as the causes of gentrification are contested, so are the effects, especially as they relate to the extent to which gentrification exacerbates racial inequality. The minimal racial impact school of thought suggests gentrification has almost no impact on African Americans. Here, scholars argue that white Americans are still moving to the suburbs and are too afraid to move into majority non-white communities, especially where pockets of inner-city poverty remain consistent.

It should be noted that not all majority-Black communities are conducive to gentrification. The share of Blacks and Latinxs matters when determining its likelihood and success, where the presence of a greater number of Black and brown people reduces the chances of white-led diversification (Hwang, 2015). Scholars like Freeman and Cai (2015) suggest that majority-Black neighborhoods are less likely to be gentrified compared to neighborhoods less than 50% Black (also see Bates, 2013; Bostic & Martin, 2003). Additionally, Maciag (2015) finds only 8% of all neighborhoods are gentrified. Thus, from this perspective, gentrification is either an outdated conceptualization of neighborhood change or its significance has been overstated. Scholars, here, stress distinctions between an increasing number of affluent neighborhoods and gentrification as a specific neighborhood change process (Hwang, 2015; Solari, 2012).

What's more, America has entered a new phase of gentrification where original middle-class white gentrifiers are themselves being displaced by those with even higher incomes. For example, Chicago's Wicker Park neighborhood during the industrial age was home to mostly Polish immigrants. Following deindustrialization, in the 1980s the neighborhood became an obscure barrio, mostly populated with Mexicans and Puerto Ricans. In the 1990s, it transformed into an epicenter of urban neo-bohemian culture, populated by white hipster artists and musicians. Currently, a three-bedroom condo in Wicker Park costs around $420,000, or about $3,200 a month to rent, considerably more than what the original gentrifying bohemian crowd can afford (Lloyd, 2010). Taken together, the minimal impact theory is useful for understanding why all neighborhood change should not be considered a gentrification effort or as being detrimental only or primarily to African Americans.

The final set of scholars suggest gentrification is highly problematic in the way it alters the character of communities and exacerbates racial equality. The perspective operates as a direct alternative to the minimal racial impact perspective previously discussed. This body of literature centers on the notion that gentrification/gentrified neighborhoods are a core facet of many contemporary cities with large African American populations and emphasizes the idea that during this process of neighborhood change African Americans, as long-term residents of inner-city neighborhoods, are disproportionately affected.

In addition to the displacement of people, gentrification often involves the displacement of culture as well as local social and commercial institutions, which tend to be viewed as problematic by those being displaced (Hyra, 2015; Zukin et al., 2009). Both Patillo (2007) and Martinez (2010) highlight tension between Blacks and Whites created by racialized neighborhood change around the use of public space, noise, and schools. In addition, this framework aligns with those who claim that as inequality increases, the distribution of wealth becomes increasingly bifurcated/divided, with an added spatial component (Moretti, 2012; Owens, 2012; Solari, 2012). This perspective is useful for understanding how gentrification becomes racialized by facilitating a racially segregated housing market, intensifying racial divisions, and disproportionately displacing African Americans.

In retrospect, existing theories offer some, but perhaps minimal, guidance for moving beyond principled positions to reach a broader understanding of the relationships between individual preference, political economy forces, and African Americans displacement. For instance, the political economy forces school of thought and the individual neighborhood preference school are both rooted in a race-neutral rationale, while racial undertones are empirically apparent. During both the height of suburbanization and gentrification, whites disproportionately held home-buying power and, thus, were more likely to benefit from both trends compared to African Americans. Nevertheless, the individual neighborhood preference theory helps to consider the possibility that places where African Americans have more home-buying power are also the places where African Americans are less likely to be victims of racialized neighborhood change and displaced by gentrification. What's more, the relationship between regional Black political economy development and specifically African American displacement remains unclear.

Relatedly, minimal racial impact theory does align with recent discussions of Black gentrification, where African Americans are both the victims and beneficiaries of gentrification. However, minimal impact theorists fail to consider a glaring fact: gentrifiers tend to be upwardly mobile and white, and gentrification still *disproportionately* involves the displacement of African Americans. A major analytical flaw is rooted in the notion that these theories do not account for the geographical concentration of African Americans. It remains unclear whether this theory holds when using the appropriate subset of localities based on where Blacks actually live.

Lastly, though I agree most with the basic premise of increasing racial inequality theory, as a sweeping perspective, it fails to acknowledge variation in types of neighborhood change and the reality of Black gentrification, especially in the wake of major demographic changes like the Reverse Great Migration. This study uses components from each of the reviewed perspectives to begin thinking about how regional and local socioeconomic context shapes the impact of gentrification on African Americans. I suggest that the effects of gentrification on African Americans differ across regions and cities based on how urban social structures are organized in alignment with local economic characteristics and individual preferences. I show that regional economic restructuring shapes Black home-buying power and neighborhood change processes like gentrification.

A Regional Political Economy Perspective

My theoretical framework begins with understanding the nature of cities where gentrification is most prominent. As previously mentioned, gentrification violates historical or traditional patterns of urban organization, making it a disruptive neighborhood change process. Urban organization refers to patterns of growth that determine the spatial organization of people and economic activities in urban spaces (Glass, 2010). To illustrate, urban organization scholars developed land use models that use concentric and polycentric zones, which provide depictions of the intersection of geography and economics as a significant factor in determining where individuals live (Burgess, 1935). In both concentric and polycentric zone models, there is a positive correlation between individual economic status and distance from the central business district, with neighborhoods becoming more affluent the further out one moves toward suburban areas (Muth, 1969). Right outside of the central business district is a transition zone, characterized by decay, old abandoned factory buildings due to deindustrialization, and poor housing conditions for low-income residents (Bates, 2013; Bluestone & Harrison, 1982). Early models depict African Americans mostly concentrated in the transition zone with neighborhoods becoming more white and less ethnically diverse the further one moves away from the central business district.

Now more than ever, metropolitan areas vary in their built environments, timing of growth, and settlement geography (Hill & Feagin, 1987; Meyer & Esposito, 2015). In regard to supply and demand for housing, the scarcity of land and timing of economic growth is important because it impacts the current age, condition, and availability of central city housing stock (Alonso, 1964). Primarily due to technological advances, some metropolitan areas have experienced increasing geographical sprawl of urban spaces, including an expansion of industrial activities and residential dwellings (Soja, 2010, 2013). Meanwhile, other metropolitan areas continue to have a dominant central business district within the city nucleus that drives economic and residential activity, making it more prone to gentrification than others. Gentrification is most prevalent in older Midwestern and Northeastern rust belt cities due to a particular pattern of urban organization. Former industrial centers are densely populated with a high concentration of African American communities historically settled around central business districts.

Despite the prevalence of that pattern of racialized concentric circles (Alonso, 1964; Burgess, 1935), there are regional distinctions in settlement patterns that influence the current concentration and clustering of African American communities within major metropolitan areas. A critique of early land use models is lack of generalizability, particularly in regard to where African Americans reside (Meyer & Esposito, 2015). During the Great Migration in the midst of a manufacturing economy, African Americans were superimposed on a preexisting urban landscape/design in Northern and Midwestern industrial centers. Local city governments were not mentally prepared or spatially situated to handle an influx of African Americans and adapted poorly to a rapidly diversifying population (Taeuber & Taeuber, 1969). As such, African Americans in the rust belt were limited in their residential choices and remain isolated in designated areas creating exasperated urban dualism, a tale of two cities.

Neglected and disinvested communities close to a central business district with a high concentration of renters are most vulnerable to gentrification. In America, because race and class remain tightly linked, these neglected and disinvested communities tend to be majority-Black neighborhoods (Wilson, 1987). Several early studies of urban organization used Chicago as a prototype (Alonso, 1964; Burgess, 1935). While Black Chicagoans have remained hypersegregated since their initial settlement during the Great Migration, and though this pattern is common throughout Midwestern and Northeastern metros, this is not a nationwide pattern.

The concentration of Black and white households within urban areas and dispersion within states varies across regions. Mostly due to the transatlantic slave trade route, African Americans have always been heavily populated throughout the South in a variety of neighborhood types, both urban and rural. Given the Reverse Great Migration, African Americans remain mostly concentrated in the South with increasing movement to booming metros such as Atlanta, GA, Charlotte, NC, and Houston, TX (Frey, 2004). Compared to other parts of the country, majority African American neighborhoods in the South are also less centralized or clustered together, which in turn means Black poverty is less concentrated. During periods of growth for Southern metropolitan areas, their sheer volume and dispersion throughout the region make it illogical for Black interests to not be considered in local planning and development efforts.

From these two anchors, urban organization and regional population concentration, my argument proceeds straightforwardly and is depicted in Figure 7.1 (see Figure 7.1). How central cities are organized, in combination with regional and subregional patterns of African American concentration, shapes local Black home-buying power. Relative local Black home-buying power, in turn, influences the likelihood of African American displacement during periods of gentrification.

Black home-buying power is shaped by three factors: local normalization of Black homeownership, housing prices, and aggregate median income for Black households. As previously mentioned, African Americans residing in the Midwest and Northeast are concentrated in densely populated rust belt metropolitan areas. These cities have been heavily impacted by economic restructuring, which refers to a shift beginning in the late 1970s away from a manufacturing-based economy to a new technology-based economy (Bluestone & Harrison, 1982). Economic restructuring opened the path for gentrification to occur by facilitating the cleared physical space for inner-city redevelopment in old abandoned factories. Gentrifying areas went from being in the bottom half of the distribution of home prices in a metropolitan area to the top half.

Most importantly, economic restructuring fundamentally changed the economic outlook of rust belt Black communities. The loss of manufacturing

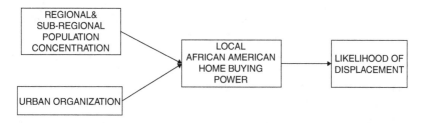

FIGURE 7.1 Regional Black Displacement Model.

jobs coupled with a decline in public sector employment abruptly limited opportunities for upward group mobility, which, in turn, depleted African American home-buying power in Midwestern and Northeastern cities (Parks, 2012). Economic restructuring had less of an impact on Southern metropolitan areas and corresponding local Black home-buying power (Karnig & McClain, 1985).

Overall, Black home-buying power is significantly less limited in Southern urban areas compared to outside the South. Home prices in Southern urban areas tend to be relatively low in comparison to major Northern and Midwestern metros (Pendergrass, 2013; Robinson, 2014; Tolnay, 2003). Outside the South, in places like New York City and Chicago, the "irresponsible Black homeowner" myth continues to be weaponized against African Americans to facilitate housing discrimination (Lipsitz, 2006; Patillo, 2007). Conversely, responsible Black homeowners across socioeconomic levels are common throughout the South. African Americans have greater home-buying power in the South due to a normalization of Black homeownership over time, relatively low housing prices, and higher than average median household incomes.

With that in mind, we can then better understand the idea that Black home-buying power influences the effects of gentrification. Home-buying power operates as a defense mechanism against the negative effects of gentrification and spatial inequality more broadly. Gentrification is a modern iteration of a long-standing history of American spatial inequality, facilitated by racial capitalism. Segregation, gentrification, urban renewal, redevelopment, and revitalization are all processes of neighborhood change. Gentrification, like other neighborhood change processes before it, is disturbing because it often involves deceptive displacement disproportionate to the detriment of Black people (Bates, 2013; Goetz, 2011; Hyra, 2015).

Making this connection is important because at the heart of all neighborhood change process is an old fight between Blacks and whites over rights to space. Regional differences in urban organization, African American concentration, and Black home-buying power that impacted the extent of local white flight from central cities in the 1950s and 1960s also impacted urban renewal in the 1970s and continuing gentrification since the 1980s (Hetzler, Medina, & Overfelt, 2006; Lipsitz, 2006). However, today, African Americans residing in the South, given their relatively unlimited home-buying power, are more likely to benefit from gentrification efforts and less likely to be displaced (Pendergrass, 2013; Robinson, 2014). Black home-buying power impacts local African Americans' access to mortgage loans, political clout, and overall inclusiveness in gentrifying efforts (Bostic & Martin, 2003). For real estate developers, selective demolition of dwellings, new housing construction, and occupancy is typically designated based on racial bias. High socioeconomic status individuals are more likely to afford housing in gentrifying areas compared to low-income individuals. Homeowners are less likely than renters to be displaced by gentrification. Given limited home-buying power, Blacks living the Midwest and Northeast are more vulnerable to the negative effects of gentrification, specifically displacement.

Analytic Approach

This study uses data from the 2015 US Census American Community Survey (5 Year Estimates) to gather descriptive statistics on African Americans at the metropolitan area and zip code level. The empirical goal of the following spatial analysis is exploratory in nature. I examine regional differences in the distribution of African Americans, the centralization of Black neighborhoods, Black home-buying power, and access to quality housing. The primary motivation of this analysis is to show that while racism and racial discrimination in the housing market are national phenomena, the effects of both vary in degree by place. First, I show where Blacks live in America in an effort to focus my analysis on the Midwest, Northeast, and the South. Next, I examine the median year homes were built at the metropolitan level to get an idea of key time periods of growth and current housing stock conditions. Theoretically, current housing conditions are connected to what is displayed in the next map, median rents, to better understand regional differences in access to affordable quality of housing. Lastly, to gauge upward group mobility and increasing home-buying power, change in African American median household income between 2000 and 2015 is mapped. Together, the collection of maps presented is meant to paint a picture that shows where Blacks are vulnerable to the negative effects of neighborhood change and where Blacks are poised to be included in neighborhood change process and benefit materially, socially, and politically.

A regional political economy perspective leads me to predict that African Americans residing in the Midwest and Northeast are more likely to be concentrated in large metropolitan areas experiencing hypersegregation, with higher than average housing costs and older built environments, than African Americans living in the South or West. This makes African Americans in the Midwest and Northeast more vulnerable to displacement during gentrification than African Americans residing elsewhere.

Results

Regional and State Level Concentration of African Americans

Figure 7.2 displays the size and percentage of African Americans by metropolitan statistical area (MSA) (see Figure 7.2). Beginning first with regional differences, Midwestern metropolitan areas with large Black populations include Chicago, IL, Detroit, MI, Cleveland, OH, and St. Louis, MO. One might note that in each of these cities, the percentage of the total MSA population that is

Black does not exceed 25%. African Americans only make up 16% of the total Chicago population, 22% of Detroit's total population, 19% of Cleveland's, and 18% of St. Louis' total population.

Northeastern cities with a large Black population include New York, Baltimore, Philadelphia, and Washington, DC. African Americans make up over 20% of the total population in Baltimore, Philadelphia, and Washington, DC. However, even with 3.4 million Blacks living in New York City, the largest number in any MSA across the country, they make up only 17% of the city's total population.

Based on historical migration patterns, it is no surprise that the US region with the fewest number of African Americans is the West. However, what is surprising is the small number and small percentage of Blacks living in the Los Angeles area given it is one of the largest cities in America. The Los Angeles MSA, which includes Long Beach, has a Black population of 888,607, which is only 6.7% of the total population. The second-largest concentration of African Americans in the western region is in Las Vegas, where 220,592 African Americans reside and make up less than 11% of the total population.

Most apparent in Figure 7.2 is the large concentration of African Americans in the South (see Figure 7.2). Dallas, TX, Atlanta, GA, Houston, TX, and Miami, FL, all have African American populations over 1 million. The Atlanta MSA, "The Black Mecca," is home to 1.8 million Blacks, and they make up over 30% of the total population. Furthermore, it is not uncommon in the South, in contrast to other regions, for small and midsize MSAs to have Blacks make up more than 50% of the total population, composing majority-Black cities. Also, now with the increased migration of Latinxs to the Southeast as a new destination, Southern metros are becoming even more likely to be majority non-white cities.

Related to regional concentration is African American dispersion at the state level. As shown in Figure 7.3, in the Midwest and Northeast, African Americans are highly concentrated in metropolitan areas with little dispersion throughout the entire state (see Figure 7.3). Illinois, Ohio, Indiana, and Pennsylvania all have large Black populations that are concentrated in two or three cities throughout the state. In comparison to Southern states, specifically Louisiana, Mississippi, Alabama, Georgia, and North Carolina, there are few rural or midsized Northeastern and Midwestern cities with large African American population.

When addressing contextual effects, the tendency is to focus on the concentration of African Americans at the neighborhood/census tract level and its effects on neighborhood change, politics, and political behavior. However, comparing the concentration of Blacks at the regional level highlights the broader social contexts in which African American communities exist. Discussions of the causes and effects of gentrification as it relates to African Americans must first consider regional concentration and how dispersed Blacks are

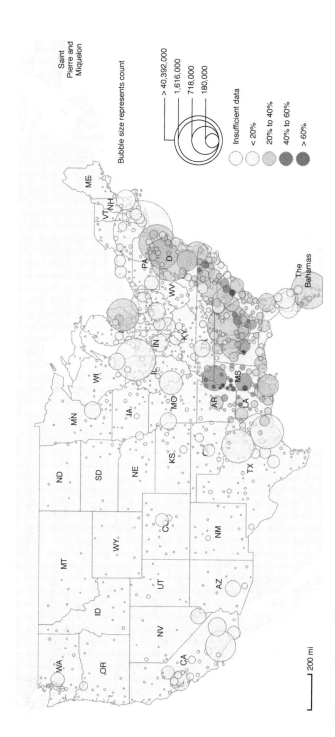

FIGURE 7.2 Nationwide African American Population Size and Proportion by Metropolitan Statistical Area (MSA).

Source: US Census Bureau, American Community Survey 2015 (5 year estimates). https://www.census.gov/acs/www/data/data-tables-and-tools/data-profiles/2015/

FIGURE 7.3 African American Dispersion Within Select States by County.
Source: US Census Bureau, American Community Survey 2015 (5 year estimates).

throughout a state. Though gentrification is just one type of neighborhood change and is not experienced uniformly throughout the country, the process is most prevalent in rust belt metros where African Americans are highly concentrated.

Centralization and Hypersegregation of African American Communities within Metros

Figures 7.4 and 7.5 present a comparison of hypersegregation and dispersion at the metropolitan area level. Specifically, Figure 7.4 compares areas where African Americans reside in Chicago, IL, and Atlanta, GA, MSAs (see Figure 7.4). The figure illustrates clearly that African American Chicagoans primarily live in only two parts of the city, a relatively small section of the Westside and a large swath of land South of the downtown area, infamously known as "the Southside." When examining Atlanta, it is harder to pinpoint a specific part or side of the city where African Americans are confined/located, as is seen in Chicago. A similar difference is shown in Figure 7.5, which compares where African Americans reside in New York City, NY, and Raleigh-Durham, NC (see Figure 7.5). Hypersegregation creates less variation in the types of neighborhoods African American home buyers have access to.

Given historical migration patterns and continuing housing discrimination, neighborhood choice for African Americans is more limited in the Midwest, Northeast, and West than in the South. Blacks in Raleigh-Durham are dispersed throughout the metro area similarly to the way Blacks are dispersed throughout Atlanta. In New York City, you see several majority-Black neighborhoods clustered together, similar to Chicago. Chicago and New York are emblematic of other Northeastern and Midwestern metros with long-standing majority-Black communities that have been historically confined to particular sections of a city via racist housing policies since the Great Migration.

Atlanta and Raleigh-Durham are emblematic of other Southern metropolitan areas that have long-standing majority-Black communities widely dispersed throughout, making it harder to isolate Black communities through displacement. The strategic clustering and hypersegregation of these majority-Black communities over time make it easier to further isolate Black communities through displacement. Though there are signs of gentrification in the South, it looks like whites are trying to carve out spaces in Black cities, whereas in the Northeast and Midwest, it feels as though Blacks are becoming further confined to limited space in white cities.

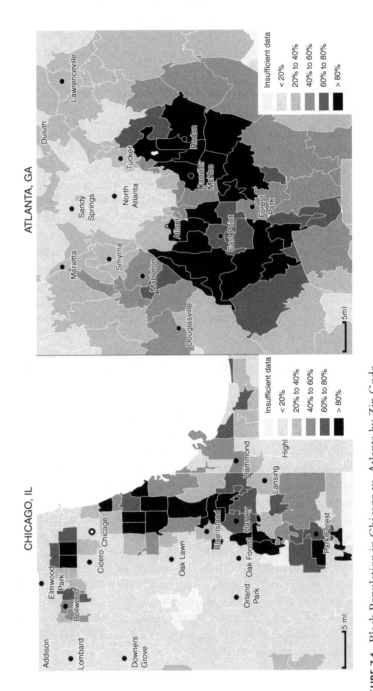

FIGURE 7.4 Black Population in Chicago vs. Atlanta by Zip Code.

Source: US Census Bureau, American Community Survey 2015 (5 year estimates).

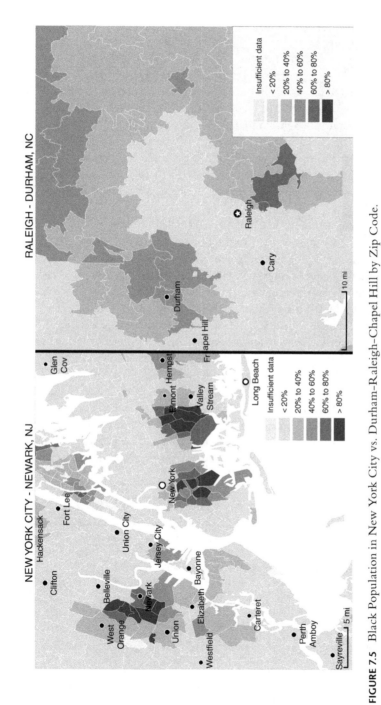

FIGURE 7.5 Black Population in New York City vs. Durham–Raleigh–Chapel Hill by Zip Code.

Source: US Census Bureau, American Community Survey 2015 (5 year estimates).

Regional Differences in Central City Demand and Age of Housing Stock

Table 7.1 points to regional differences in the condition of housing available to African Americans (see Table 7.1). In regard to the median age of housing stock, the majority of dwellings in the Midwest and Northeast were built prior to 1960, whereas in the South most structures were built in the late 1980s and early 1990s. According to the 2015 US Census, over 50% of housing units in the South and 46% of housing units in the West were built after 1980, compared to only 26% in the Northeast and 36% in the Midwest. Looking at city-specific housing stock, 1958 is the median year structures in New York City were built, compared to 1990 in Atlanta. Despite increased access to newer housing in the South, median gross rents tend to be lower in the South.

In the South, there is less of a direct correlation between the age of housing units and the cost of the housing, compared to the Midwest, Northeast, and West. Large MSAs in the Northeast and Midwest, particularly Chicago, New York City, and Washington, DC all have median gross rent levels quickly approaching $1,500 per month. There are small and midsize MSAs in the Midwest and Northeast with affordable housing options—think Des Moines, Iowa, or Rochester, Minnesota. However, those are not places where African Americans have established communities or feel welcomed to reside in racially integrated communities. There are few majority-Black cities in the South with median gross rent over $1,000 per month.

Comparing the age of housing stock and median rent levels highlights two particularly noteworthy regional differences. First, densely organized older housing stock in the central city makes large Midwestern and Northeastern cities more susceptible to gentrification. Increasing demand for central city housing combined with limited space to increase the supply of central city housing

TABLE 7.1 Age of Housing Units by Region

	Northeast	Midwest	South	West
Occupied housing units	20,937,102	26,161,479	43,399,427	25,793,025
Year structure built				
Built 2010 or later	1.00%	1.20%	2.30%	1.40%
Built 2000 to 2009	7.90%	12.10%	19.20%	15.90%
Built 1980 to 1999	18.30%	23.30%	34.30%	29.80%
Built 1960 to 1979	23.90%	26.70%	26.70%	29.20%
Built 1940 to 1959	22.00%	18.70%	12.20%	15.60%
Built 1939 or earlier	27.00%	18.00%	5.40%	8.20%

Source: Data from US Census Bureau, American Community Survey 2015 (5 year estimates).

pushes prices up for renters and homeowners. Second, the cost of living in the Midwest and Northeast is higher for Blacks than non-Blacks given rapidly rising rents in established Black communities and limited housing options in a hypersegregated housing market.

There continues to be a reduced supply of housing available to African Americans, particularly for those residing outside of the South. The rapid increase in rent and the cost of central city housing in large Northeastern and Midwestern MSAs where African Americans are historically concentrated makes them more likely to be displaced during the process of gentrification than Blacks residing in the South.

Black Home-Buying Power as a Defense Against Gentrification

The high cost of central city housing in select Midwestern and Northeastern central cities, combined with African American economic decline, has severely crippled Black home-buying power in those regions over time. According to a Zillow Group (2017) monthly report, for over a century, there has been about a 27 percentage-point gap in Black and white homeownership rates (Zillow, 2017). However, though a lot of attention has been given to interracial differences in levels of homeownership, intragroup differences in African American homeownership levels are just as striking.

Table 7.2 shows the percentage of African American homeowners by region, along with other measures of aggregate socioeconomic status (see Table 7.2). In 2016, about 45% of African American residing in the South own their homes, compared to 35% in the Northeast, 36% in the Midwest, and 32% in the West. The largest gap in Black homeownership is between the South and the Midwest, and it is particularly interesting, given recent regional migration patterns which scholars have shown are in part due to increased homeowning opportunities.

TABLE 7.2 Select Socioeconomic Status Indicators for African Americans by Region

	Northeast	Midwest	South	West
Homeowners	34.91%	35.96%	45.08%	32.5%
Unemployed (2015)	11.60%	14.20%	10.4%	11.3%
Median household income in the past 12 months	42,824	32,749	38,430	45,473
(in 2016 inflation-adjusted dollars)				
Bachelor's degree or higher	22.57%	18.33%	20.65%	23.83%
Income in the past 12 months below poverty level	17.87%	24.29%	19.65%	17.61%

Source: Data from US Census Bureau, American Community Survey 2015 (5 year estimates).

Compared to African Americans residing in other parts of the country, Blacks in the Midwest have the lowest median household income ($32,749) and the highest poverty level (24%). Furthermore, based on the previously mentioned analysis, we know Black poverty in the region is highly concentrated due to a lack of dispersion throughout at the state and metropolitan level. Stagnant upward group socioeconomic mobility across the rust belt is primarily due to declining employment opportunities and continued systemic racial discrimination. Economic decline helps facilitate a depletion of Black political power, making it harder for Midwestern and Northeastern African Americans to combat the forces of gentrification.

Home-buying power for African Americans is based not solely on individual economic fortunes. One must also consider local housing markets and the normalization of African American homeownership. According to the 2010 US census, Atlanta, Chicago, New York, and Philadelphia have over 200,000 urban-area (central city) Black homeowners. However, when one looks closely at the average age of urban Black homeowners in each of these cities, Atlanta stands out. Over 40% of urban Black homeowners in Atlanta are under the age of 45, compared with only around 20% in most major cities. Relatedly, only 19% of urban Black homeowners in Los Angeles and 24% of urban Black homeowners in Chicago are under the age of 45. Atlanta's high percentage of relatively young inner-city Black homeowners is in alignment with other Southern cosmopolitan cities. Further, though compared to Atlanta they have an overall smaller number of total Black urban households, Charlotte, NC (41%), Durham, NC (33%), Houston, TX (33%), and Jackson, MS (34%), all have a high percentage of young Black homeowners.

As previously mentioned, the majority of dwellings in the Midwest and Northeast were built prior to 1960, whereas in the South, most structures were built in the late 1980s and early 1990s (see Figure 7.6). Figure 7.7 shows regional and metropolitan area differences in the cost of housing available; despite increased access to newer housing in the South, median gross rents tend to be lower in the South (see Figure 7.7). Thus, within the region there is less of a direct correlation between the year housing is built and the cost of the housing. In contrast, large MSAs in the Northeast and Midwest, particularly Chicago, New York City, and Washington, DC all have median gross rent levels quickly approaching $1,500 per month. There are small and midsize MSAs in the Midwest and Northeast with affordable housing options, such as Des Moines, Iowa. However, those are not places where African Americans have established communities or feel welcomed to socially integrate.

Relatedly, there are few majority-Black cities in the South with median gross rent over $1,000 per month. Together these two maps, comparing the age of housing stock and median rent levels, highlight two particularly noteworthy regional differences. First, densely organized older housing stock in the central

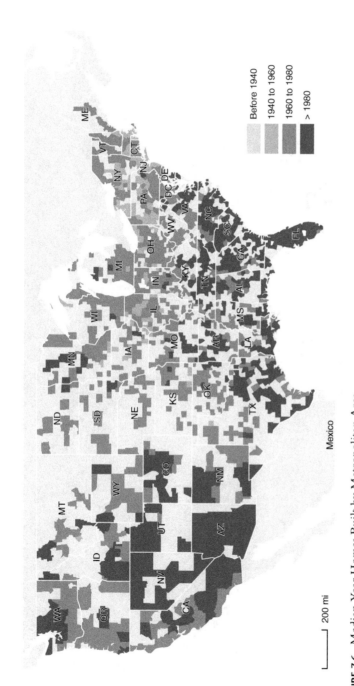

FIGURE 7.6 Median Year Homes Built by Metropolitan Area.

Source: US Census Bureau, American Community Survey 2015 (5 year estimates).

Before 1940
1940 to 1960
1960 to 1980
> 1980

200 mi

Mexico

FIGURE 7.7 Median Rent by Metropolitan Area.

Source: US Census Bureau, American Community Survey 2015 (5 year estimates).

< $400

$400 to $600

$600 to $800

$800 to $1,000

> $1,000

500 mi

Mexico

city makes large Midwestern and Northeastern cities more susceptible to gentrification. Due to African Americans' concentration in large Northeastern and Midwestern MSAs, they are more likely to be displaced during the process of gentrification than Blacks residing in the South. Second, the cost of living in the Midwest and Northeast is higher for Blacks than non-Blacks given rapidly rising rents in established Black communities and limited housing options in a hypersegregated housing market.

Discussion

This chapter has shown that there is regional variability in the prevalence of gentrification and its effects on African Americans, the widest difference of which is the likelihood of displacement for Blacks in the Midwest and Northeast versus Blacks residing in the South. African Americans residing in the South Atlantic (i.e., Maryland, Georgia, North Carolina, Virginia, Florida) have considerable home-buying power, which operates as a defense against gentrification efforts. African Americans living in the Northeast and Midwest, in addition to depleted home-buying power, are concentrated in older cities that are riper for gentrification efforts.

The goal of this chapter was to consider the necessity of a regional political economy perspective of gentrification. Though evidence presented in this chapter suggests there are regional, subregional, and local variation in the potential for and possible effects of gentrification, the optimal method for a systematic analysis of contextual effects at any geographic level is a mixed methods approach; the exact causal mechanism underlying the causes and effects of gentrification require additional exploration. Nevertheless, what has been made clear here is that scholars must undertake the delicate task of qualitatively analyzing local distinctions in Black home-buying power, political engagement in development efforts, interracial dynamics, and opportunities for economic mobility.

Hopefully, the theory put forth makes scholars pause in their thinking of gentrification and consider nuanced types of gentrification, followed by the regional distinctions in its causes, effects, and prevalence. Neighborhood change in America is more often than not plagued by government intervention that promotes white privilege in the housing market, if not outright racial discrimination, often evidenced by continued racially inequitable neighborhood investments (i.e., triggering white flight with government subsidization of American suburbs), and in rare though substantial cases, disinvestment and the displacement of African Americans.

Though not a widespread national trend, given their geographical concentration, displacement during gentrification remains a substantial problem for African Americans. It is easy to say African American displacement has minimal impact when you are not the one being displaced. Analytical focus must also be placed on the common narrative connecting the array of neighborhood change processes, the fight for Black space, and the right to reside without fear of disruptive and detrimental government intervention still exists. African Americans continue to desire access to quality neighborhoods that include the same quality of public goods afforded to other citizens: good, safe schools for their kids and nice homes for a decent price. African American men and women continue to want to live the American Dream. Though not enough, some do, and shockingly mostly in the South.

African American movement (back) to Southern cities reflects their preference for the mix of public goods and local governments the region offers, in particular, many relatively safe majority-Black neighborhoods, moderately priced homes, and access to quality educational institutions. Consequently, education spending and housing costs factor into their moving decisions, in addition to noneconomic variables such as social climate (Pendergrass, 2013; Tiebout, 1956). Blacks and Latinxs are leaving subtler prejudice, higher levels of racial residential segregation, and greater constraints on Black economic opportunity in the Northeast and Midwest, for more overt prejudice, increased employment opportunities, and easier access to homeownership in the South (Pendergrass, 2013, p. 2).

In addition, displacement and disinvestment have made conditions for inner-city Blacks in the Midwest and Northeast decline rapidly over the past three decades (Parks, 2011). Worsening conditions in minority communities contrasted against flourishing gentrified neighborhoods within the same city create exasperated urban dualism and may breed feelings of racial resentment and racial threat. Upwardly mobile Blacks are showing their discontent with local city government public expenditures by moving either South or to the suburbs.

Southern sociopolitical culture in combination with Southern opportunity is fostering a racial synergy of sorts in major Southern cities that remains intimately connected with notions of struggle and progress. I suspect white political leaders and business elite in the urban South are more racially enlightened than their Northern counterparts due to greater exposure to strong African American institutions, minority homeowners, and minority conservative values (Hyman & Sheataley, 1956). That may explain a majority white anti-racism protest in Charlottesville, Virginia, and multicultural Black Lives Matter protest in Dallas, Texas. However, the racial enlightenment experienced by some whites in South Atlantic metros is contrasted against growing feelings of racial resentment and racial threat by whites isolated outside of these progress pockets. This isolation from meaningful interaction with Blacks in the rural South and in hypersegregated Midwest/Northeast cities may foster white disillusionment, which makes engaging in conversation about targeted policy to address racial discrimination so difficult.

Also, potentially complicating conversations of a national Black agenda are the local experiences of Black gentrifiers and Black migrants versus long-term Black residents in cities nationwide, as intragroup socioeconomic inequality increases. Regional distinctions in neighborhood change lead to a disjointed geographic landscape with pockets of inter- and intragroup resentment, which creates a plurality of American communities steeped in alternative realities.

The next step in this line of analysis is to see how regional differences in neighborhood change shape African American views about local quality life, upward group mobility, and social policies. I suspect regional differences in gentrification are shaping racial progress attitudes and creating more spatialized nuance in Black public opinion. More broadly, I am curious to see if varying susceptibility to detrimental neighborhood change process creates divergent African American attitudes about local quality of life and upward group mobility. Putting individual circumstances aside, I expect African Americans living in booming South Atlantic metros to have more positive views of local neighborhood conditions and upward group mobility than African Americans living in old industrial centers where white gentrification is more prominent.

Not within the scope of this chapter, but still a connected concern is how local changes after major natural disasters impact majority–Black neighborhoods. Racial inequities in rebuild efforts after natural disasters ought to be viewed at the intersection of environmental racism and neighborhood change issue. Specifically, in the age of climate change, we also must pay special attention to neighborhood change following hurricanes and major flooding that cause catastrophic damage to property triggering massive displacement for southern Black residents. Is it still gentrification if Blacks are displaced by a flood and then priced out of newly developed central city housing? Knowing how Black neighborhoods in New Orleans were disrupted by Hurricane Katrina, and the lopsided effort to make affected African Americans whole, will Houston's rebuild efforts after Hurricane Harvey be racially inclusive or simply shift impacted low-income African Americans to other cities nearby?

Future research must continue to wrestle with new ways in which African Americans are benefited or harmed by neighborhood change. Additionally, greater exploration of ways Blacks are adapting and resisting neighborhood change is needed, paying particular attention to whether socioeconomic factors foster aggressive or passive collective responses.

Conclusion

Gentrification often feels like a personal assault on African Americans, involving disrespect of Black history coupled with disingenuous attempts to recreate through a white lens Black culture that was destroyed. Gentrified neighborhoods resemble store-bought frozen macaroni and cheese, inauthentic and void of taste, nothing like the remembered real thing. Though not all instances of neighborhood change are examples of gentrification, its devastating effects on select African American communities remain. Like other dominant neighborhood change processes that came before gentrification, the intersection of race, place, and political economy continues to be an important point of analytical focus. The relationship between where someone lives and the color of their skin is an American tradition. However, over time, with uneven racial progress, additional nuances arise. This chapter has addressed one of those nuances, the diverging impact of gentrification on African Americans by region. I stress how the complexity of neighborhood change, specifically gentrification, is emblematic of larger economic, racial, and spatial shifts in America's post-Civil Rights era. Though American society has come to normalize and accept gentrification as inevitable, we must consider the possibility of different processes of neighborhood change occurring in other localities. As African Americans continue to fight for racial equality, conflicts over land to claim as one's own, access to housing, and space to freely exist will remain at the forefront.

References

Alonso, W. (1964). *Location and land use. Toward a general theory of land rent.* Cambridge, MA: Harvard University Press.

Bates, L. K. (2013). *Gentrification and displacement study: Implementing an equitable inclusive development strategy in the context of gentrification.* Urban Studies and Planning Faculty Publications and Presentations. https://doi.org/10.15760/report-01

Bluestone, B., & Harrison, B. (1982). *The deindustrialization of America, plant closings, community abandonment, and the dismantling of basic industry.* New York, NY: Basic Books.

Bostic, R. W., & Martin, R. W. (2003). Black home-owners as a gentrifying force? Neighbourhood dynamics in the context of minority home-ownership. *Urban Studies, 40*(12), 2427–2449.

Brown-Saracino, J. (2017). Explicating divided approaches to gentrification and growing income inequality. *Annual Review of Sociology, 43,* 515–539.

Burgess, E.W. (1935). *The growth of the city: an introduction to a research project.* London, UK: Ardent Media.

Freeman, L., & Cai, T. (2015). White entry into black neighborhoods: Advent of a new era? *The Annals of the American Academy of Political and Social Science, 660*(1), 302–318.

Frey, W. H. (2004). *The new great migration: Black Americans' return to the South, 1965–2000.* Center on Urban and Metropolitan Policy, the Brookings Institution. https://www.brookings.edu/research/the-new-great-migration-black-americans-return-to-the-south-1965-2000/

Gale, D. E. (1984). *Neighborhood revitalization and the postindustrial city: A multinational perspective.* Lexington, MA: Lexington Books.

Glass, Ruth. (2010). Aspects of change. *The gentrification debates: A reader,* Brown-Saracino, J. (ed). 19-30

Goetz, E. (2011). Gentrification in black and white: The racial impact of public housing demolition in American cities *Urban Studies, 48*(8), 1581–1604.

Hetzler, O., Medina, V. E., & Overfelt, D. (2006). Gentrification, displacement and new urbanism: The next racial project. *Sociation Today, 4*(2).

Hill, R. C., & Feagin, J. R. (1987). Detroit and Houston: Two cities in global perspective. In M.P. Smith & J.R. Feagin (Eds.). *The Capitalist City: Global Restructuring and Community Politics*, (pp. 155–177). Oxford, UK: Blackwell.

Hunt, M. O., Hunt, L. L., & Falk, W. W. (2013). Twenty‐first‐century trends in black migration to the US South: Demographic and subjective predictors. Social Science Quarterly, 94(5): 1398-1413

Hwang, J. (2015). Gentrification in changing cities: Immigration, new diversity, and racial inequality in neighborhood renewal. *The Annals of the American Academy of Political and Social Science, 660*(1), 319–340.

Hyman, H. H., & Sheatsley, P. B. (1956). Attitudes toward desegregation. *Scientific American, 195*(6), 35–39.

Hyra, D. (2015). The back-to-the-city movement: Neighbourhood redevelopment and processes of political and cultural displacement. *Urban Studies, 52*(10), 1753–1773.

Iceland, J., Sharp, G., & Timberlake, J. M. (2013). Sun belt rising: Regional population change and the decline in black residential segregation, 1970–2009. *Demography, 50*(1), 97–123.

Karnig, A. K., & McClain, P. D. (1985). The new south and black economic and political development: Changes from 1970 to 1980. *The Western Political Quarterly, 38*(4) 539–550.

Key, V. (1949). *Southern politics in state and nation.* Knoxville, TN: University of Tennessee Press

Ley, David. (1978). "*Prisoners of Space? Exploring the Geographical Experience of Older People.*" Economic Geography, 54(4), 355–356

Lipsitz, G. (2006). *The possessive investment in whiteness: How white people profit from identity politics.* Philadelphia, PA: Temple University Press.

Lipton, S. G. (1977). Evidence of central city revival. *Journal of the American Planning Association, 43*(2), 136–147.

Lloyd, R. (2010). *Neo-bohemia: Art and commerce in the postindustrial city.* New York, NY: Routledge.

Maciag, M. (2015). Gentrification in America report. Governing the States and Localities.

Martinez, M. J. (2010). *Power at the roots: Gentrification, community gardens, and the Puerto Ricans of the Lower East Side.* Lanham, MD: Lexington Books.

McClelland, Edward (2013, May 6). *White Flight, By the Numbers.* NBC 5 Chicago, Retrieved from www.nbcchicago.com

Meyer, W. B., & Esposito, C. R. (2015). Burgess and Hoyt in Los Angeles: Testing the Chicago models in an automotive-age American city. *Urban Geography, 36*(2), 314–325.

Mills, E. S. (1972). *Studies in the structure of the urban economy.* Baltimore, MD: Johns Hopkins Press.

Moretti, E. (2012). *The new geography of jobs.* Boston, MA: Houghton Mifflin Harcourt.

Muth, R. F. (1969). *Cities and housing; the spatial pattern of urban residential land use.* Chicago, IL: University of Chicago Press.

Owens, A. (2012). Neighborhoods on the rise: A typology of neighborhoods experiencing socioeconomic ascent. *City & Community, 11*(4), 345–369.

Parks, V. (2011). Revisiting shibboleths of race and urban economy: Black employment in manufacturing and the public sector compared, Chicago 1950–2000. *International Journal of Urban and Regional Research, 35*(1), 110–129.

Parks, V. (2012). The uneven geography of racial and ethnic wage inequality: Specifying local labor market effects. *Annals of the Association of American Geographers, 102*(3), 700–725.

Patillo, M. (2007). *Black on the block*. Chicago, IL: University of Chicago Press.

Pendergrass, S. (2013). Perceptions of race and region in the black reverse migration to the south. *Du Bois Review: Social Science Research on Race, 10*(1), 155–178.

Robinson, Z. F. (2014). *This Ain't Chicago: Race, class, and regional identity in the post-soul South*. Chapel Hill, NC: UNC Press Books.

Smith, N. (1979). Toward a theory of gentrification a back to the city movement by capital, not people. *Journal of the American Planning Association, 45*(4), 538–548.

Soja, E. W. (2010). *Seeking spatial justice, Vol. 16*. Minneapolis, MN: University of Minnesota Press.

Soja, E. W. (2013). Regional urbanization and third wave cities. *City, 17*(5), 688–694.

Solari, C. D. (2012). Affluent neighborhood persistence and change in us cities. *City & Community, 11*(4), 370–388.

Taeuber, K. E., & Taeuber, A. F. (1969). *Negroes in cities: Residential segregation and neighborhood change*. New York, NY: Atheneum.

Tiebout, C. M. (1956). A pure theory of local expenditures. *Journal of political economy, 64*(5), 416-424.

Tolnay, S. E. (2003). The African American "great migration" and beyond. *Annual Review of Sociology, 29*, 209–232.

Wilson, W. J. (1987). *The truly disadvantaged: The inner city, the underclass, and public policy*. Chicago, IL: University of Chicago.

Zillow Group Inc. (2017). *Consumer Housing Trends Report 2017*. Retrieved from www.zillow.com/report/2017/

Zukin, S. (1987). Gentrification: culture and capital in the urban core. *Annual Review of Sociology, 13*(1), 129–147.

Zukin, S., Trujillo, V., Frase, P., Jackson, D., Recuber, T., & Walker, A. (2009). New retail capital and neighborhood change: boutiques and gentrification in New York City. *City & Community, 8*(1), 47–64.

8

"PEOPLE WERE NOT AS FRIENDLY AS I HAD HOPED"

Black Residential Experiences in Two Multiracial Neighborhoods

Sarah Mayorga-Gallo

Residential segregation and concentrated poverty are clear manifestations of structural racism. As such, expanding the geography of opportunity for Black Americans is often associated with access to racially mixed neighborhoods. Multiracial neighborhoods, where white and non-white groups live together, are on the rise (Ellen, Horn, & O'Regan, 2012; Fong & Shibuya, 2005; Hyra, 2017). Scholars point to dynamic processes, such as post-1965 immigration from Asia and Latin America; white (upper) middle-class cultural shifts that seek out diversity and urban living; increasing non-white suburbanization; and a growing Black middle class to explain these new multiracial configurations (Ellen et al., 2012; Fong & Shibuya, 2005; Frey, 2001, 2014; Ley, 2003).

Some scholars view these changes optimistically, asserting that these neighborhoods are markers of increasing white tolerance and civility toward people of color (Anderson, 2011; Maly, 2005). An underlying assumption of this view is that increased racial diversity in neighborhoods marks an openness or cosmopolitanism that residents of segregated neighborhoods do not have; therefore, these new opportunities for interaction will be positive and tolerant. Meanwhile, others whose research focuses on power relations in multiracial spaces highlight the evolving nature of racial inequities when spatial distance is no longer a barrier to interracial interactions (Aptekar, 2015; Berrey, 2005; Mayorga-Gallo, 2014). Given these contrasting views, how are scholars of Black life in the United States to make sense of multiracial neighborhoods and their relationship with racial inequality? Predominantly Black neighborhoods have been disinvested in by banks, corporations, and federal housing policies, so gaining access to neighborhoods where white residents live has long been framed in the literature as a fundamental step toward racial equity (Massey & Denton, 1993; Wilson, 1987/2012). Given the common belief that Black people would be better off economically in racially mixed neighborhoods, it is important to empirically determine the economic as well as social implications of these neighborhoods for Black residents, whose exclusion in the housing market is a cornerstone of American racism and wealth inequity (Massey & Denton, 1993; Oliver & Shapiro, 1995–2006).

In this chapter, I study two multiracial neighborhoods—Creekridge Park[1] in Durham, NC, and Carthage in Cincinnati, OH—to understand the racial structure of these racially mixed spaces. I use the term multiracial to refer to neighborhoods with more than two racial–ethnic communities. I opt for multiracial rather than integrated—which is more common in the sociological literature—because multiracial is descriptive without assumptions about the social patterns of a place. The term integrated, which is usually designated by the percentages of racial–ethnic groups, often presumes an inclusive environment. Rather than make assumptions about social life in these spaces, the social patterns of multiracial spaces must be documented using qualitative data.

While living in Creekridge Park and Carthage should be a boon to the economic bottom-line of Black homeowners and opportunity structure of Black renters, what I find is a complicated story of social support, social isolation, and social control across both sites. Moving forward, I provide details about each neighborhood and the demographic and sociopolitical characteristics of Creekridge Park and Carthage residents. Thereafter, I analyze residents' social interactions with their neighbors, taking time to highlight both the affirming aspects of their relations as well as the fraught ones. Although I find that there are supportive relationships that develop in these neighborhoods, I also identify how living in multiracial neighborhoods presents new challenges to Black residents, as whiteness—a system where whites are socially, politically, and economically advantaged—prevails despite demographic shifts.

A Closer Look at Carthage and Creekridge Park

Why Compare Carthage and Creekridge Park?

Much new work on multiracial neighborhoods and the microsegregation that takes place within focuses on gentrifying spaces (Hyra, 2017; Tach, 2014). By studying Carthage and Creekridge Park, I am able to investigate relationships across race and class outside of the narrative of (white) upper-class residents changing (Black and Latinx) working-class or poor neighborhoods in the United States. Creekridge Park and Carthage are both historically white neighborhoods with middle- and working-class residents, respectively. Ellen, Horn, and O'Regan (2012) find that formerly predominantly white neighborhoods, which they define as neighborhoods where Black, Latinx, and Asians each comprise less than 20% of the population, were the most likely to become integrated between 2000 and 2010. The definition of integration they used relied on a threshold (at least 20% of the population was Black, Latinx, or

Asian), rather than city–neighborhood proportionality. Multiracial neighborhoods are sometimes opportunities for affordable homeownership, as we see in Creekridge Park and Carthage. While Creekridge Park's housing prices have increased over the last ten years, Carthage's housing market has experienced major devaluation due to the Great Recession. A few homeowners mentioned the decrease in their housing values keeping them in the neighborhood, with some now owing more than their house is worth.

An important distinction between the residents of Creekridge Park and Carthage is how many Carthage residents are Cincinnati natives. Of the 43 residents interviewed, 40% were from Cincinnati, while another 21% were from surrounding Cincinnati suburbs (e.g., Fairfield, West Chester, Anderson Township). Five residents or 14% were from other states, but three of those five were from nearby Kentucky and Illinois (e.g., Louisville and Chicago). In deep contrast, only 12% of survey respondents in Creekridge Park were Durham natives, while 24% were from North Carolina. The origin of the remaining respondents was wide-ranging, including neighboring Virginia and South Carolina, as well as New York, Pennsylvania, and Massachusetts, among other states and countries.

These differences reflect larger stereotypes about both cities, with Durham being home to many transplants, particularly young professionals, and Cincinnati being seen as a very insular city. When I first moved to Cincinnati, the comment I heard from many is that the first question locals will ask upon meeting you is "Where'd you go to school?" inquiring after the high school you attended. This practice is so ubiquitous that it was the center of a Cincinnati Magazine article titled "The Question." As the author puts it, "In a town where the vast majority of residents are lifers, The Question is just plain handy" (Powell, 2012). It is important to note that Cincinnati is also one of the most racially and economically segregated cities in the nation (Swartsell, 2015); as such, your high school location also tells people a lot about your family background.

Both of these neighborhoods are also located in new destination cities for Latinx migration but are in different phases of population change. In 2010, 14% of Durham's population was Latinx, while only 3% of Cincinnati's population was Latinx. Both of these neighborhoods, however, are at least 20% Latinx (see Table 8.1). These similar but differing contexts allow us to see how shifting racial dynamics—at both the neighborhood and city levels—shape contemporary racial constructions and influence interracial interactions. Lastly, these two cases dovetail with Jessica Stewart's chapter in this volume, which reiterates the importance of geographic context on Blacks' attitudes toward their neighborhood and outlook on political institutions.

Methods

The purpose of my Creekridge Park study was to understand the social relationships in a multiracial neighborhood given the dominant theoretical narrative that neighborhood racial integration leads to positive interracial interactions. I wanted to see how low spatial proximity shaped interactions across race between Black, white, and Latinx residents. My Carthage study is part of a larger two-neighborhood comparison in Cincinnati between two small, working-class residences with different racial compositions; one is a predominantly white neighborhood (Riverside) while the other is a multiracial neighborhood (Carthage). I was interested in studying how race and class intersected to shape neighborhood interactions. In short, are homeowners and renters more likely to interact in a predominantly white neighborhood than in a multiracial neighborhood? Taken together, these projects elucidate processes of inclusion and exclusion across race and class lines.

I conducted research in Creekridge Park over an 18-month period between 2009 and 2011. I conducted semi-structured interviews with 63 area residents (49 white; 7 Black; 6 Latinx). These interviews ranged from 30 minutes to over 2 hours and took place either at the respondent's home or a neighborhood business. I conducted interviews in both English and Spanish, depending on the respondent's preference (I am a native Spanish speaker). I first entered Creekridge Park social life via a key informant who I knew from Duke University. He introduced me to a Creekridge Park Neighborhood Association board member, who put me in touch with a handful of residents. Then all of my recruiting came via snowball sampling of interviewees, solicitation via the neighborhood association LISTSERV, and introductions at neighborhood events. I did not pay participants, but I did buy a meal or coffee if we were at a restaurant or brought some baked goods from Stella's Café, a local bakery, if we were meeting in their home. I also conducted participant observation at neighborhood events and informally around the neighborhood. Lastly, I completed a household survey ($n = 85$; 64 white; 11 Black; 6 Latinx) to assess attitudinal trends and other patterns, such as grocery store preferences and friendship networks. These surveys were completed either online or via paper mailing. Each household received an advertisement for the survey at least once; I targeted certain neighborhood areas twice if there was low participation from those streets. For more on my methodology and field experience, see Mayorga-Gallo (2014) and Mayorga-Gallo and Hordge-Freeman (2017).

My data from Carthage are based entirely on in-depth interviews with 43 residents (23 white; 11 Black; 9 Latinx) conducted during early 2015. To recruit participants, I used the USPS Every Door Direct Mail service, which allows you to send mail to every residential and/or business address in a zip code for a reduced postage rate. I created a postcard with my information on it, including what the study was about, that I was paying $15/hour, and where residents could call to set up an interview. I first mailed the postcard in Spanish and then in English. Interviews ranged from 30 to 90 minutes and were conducted in English and Spanish, depending on the respondent's preference. At the end of the semi-structured interview questions, I asked residents a handful of survey questions as well, such as describing their close friendship networks. Many of these questions are duplicated from my Creekridge Park study for comparability and are also used in national survey instruments (e.g., General Social Survey).

While white respondents are overrepresented in my Creekridge Park sample, all three groups are proportionately captured in the Carthage sample.

Neighborhood Demographics

Creekridge Park,[2] home to about 1,500 residents, is located in Durham, NC; Carthage, home to about 2,700 residents, is located in Cincinnati, OH. Both neighborhoods are home to white, Black, and Latinx residents, although their percentages differ (see Table 8.1).

The neighborhoods are also economically distinct. Creekridge Park is a mixed-income, primarily middle-class neighborhood, while Carthage is a mixed-income, primarily working-class neighborhood. In 2015, when I was in the field, the median household income for Carthage was $26,509. The median household income for the Census block group that includes Creekridge Park was approximately $55,000 while I was in the field.[3] Regardless of race, the majority of Carthage residents identified themselves as working class (56% of the neighborhood), while in Creekridge Park, Black and Latinx residents were more likely to identify as working class than whites. In fact, 72% of white Creekridge Park residents identified as middle class. This identification is likely connected, in part, to educational attainment, as white Creekridge Park residents were much more likely to have a college (44%) or graduate degree (38%) than any other group across both neighborhoods.

The Latinx populations in both neighborhoods are mostly from Mexico and Central America, as Cincinnati and Durham are both new destination

TABLE 8.1 Neighborhood Demographics

	2015 Demographics		2010 Demographics	
	Carthage	Cincinnati (Hamilton County)	Creekridge Park	Durham County
White, non-Hispanic	60%	49% (67%)	34%	42%
Black	17%	43% (36%)	39%	38%
Hispanic	21%	3% (3%)	26%	14%
Total (*n*)	2,864	297,397	1,570	169,498

Note. Percentages of each racial group living in each neighborhood and its corresponding city/county context.

Source: 2010 data are 2010 US Census Bureau data; 2015 data are 5-year American Community Survey estimates.

TABLE 8.2 Housing Tenure by Race

	Owner-Occupied		Renter-Occupied	
	Carthage	Creekridge Park	Carthage	Creekridge Park
White, non-Hispanic	63%	50%	37%	50%
Black	44%	17%	56%	83%
Hispanic	18%	13%	82%	87%

Note. Percentages of each racial group living in a unit they own or rent across both neighborhoods.

Source: Data from 2010 US Census Bureau.

cities for Latinx migration. Latinx residents are more likely to be renters than owners across both neighborhoods. Black residents are about as likely to rent as they are to own in Carthage, while they are more likely to rent than own in Creekridge Park. Inversely, white residents are equally likely to be renters and owners in Creekridge Park but are more likely to own than rent in Carthage (see Table 8.2). The intersection of housing tenure and race is important in shaping neighborhood dynamics across both neighborhoods as homeowner attitudes toward renters are generally negative.

Changing Landscape

Both of these neighborhoods are historically white neighborhoods that are now multiracial, but the residents view these changes and characterize their neighborhoods in different ways. In Creekridge Park, Black residents have been living in the neighborhood in significant numbers since the 1990s. Around this same period, Latinx migration also started to increase in the city and state. The neighborhood's Black and Latinx populations increased over the next 20 years, reaching their current statistically integrated[4] state in 2010 (see Figure 8.1). Carthage also has experienced recent demographic changes, although the neighborhood is still predominantly white. In twenty years, the white population has decreased by about one-third and both the Black and Latinx populations have grown to about 20% each. This is, in fact, why I chose to study Carthage. Carthage is one of the only neighborhoods in the city of Cincinnati with a substantial Latinx population, and I was interested in capturing this growing population.

When asked whether they considered their neighborhood stable or transitional, Creekridge Park survey respondents were pretty evenly split; 51% answered transitional, while 49% said stable. Their reasons for the transitional characterization relied on common understandings of renters as inherently transitory, although the number of young families living in "starter homes" was also mentioned multiple times. One respondent, capturing the ambivalence

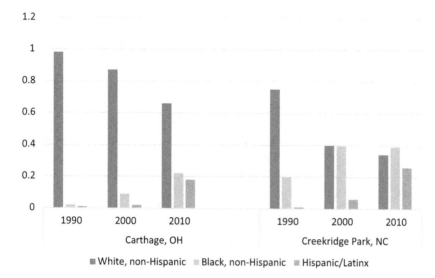

FIGURE 8.1   Demographic Change, 1990–2010.
Source: Data from US Census Bureau.

of residents on this topic, explained Creekridge Park was "more on the stable side of transitional." This comment also highlights how transitional does not necessarily mean instability in this neighborhood.

In contrast, long-term Carthage residents characterized the neighborhood as changing but clearly saw this transition as a decline. For example, Deacon, a white resident who was living with his grandmother in affordable housing for elders, said, "I hate to use the word ghetto, but it seems like it's kind of turned into that." He explained this meant drug dealing and fewer businesses in the area. He blames the change on an increase in Section 8 properties, the federal housing program that provides vouchers for poor and low-income families, and lack of employment. Ironically, Deacon's grandmother's building is classified as a "Low-Income Housing Tax Credit affordable community," which means it is partially funded by government subsidies. Carthage residents across racial groups most often cited drugs and rental properties—Section 8, or otherwise—as the causes of neighborhood decline and criminal activity. However, white and Latinx residents were more likely to see crime as a problem in Carthage than Black residents.

Neighborhood Descriptors

I asked respondents from both neighborhoods what three words they would use to describe their neighborhood. Those results are detailed in Figure 8.2 (see Figure 8.2). In Creekridge Park, "diverse/mixed" was the most common set of

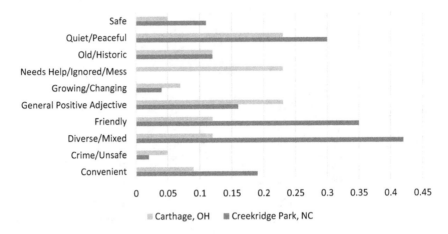

FIGURE 8.2   Common Neighborhood Descriptors.

Source: Data from Household Survey (Creekridge Park) and Interviews (Carthage).

descriptors, followed by "friendly/neighborly." Carthage residents were more varied and ambivalent in their characterizations than Creekridge Park residents. General positive adjectives, such as "charming" and "nice," were just as common as "needs help/ignored/mess." Interestingly, despite all the discussion of prostitution and drug abuse by residents, "peaceful/quiet" were also top descriptors. Overall, there was much more agreement in Creekridge Park than in Carthage in the top neighborhood descriptors; no Carthage descriptor cracked 25%, while three Creekridge Park descriptors did: "diverse," "friendly," and "quiet."

Racial and Sociopolitical Attitudes

What is the sociopolitical context of Creekridge Park? Although electoral data are not available at the block level, state and county data give some insight into the neighborhood. On the one hand, historically speaking, North Carolina is a conservative state. Its electoral votes were won by President Trump and Vice President Pence in 2016 (49.8% of the popular vote) and Romney/Ryan in 2012 (50.39% of the popular vote). Although the state went blue in 2008 (52.87% of the popular vote), it was only the second time in contemporary elections that a Democratic presidential nominee won the state (President Carter was the first in 1976). On the other hand, Durham is a consistently Democratic county. In 2016, 77.7% voted for Clinton/Kaine; President Obama and Vice President Biden won about 75% of Durham County in both 2008 and 2012 (Leip, 2012).

Similarly, Cincinnati is the blue dot in red southern Ohio. In 2016, President Trump and Vice President Pence won the state of Ohio with 51.3% of the popular vote. Hamilton County, where Cincinnati is located, went Democratic with 52.7% voting for Clinton/Kaine. All the surrounding counties went for

Trump/Pence. In 2012, Ohio's electoral votes went to President Obama and Vice President Biden (50.6% of the vote), yet blue Hamilton County (52.5% of the vote) was still surrounded by Republican-voting counties. The same pattern emerged in 2008.

Creekridge Park residents rate more liberally than both the national average and Carthage residents on racial attitudes. I asked residents how they would explain ongoing socioeconomic inequality between Blacks and whites in the US given four possible options: lack of opportunity for Blacks, racial discrimination, lack of Blacks' willpower or motivation, or less in-born ability.[5] Of Creekridge Park respondents, 57% said it was because of lack of opportunity, while 43% of Carthage residents and 47% of a national sample, respectively, acknowledged lack of opportunity as an issue. In Carthage, however, residents were almost as likely (40%) to say that African Americans do not have the motivation or willpower to pull themselves out of poverty. This number was driven mostly by white and Latinx resident responses; lack of motivation was the most popular response from Latinx respondents. None of my respondents from either neighborhood said it was because of less in-born ability, while 10% of a 2010 national sample did. Interestingly, a handful of white respondents from Carthage rejected the premise of the question. For example, Erin, a 22-year-old homemaker with no kids who identifies as middle class (her family's income was between $15,000 and $19,999), said she did not agree with any of the responses and then went on to explain,

> I believe that you have your own choice. You have the choice to either get up and go and pick up a phone and pick up a pipe, live the street life, or you have the choice to pick up a book and read it and go to school. There are grants; there are all kinds of things to get you out. There are Boys and Girls Clubs, all kinds of things that you can get yourself involved in at a young age that you stay out of the streets, you stay out of trouble. It's not that they don't have the willpower, that they don't want to, it's that they feel that they can't because they're Black.

Erin's response is that Black folks need to make better choices, echoing a culture of poverty framework. Specifically, they need to stop doing drugs. This, of course, is contrary to empirical data: national data show that Black people are less likely to be drug users than white people (Alexander, 2010). Erin also highlights the choice Black folks make to discuss and notice race and historic racial subordination; this is holding them back in her view. The idea that Black people are fixated on race was something other white Carthage residents also discussed.

On race relations, 72% of Creekridge Park respondents and 74% of Carthage respondents said the issue was either important or extremely important to them, although Latinx residents in Carthage were an outlier with just 38% agreeing it was important or extremely important. Lastly, over 66% of Creekridge Park respondents believe that undocumented migrants help rather than hurt the economy, while an NYT/CBS News poll (2010) from the same period shows that over 74% of Americans believe undocumented migrants are detrimental to the economy. Similarly, 64% of all Carthage residents also agreed that undocumented migrants help rather than hurt the economy, although Black residents were the outlier here with 78% saying they hurt the economy. This pattern differs from Tatishe M. Nteta's (2014) study on Black Americans' attitudes toward undocumented immigrants; he found that only 32% of Blacks sampled have unfavorable views of undocumented immigrants. Nteta also found that residential proximity to new immigrants significantly predicts support for the DREAM Act. As we will see below, despite residential proximity, interactions between Black and Latinx residents in Carthage were very limited.

Findings

Given the theoretical importance of access to multiracial spaces for Black mobility, what does social life look like for Black residents in Creekridge Park and Carthage? In the following sections, I discuss the social relationships of Black, white, and Latinx residents, with a particular focus on Black residents. These relationships and the way residents are able to wield power—or not—help outline the racial structure of these two neighborhoods. I find that while some experience social support, Black residents are more likely to describe social isolation in the neighborhood than close ties. They are also more likely to be victims of social control practices than other residents, which entangles them with landlords, lawyers, and the police. In this way, multiracial spaces are extensions of larger systems of racial inequality rather than respites from them. Lastly, Black residents can be met with limited engagement and social control practices, even at the hands of white renters. This points to the importance of not just a racial lens, but an intersectional race and class lens to investigate processes of inclusion and exclusion within multiracial neighborhoods.

Social Support

Friendships

One of the ways that social scientists measure social support is through friendship data. Bridging social capital, which emerges from relationships that cross status differences, is said to be a potential outcome of economically and racially mixed living (Putnam, 2007). I first focus on the friendship data of white, Black, and Latinx residents to show the divergent access they have to neighborhood social support.

Forty-five percent of survey respondents in Creekridge Park replied that they have at least one friend in the neighborhood. The features of neighborhood friendships differed across individuals. Some people got together regularly for drinks, while others vacationed together. These examples of neighborhood friendships, however, were all shared by white residents. This pattern of segregated friendship networks is corroborated by survey data; as Table 8.3 shows, 86% of surveyed whites in Creekridge Park list other white people as their closest friends (see Table 8.3). In short, white residents are well-connected, but mostly to each other. This is particularly noteworthy because most residents in Creekridge Park are not white, and previous research has shown whites claim lack of opportunity explains their racially segregated networks (Bonilla-Silva, 2003/2017; Ingraham, 2014).

White residents in Carthage, both renters and homeowners, shared how they met their neighbors and became friends. Previous connections mattered for some, including Todd, who is a homeowner. When I asked him how he met his neighbors, he explained that he met Vicky from across the street because he was checking out his house before moving in. Vicky was suspicious of his canvassing of the house, so she came over to "confront" him. In her interrogation, she found out that she knew Todd's wife's cousin. As Todd put it, Carthage is like "a big family... everybody knows everybody." Knowing the same person turned what could have been a conflict into a new social tie.

Others, like longtime homeowner Gwen, met neighbors through activities such as a garden club started by Gwen's neighbor Eve, also a white homeowner. When asked how often she spent time with her neighbors, Gwen described how she spoke with her next-door neighbor Sherry every day and that they are "very close." They check in over the phone and in person and do favors for one another, such as call each other before they head to the store in case they can save the other a trip. Gwen is in her eighties, while Sherry is in her seventies. Gwen also spends time with Eve, who is in her sixties, and will accompany her on trips to the grocery store and dress shopping. Some residents who said they

TABLE 8.3 Race of Five Closest Friends Across Neighborhoods

Respondent race	Creekridge Park			Carthage		
	White	Black	Latinx	White	Black	Latinx
White	86%	23%	45%	73%	30%	33%
Black	4%	70%	5%	18%	59%	8%
Latinx	5%	3%	45%	7%	3%	58%
Other	5%	3%	5%	2%	8%	0%
Total friendships	305	40	20	45	37	12

Source: Creekridge Park data derived from Mayorga-Gallo's 2011 survey data. Carthage data from author's 2015 face-to-face interviews.

did not have a lot of friends, such as 22-year-old Erin, still spent some time with their neighbors. Erin mentioned her neighbor Annie, who is 30 years her senior, various times during her interview. The friends Erin grew up with were now too busy raising children and working, so they did not have time to do activities with Erin. As such, Erin plans movie days with Annie and helps Annie with her medical issues.

My Creekridge Park data included a few accounts of Black residents with neighborhood-based friendships. Connie, for example, occasionally got together with her white next-door neighbors, Lilith and Frank. She even described one scenario in which she stayed at their house for a week when her own house lost power after a storm. During our interview, Connie described how she befriended Lilith and Frank. It seems Connie shared a connection with Lilith and Frank before they even moved next door. Their proximity to each other provided support for their friendship, but the catalyst was their pre-Creekridge Park hiking club association. Connie also knew Frank's cousin. This type of neighborhood relationship, where residents knew each other beforehand, was also common among white homeowners.

In Carthage, Angelina, a Black homeowner, mentioned that she had a good friend in the neighborhood who lives at the end of her street and is also a Black woman. She describes how their husbands get together and,

> me and her we hang out, go have dinner, and we hang with some of the same other people, or they invite me to birthdays, family gatherings, the kids' birthdays and stuff, so yeah, I hang out with her. She's nice, and she calls me regularly.

The majority of Black resident friendships in Carthage were intraracial (59%), while 30% of Black resident friendships were Black–white dyads. For example, Colleen, who is a Black renter and identified as having "Caribbean roots," said that most of her friends were white. Shaun, a Black renter in Carthage and a truck driver, described occasionally inviting other residents of his apartment building to join him if he was grilling out; they sometimes did. He said he had one good friend in the building, James, a white renter:

> My neighbor, James, used to ride with me sometimes. In fact, I used to take him with me out of town when I was in the big trucks. He's a real good old guy. Knowing him has made life real bearable in that building.

Based on the survey and interview data, it seems Black Carthage residents have somewhat looser networks, in the sense that they are more likely to have non-Black friendship ties. I do not, however, want to overstate the significance of these quantitative differences (11%) across small samples. Given that I am often read as white in Durham and Cincinnati, it is also possible that Black respondents in Carthage were more likely to share their white friendship tie information with me than in Creekridge Park because I collected the Carthage data during face-to-face interviews instead of an anonymous survey as I did in Durham.[6] Also worth considering is that both Shaun and Colleen are renters. Although not all Black renters had close ties with white neighbors (see Andrea and Bernice below), my Cincinnati and Durham data both had a couple of examples of cross-racial relationships between renters in the same apartment building.

Most Latinx residents had friendship ties with family, compatriots, or other Latinx folks. For example, Juliana said she moved to Creekridge Park due to her cousin's suggestion; her cousin lives just down the street from her. Ramona, a Latina renter in Carthage, also has family in the neighborhood and surrounding communities, including her brother, two sisters, and in-laws. Only two Latinx interviewees cited a non-Latinx person as a close friend. Both live in Carthage. When asked if she has any friends she feels close to, Carmen—who owns her home in Carthage—said, "We have a large family of Americans (whites) who we spend holidays with, such as Christmas, Thanksgiving, their birthdays, my kids' birthdays. With them we are very friendly." Diego, also a homeowner, said that his close friends were both Latinx and white. His white friends, with whom he has a "very deep" connection, are landscaping clients that live in Indian Hill, one of the wealthiest neighborhoods in Cincinnati. The closeness of this relationship is an interesting contrast to how Diego describes his relationship with his neighbors below.

Helping Behaviors

While some residents did not specifically call their neighbors friends, they did talk about how they "look out" for each other and provide support for one another. I interviewed Andrea and Bernice together; both are elderly Black women who rent in the same apartment building. Bernice shared a story of when she hurt herself and came down to ask Andrea for help:

> One time I hit my head and I came down here because I was bleeding and I couldn't see. I kept saying "Am I cut enough to call 911?" She said, "Call 911, fool." So I called them, they stopped the bleeding, and I didn't have to go nowhere. We kind of look out for each other. I call her if I haven't talked to her in a few days or if I know she's not feeling well or something. I call her and see how she's doing.

When explaining their relationships with others in the building, who are mostly white, Andrea shared, "As far as the people here, I stay to myself. That's the best way to be. When she [Bernice] gets mad at me, I just get so depressed because she's the only one that I truly believe has my back." Andrea described the cliquishness of the other building residents and the gossiping that goes on, deciding that it's better if she just keeps to herself. Here we see how sharing an apartment building does not necessarily lead to social ties between Black and white residents.

For some, there was an important distinction between neighborship and friendship. Seth, a white homeowner from Creekridge Park, explained that friends and neighbors do not have to be the same thing:

> I mean, my next-door neighbors here, we've had a key to their house for 12 years now. I can go into their house any time I want to. They'll let me borrow anything I want to. [...] I turned 40 last year and I had a fortieth picnic and stuff and of course my neighbors were invited, but as far as eating together regularly and talking about non-neighborhood stuff, no.

Clare, a Black homeowner in Carthage, captured her relationship with neighbors as follows:

> I do know my neighbors, and they know me. And what I love about it is we all got our own lives. We speak. We invite each other over if we're having something like a barbecue or something like that. We got your back. We're like a little neighborhood watch type of thing, but everybody minds their own business.

The juxtaposition of knowing each other but minding your own business reflects a neighborship ethos rather than a friendship ethos. Clare describes her street as majority "middle-class Caucasians" and four to five "working Black families." Interestingly, when I asked Clare if she had any friends in the neighborhood she responded,

> In the neighborhood, we're all old school. So as far as friendships I think we're friendly but as far as a—for me to call someone a friend you have to have a long—you have to have a certain spiritual bond with that person. So we're friendly but I wouldn't say we're all friends.

This parallels Black homeowner Cheryl's point of view on her neighbors and friendship in Creekridge Park. Cheryl described having neighbors who would let her know if an unknown person was on her property, clarifying, "I had people who looked out for my house. I didn't have any relationships in this neighborhood for the most part." When I asked Cheryl if she had any friends in the neighborhood, she responded, "Absolutely not. Absolutely not. I think too much of the term friend to use it lightly. So, I absolutely would not say that I have any friends in this neighborhood, absolutely not." Although she acknowledged that the neighbor role has obligations, she also saw a clear distinction between friendship and neighborship.

Despite this distinction between neighbors and friends, Clare and Seth had social ties to their neighbors that they appreciated, which is what Cheryl was looking for. In this way, being a (good) neighbor comes with social obligations outside the parameters of property protection for many residents. Mary, a Black renter in Creekridge Park, was looking for the same thing. Although Mary's previous neighbor was not home much and did not chat with Mary as often as her current neighbors Luke and Emma, Mary said her old neighbor was somewhat friendly because he offered her a ride one day. This was a particularly kind and neighborly act for Mary since she relies on public transportation for her grocery shopping and other activities. It is clear from our conversation, however, that Mary preferred it when people regularly spoke with her. Unlike her Latinx counterparts whom we hear from below, a hello did not constitute friendliness for Mary. We hear more from Mary and Cheryl below.

Greetings

Most Latinx respondents indicated that they thought Creekridge Park was a very friendly place. They based their characterization of friendliness on greetings, as very few Latinx residents engaged in full conversations with neighbors. Juliana, a Latina renter, revealed that the basis of her interactions with other neighbors were *saludos* (greetings). I asked her if there were neighbors who spoke Spanish, and she explained that her neighbors' Spanish was limited to *hola* (hello) and *¿cómo estás?* (how are you?). Therefore, so were their conversations. Héctor's experience echoes Juliana's; as a renter in Creekridge Park, he stated that his neighbors were generally friendly, but there were limits to their interactions. As he put it, "we halfway greet each other." Although they cannot communicate beyond preliminary greetings, he appreciates their hellos. Martín, a Latino renter in Creekridge Park, also identified similar practices, which provides some evidence that this mode of interaction between Latinxs and non-Latinxs is normative in Creekridge Park. The hellos Martín received from his white neighbors pleased him very much, particularly since he saw these short interactions as a reflection of Creekridge Park's quiet and peaceful nature. He thought these moments of acknowledgment were "*perfecto.*"

The characterization of Creekridge Park and its residents as friendly by Latinx migrants echoes claims by white respondents. In fact, 35% of those surveyed used "friendly" to describe Creekridge Park. While the neighborships that whites describe differ significantly in their intimacy, Latinx residents do not identify this difference. Their experiences of Creekridge Park and its American residents are greatly shaped by their social positions in the United States as Latinx migrants—some of whom are undocumented. Within an unreceptive national context (as Latinx respondents described), the greetings they receive are perceived as a stark, "friendly" contrast.

Mary, who had positive relationships with a few of her neighbors, described her displeasure with her new neighbors across the street. She stated a couple of times during the interview that this new couple was not as friendly as Luke and Emma, her other neighbors, because they did not say hello or speak to her when she and they were outside at the same time. She was clearly unhappy about it, although she did remark toward the end of the interview that they were not doing anything harmful. Mary pointed to age differences to rationalize why her new neighbors did not speak to her but did socialize with Emma and Luke. The survey and interview data indicate, however, that very few of my Creekridge Park respondents did not speak to their neighbors. Mary's initial reaction to her neighbors' lack of communication indicates that at least acknowledging your neighbor is normative in Creekridge Park and that her neighbors' failure to do so was undesirable for Mary.

These greeting relationships were also common among Latinx residents and non-Latinx residents in Carthage. Diego, who said he had close ties with some white folks, explained that with his neighbors he mostly stuck to greetings. When I asked him if he did these greetings in English, he responded, "Not very fluently, but yes. '*Hola*, how are you? Good morning, good night.' They say lots of things to me and I don't understand them, but I smile anyway." Given how he characterizes the depth of his friendship with other white folks, his limited engagement with his Carthage neighbors is a noticeable difference. Ramona also says she has limited interactions with neighbors, mostly just "hellos" and "how have you been," since she does not speak much English. Raúl, a Latino homeowner, says that he always greets and is greeted by his white neighbor across the street, but that they do not get together socially. He also states that he has a Black neighbor next door but gives no indication that they communicate—even via greetings.[7] Carmen and Lourdes—both homeowners—also said they mostly just greet their neighbors, but they blamed it on their busy work schedules and not having much time for socialization, not a language barrier.

Overall, we see that Black residents experience some social support—from Black, but also some white neighbors. Whites are very well-connected in these neighborhoods, but mostly to each other. Latinx residents, largely for language reasons, have mostly greeting relationships with white residents, but do not share much intimacy with Black residents. They are mostly in community with other Latinx migrants. This echoes research on recent Latin American migrants and their native-born counterparts that finds a sense of commonality with Blacks is more likely to emerge among Latinxs who speak English and are US citizens (Jones-Correa, 2011).

I highlight friendship and neighborship data, as they are good indicators of the kinds of resources and support Black residents have available to them through their neighborhood. Contrary to the sociological theory on the benefits of racially and economically mixed neighborhoods, Black residents do not

benefit from bridging social capital because they do not have close or reciprocal ties with white and or Latinx residents for the most part. This is also why
studying multiracial neighborhoods matters; it allows us to fully interrogate the
underlying assumptions of integration research and flesh out a more complex
reality.

Social Isolation

Unlike their white and Latinx neighbors, Black residents were much less likely
to see Creekridge Park as a friendly neighborhood. Cheryl indicated that she
had hopes that more substantial neighborhood interactions would be a part of
her life in this neighborhood. She explained, "People were not as friendly as
I had hoped and thought that they would be or at least this image I had in my
head of what friendly would be like." Cheryl recounted how she was ignored
by her neighbors for the first 5 years of her tenure in Creekridge Park. This
changed when she began to plant a garden in her front yard. Cheryl's disappointment with the social interactions in Creekridge Park is particularly conspicuous when compared with the overwhelmingly positive characterizations
and social experiences of white homeowners.

Black residents Miriam and Harry are married and own their home, having
lived in Carthage for 11 years. They described how the neighborhood, in general, did not produce many social interactions. Miriam thinks folks are just not
as friendly as they used to be, while Harry thinks it is about trust:

> They just don't have the trust and stuff that we grew up with, ya know,
> doors open. I was selling papers on the corner at nine years old. [...] And
> people were always outside. And you knew everybody. [Now] The doors
> close up when people come home and they don't come out. I think it's
> pretty much that way where my brother stays in Fairview [near down-
> town Cincinnati]. They know their neighbors enough to wave. But it's
> not that much interaction. I can't say it's just like this in Carthage. I think
> it's just a country[-wide] problem. People get their news. And they feel
> like that's the way it is. And they don't wanna try to change anything.
> You can't change anything if you don't come out and interact with people
> because you don't know what to change.

Harry explained that he and Miriam are the only ones that use their porches
and spend time outside on their street. Rather than particular to Carthage,
Harry saw this social isolation as a national problem and clear shift from practices of his youth. Harry's assessment of dissipating trust and the social effects of
technology are in line with Robert Putnam's (2000) book *Bowling Alone*.

Margaret, a Black Carthage resident whose boyfriend owns the home she
lives in, said she had almost no interactions with her neighbors. Only the older

couple next door says hello to her. She explained that her other neighbors have a young child her son's age and that "they don't even play together." Her son tried but complained afterward that they were mean and picking on him. She has never spoken to the parents or seen them outside, she said. It seems like she did not have any interest in building a relationship with them either. That disinterest in neighborhood ties differs from Cheryl, who hoped to connect with folks.

Sue, a white female renter, described how the Carthage she knew growing up no longer exists. Similar to Harry and Miriam, she thinks people are more closed off then they used to be. She ties this to the amount of time that folks spend working and inside their homes. She also said that old Carthage was homogeneous:

> There's such a mixture of people now that used to be all—no culture mixes[8] back then. And there's so many preconceived notions now about what people are like without waiting to find out what they're like. If a Mexican family moves in, nobody's willing to find out what they're like.

She goes on to explain that in her building, she is a minority and has witnessed anti-Latinx racism from Black residents. She argues that the way that whites used to talk about new Black residents is how Black residents now talk about new Latinx residents. She says that she's learned "everybody's prejudiced against somebody else." After lamenting that her Black neighbors have misinterpreted her shyness as snootiness and characterizing this as possibly reverse discrimination, Sue reported that she presently feels included: "They invite me to bingo now."

Only one Latinx resident seemed to experience social isolation. Adolfo, a Latino homeowner, shared that he had no friends in Carthage or Cincinnati that he felt close to, despite having lived in Carthage for 11 years. His friends are located across the US and they see each other maybe once a year. He lives in Carthage with his two sons, ages ten and thirteen, and lives on a predominantly white street with no other Latinx residents. While he speaks English, he also works the night shift, which means he spends his days sleeping.

In this section, we saw how some Black residents wanted to have deeper connections with their neighbors but were met with silence. While Harry and Miriam blame this on American cultural shifts, it is easy to see Cheryl's experience as a result of her social position as a Black homeowner. The economic decision she made to live in a mixed neighborhood—to avoid, as she put it, "the depressed values of homes in all-Black neighborhoods"—came with social costs. Unlike her white neighbors who had a lot to gain socially, Cheryl was disappointed by a lack of social cohesion in Creekridge Park. She wanted to replicate the neighborhood-based social relationships she had when she was growing up in all-Black neighborhoods, but Creekridge Park had not delivered. Although being ignored by your neighbors may seem like a mild example of racial inequality, we should not underestimate the psychological costs of multiracial spaces. In the following section, I discuss how this kind of interracial social distance could also aggravate other situations.

Social Control

When You're the Target

Life in Creekridge Park parallels Carthage in some ways; for example, you are more likely to characterize each neighborhood as friendly and call the police with complaints if you are white. There are, however, important differences. For instance, local police and city government seem to be more responsive to Creekridge Park resident complaints than those of Carthage—unless you are Black, in which case you are out of luck in Creekridge Park, too.[9] Needless to say, not all neighbor relationships were marked by barbecues or even waves hello. When asked what they would do if they had a problem with a neighbor, residents across Carthage and Creekridge Park said they would speak with the appropriate neighbor first. I found, however, that when white Creekridge Park residents described specific conflicts with non-white neighbors, white residents usually involved the police or another authority. In part, this occurs because, as we established, white residents are less likely to know their non-white neighbors. As one white homeowner described,

> I would say if they were people that we knew, could trust, and feel safe talking to, probably most people for one, would've already talked to them if there was gonna be an issue that would bring, potentially bringing up a problem. But then for people that I didn't know I'd probably just call the police [laughs].

When white residents are more likely to know and be friendly with other white residents, however, these social control practices reinforce high interracial social distance.

Mary described an incident that escalated quickly due to her neighbor Mark's actions. After her son littered in Mark's yard, Mark, a white homeowner, called her landlord in an attempt to get Mary and her son evicted. Mary lamented,

> I didn't like that because, what kind of neighbor is that? He could've came and talked to me and told me and I could've made my son stop doing that, you know, so, but I didn't like the fact that he went behind my back and he supposed to be a neighbor. And he's gonna go behind my back, and he called [the property manager]... 'Cause to me that, that to me was being mean and hateful. I mean, it was being very mean.

Mary said that she did not think this incident with Mark was racially moti-vated, but she went on to describe another incident where Mark, unlike her other neighbors, never stopped to give her a ride when she walked home from the bus, regardless of how many packages she was carrying. He saw her and waved as he drove to his house, which was directly across the street from hers. Mary speculated that this interaction was likely fueled by Mark's desire to not have Black people in his car. Mark has since moved down the street because, according to Mary, "he don't want to live across the street from us no more." She explained that her landlord did not kick her and her son out because she always pays her rent on time, but Mary was dismayed with her neighbor's actions. Since Mary did not have a particularly close relationship with Mark, which at least on his part seemed intentional, his procedure to address the trash issue maintained their high interracial social distance.

Denise, who is a Black homeowner, talked about how much she loved liv-ing in Carthage—which made her an outlier, as many residents shared at least some complaints about life in Carthage. She explained, "Carthage has put their arms around us as 'welcome home' and everything we need is right here. [...] I've been so happy because my neighbors have just been the greatest neigh-bors except for one." She went on to describe how two white homeowners who bought the property next door to rent it out did not want her using their shared driveway despite Denise having an easement in her deed. Lawyers were involved and eventually the situation ended, despite threats to sue, a house egging, and shouting matches. As Denise described it,

> I can't even come up with a word for the hatred that these people just had for us. They thought that we were just kind of trash, just secondhand citizens is how they—"We have a house. This is just another property. We're not even here six months out of the year; we live in our vacation home in Florida."

There were clear class dimensions to how these neighbors framed their supe-riority over Denise, but their emphasis on not being from Cincinnati (they were from Kentucky) also has racial connotations. One of the cornerstones of understanding race as a social construct is how it is created and reinscribed via social interactions. How one characterizes and responds to an action depends on how one views the other actor—in regard to race, gender, class, and other markers. White folks from surrounding areas see Cincinnati as a dangerous (Black) city that differs from its neighboring areas. This is likely due to an interplay between dominant stereotypes of Blackness and the demographics of the city; in 2010, Cincinnati was 44.6% Black, while Hamilton County, where Cincinnati is the county seat, was only 25.5% Black. 2015 estimates put the Black population in Hamilton County at 36%. It is also, however, likely related to the 2001 uprisings in the predominantly Black downtown neighborhood of Over-the-Rhine, prompted by the deaths of fifteen unarmed Black men at the hands of white police officers between 1995 and 2001.[10]

When You Target Others

In both Carthage and Creekridge Park, white residents employed their standards of good parenting among other behaviors when determining whether and the extent to which they would police their neighbors of color. For example, white homeowners Paul and Kay, who were the most affluent residents I interviewed in Carthage, stated that "Unfortunately, from the comments of the community, I guess I've never heard positive things about our Black neighbors, but usually I don't hear anything." This was in response to my question about interracial interactions in the neighborhood. While their block was predominantly white, they said that they saw Black and Latinx folks on their walks. They then proceeded to describe how one of their neighbors, a Black mother, was visited by Child Protective Services (CPS). The specifics of why are unclear; they said,

> I think they had a grill on their back porch and then she has a lot of kids that are hard to kinda manage and so the kids, I don't know what they've gotten into, but yeah, she had—Child Protective Services comes in every once in a while.

It seems as if neighbors keep a close eye on this family and may call CPS when they suspect something is awry. Paul and Kay are unable to say what this mother has done wrong but are certainly aware of how CPS is in and out of her home. This policing of a Black mother for no reason besides she has "lots of kids" is dependent, at least in part, on stereotypes of single Black mothers as deficient and her Black children as troublemakers with no positive role model.

This kind of general discussion of Black families and poor parenting was also how some white Creekridge Park residents referred to different rental properties in the neighborhood. Childrearing and animal care practices that differed from what white residents believed to be appropriate were particularly scrutinized and critiqued during interviews and neighborhood events. Emma, a white homeowner, described how there was one neighbor she did not know, but on whom she called animal control. She continued,

> I don't really wanna know them if you're the kind of person that you're gonna beat your dog and scream at your children at 11 o'clock at night. It's just, you know, um, […] I walk my dogs regularly and frankly they yell so loudly that we can hear them most of the time.

Another white homeowner, Terry, mentioned, "we have a lot of dysfunctional parenting and behavior in the parking lot of the apartments behind us, and there has been a lot of drug activity there and gang activity there." He indicated that he and his wife, through an adjacent neighborhood's association, were in contact with the property manager and that the manager was making efforts to "kick people out who are problems." What is important is how white residents have no relationship with these neighbors yet feel entitled—perhaps obligated—to call the police on what they see as pathological behavior. Again, our social realities are always filtered through a racialized lens. Calling the police on neighbors you do not know is not the only approach to neighborhood life, as Cheryl commented,

> I just think it's an interesting dynamic to have white, upwardly mobile professionals moving into a neighborhood and creating or having an expectation that the standards that get met are those that they set when they new to the neighborhood.

To wit, Emma, Brendan, and Elisabeth, who we hear from below, were all recent additions to Creekridge Park and Carthage.

Some white Creekridge Park residents saw themselves as helping Black and Latinx neighbors by calling the police and relevant city services. For example, Brendan, a new homeowner in the area, spoke about how recent phone calls to the police in regard to pit bulls and a gunfight at a Latinx neighbor's house benefitted the children in that home. He cited their playtime activities, including jumping out of a window and into a garbage can, as evidence that a change in the living situation would be beneficial. Brendan shared this story after Emma said calling the police helps everyone, but probably not the families involved. This kind of ambivalence was also shared by one Carthage resident, Elisabeth. Elisabeth, a white female renter, described Carthage as "sad." Rather than conflicts with specific neighbors, she described a general feeling of depression in the neighborhood:

> I feel like I've called the police more times in this neighborhood than I ever did, even in Los Angeles. Like, it just feels like somebody is miserable every day, and they're kind of taking it out—whether it's on their kids, whether it's on their spouse. It just seems to be going on a lot. There's a guy next door who gets really drunk and cries all the time. Like, he'll cry for hours outside, and I feel helpless, like I can't help. I also don't really wanna call the police, but it's also—I don't know, tough to live there sometimes.

She then explains that she does not like to call the police because they have had "lousy attitudes" in the past and she knows that there are undocumented residents in the neighborhood. But she calls when she feels like someone is "endangered." While she does not give a specific example of what the threshold is for endangerment, she repeats "It just doesn't seem worthwhile unless it's a safety issue." Despite their ambivalence about the possible negative effects, Emma and Elisabeth still call the police.

Whether there is enough police presence in Carthage depends on whom you ask, where they live, and their general view of Carthage. Drugs and prostitution were the two largest neighborhood issues that residents complained about and in which they tried to involve police. Most residents said that they felt safe in the neighborhood, although 71% of those who said they did not were white residents. When answering whether they thought Carthage had a crime problem, white and Latinx residents both agreed there was (68% and 88%, respectively), while most Black respondents did not agree (only 38% said yes).

Angelina, a Black homeowner who has lived in Carthage for almost 12 years, talked about how the neighborhood had changed since she moved in. She details how neighbors were very nice and welcoming to her and her daughter when she first moved in and how most of her neighbors are older than her and have lived in Carthage for at least 25 years. More recently, her street has had a few foreclosures as well as elderly residents passing away or renting their houses out. As a result, "the type of people that's coming in renting, we started having a little drug problem. But, a lot of our neighbors, we got together, got with drug enforcement, and they actually came out and started helping us get it cleaned up." Angelina points to the renters on her street as the culprits who brought in drugs, but the police were called to handle it—and they did. Angelina's diminutive characterization of "a little drug problem" differs greatly from how some white residents, including long-term ones, described the drug situation in Carthage. For instance, Deacon lamented how drugs "just destroyed everything."

Hugh, a white male owner, also agreed that the shift from ownership to rentals has changed the neighborhood for the worse. He describes, "I've lived next door to an abandoned house for over 5 years. You know what I'm saying? So you have to fight the city to get them to even cut the grass." Despite his disapproval of renters, which he says are "a lot of Hispanics," his example of neighborhood apathy chronicles the city's failure. Their response has been to say it is too expensive for the city to cut overgrown lawns, which he found unacceptable. "I'm done with the city," he said. He explains that as soon as his dog passes—since his Carthage home provides him a necessary yard—he will move north to Butler or Warren counties. Both of these counties are far less populated and racially diverse than Hamilton County, where Cincinnati is located.

When Social Control Backfires

While these examples of social control certainly show how residents can shape their neighborhood in their vision, not all attempts to influence a neighborhood are enacted without personal costs. Over the course of our conversation, Jerry, a Black Creekridge Park homeowner, discussed his run-ins with the Black residents of a small multi-dwelling rental property behind his home. According to Jerry, these neighbors were noisy and even came into his backyard, which prompted him to put up a fence. Although the fence is up, he complained to the police that his neighbors would come up and hang out behind his fence, "smoking reefer and all that type of situation," as well as play their music very loudly. Although he says those living in these rentals are very transient, he did state that some of his neighbors had walked by his house in an attempt to intimidate him. After asking the police to address the threats the neighbors made to him ("[they said] they're going to shoot me"), Jerry felt frustrated with the authorities' lack of action. His antagonistic interactions with the neighbors culminated in him firing his gun in the direction of the rental property. Jerry explains:

> I did it [fire my gun] for a message to the fools [who live in the rental property behind my house] that was threatening me saying they was going to kill me. And they're going to shoot me, and they're going to do all this. I just let them know "you got the wrong one because I'm not going to be a sitting little duck here." But [after I fired my gun] that's when I got in trouble—when the policemen came. They came, I didn't run and hide. I was sitting out on my car when they came in. He asked me whether I did it. I said "yeah." And I said, "You know why I did it? Because every time the bad guys do it or whatever, you don't do nothing. I've been telling you all for the last—what, for the longest, you never arrested anybody. But look who you arresting now. You arresting me."... [Let me clarify,] they didn't arrest me. They took my weapons.

So, while white homeowners and renters successfully called upon the police to take care of issues in Creekridge Park, Jerry fired his gun in the city to get the attention of the police, who he felt were failing to address his concerns as well as warn his neighbors not to underestimate him. Shooting his gun was a strategy Jerry adapted from the resources available to him. Jerry's experience with the police is even more striking when we see how white resident concerns were treated by police officers in Creekridge Park. For example, Captain Hanks, the district commander, attended multiple resident-organized meetings about traffic accidents in Creekridge Park. The city councilor for Creekridge Park's district also attended some of these meetings. These were meetings organized by white homeowners independently of the neighborhood association. The ad hoc homeowner meetings eventually led to a new traffic light and new traffic pattern. The neighborhood association, led by white homeowners as well, also had the ear of city officials to get protections against tree removal during new construction projects in their neighborhood.

Conclusion

In this chapter, I analyzed the neighborhood relationships and interactions of Black, white, and Latinx residents of Carthage and Creekridge Park. I highlighted similarities and differences across these two multiracial neighborhoods finding that while some Black residents experienced the social support and friendship characteristic of white residential experiences, they were also met by social isolation and social control. In these multiracial neighborhoods, while there are some interracial friendships, racially homogeneous social networks prevail. Contrary to sociological theory, Black residents did not experience the benefits of bridging social capital because they generally did not have reciprocal and close relationships with their white neighbors. Rather than ambivalence on the part of Black residents, there was an unmet desire to connect more intimately with neighbors. My analyses point to the need to move beyond liberal ideas about multiracial and statistically integrated spaces being a harbinger of a utopian racial future. Without acknowledging racial structures that function outside a segregationist model, we miss the boat on how white supremacy continues to replicate itself in our shared spaces.

Racially mixed neighborhoods present new challenges because while Black residents are able to exercise preferences unlike in eras past, these moves do not necessarily mean that they are treated as full members of the community by their neighbors. In some ways, it is harder to showcase how neighborhoods are not necessarily places of equity due to racial covenants being replaced with social isolation and social control practices. In truth, while a wave hello may not seem unfriendly, when compared to the intimacy and reciprocity of white intraracial relationships, it is noteworthy.

In effect, multiracial neighborhoods are a good example of how upward mobility for Black people does not lead to the same outcomes as it does for whites. While they may gain the opportunity for homeownership, for example, they also experience social losses. In fact, Black homeowner Cheryl identified this dual process. She explained,

> I was very clear that I wanted a racially mixed neighborhood. But the reason I wanted a racially mixed neighborhood was because of what I understood about the depressed values of homes in all-Black neighborhoods. But it was very important that I not be in an all-white neighborhood because... I was specifically interested in recapturing the kind of neighborhood that I had when I grew up, a neighborhood where there were close relationships, where everybody knew each other, where people spoke to each other when they were in their yard.

So, while she avoided the segregation tax associated with Black neighborhoods, she is now paying a social tax as a Black homeowner in a multiracial neighborhood that is shaped by white residents and their interests.

Forty years ago, sociologist David T. Wellman highlighted the limitations of prejudice measures as "middle-class, liberal" views of race and racism (1977, p. 29). His argument is still resonant today, particularly for the study of multiracial neighborhoods. While arguably most sociologists who study housing inequality would agree that racism is structural—in fact, residential segregation is a great illustration of that fact—they fail to understand structure beyond that particular construct. An emphasis on concentrated poverty and residential segregation has created a void in regard to theorizing the complexity of racially integrated or multiracial neighborhoods. While yes, multiracial neighborhoods are usually economically advantageous for the residents of color who live there, particularly in comparison to the segregation tax associated with racial isolation, these neighborhoods are still shaped by an inequitable racial structure. This leads to social isolation in the midst of spatial proximity and the loss of social resources that racially segregated neighborhoods, despite their economic limitations, provided. To state that multiracial neighborhoods are the sign of a new era may be true, but it is an era marked by a rearticulation of old processes of exclusion and dehumanization.

Notes

1 Creekridge Park is a pseudonym, while Carthage is not. These distinct naming protocols are based on different IRB agreements in regard to confidentiality. All participant names, however, are pseudonyms.

2 Some of the findings from Creekridge Park have previously appeared in *Behind the White Picket Fence: Power and Privilege in a Multiethnic Neighborhood* (Mayorga-Gallo, 2014).

3 The Block Group is slightly larger than the boundaries of Creekridge Park and the estimate for Creekridge Park is based on 5 years of data from the American Community Survey (2009–2013).

4 Statistically integrated refers to areas that qualify as integrated according to sociological measures of integration, such as the dissimilarity index, that compare racial–ethnic population percentages at the neighborhood and city level. I use the term statistically integrated rather than integrated to highlight how proportionality is not necessarily indicative of the social patterns that the concept of integration implies.

5 This question and the national survey responses are from the General Social Survey (Smith, Marsden, Hout, & Kim, 2011).

6 I am, however, Latina. I was born in Puerto Rico and am the daughter of Nicaraguan immigrants. For more on my experience conducting research in Durham as a light-skinned Latina, please see Mayorga-Gallo and Hordge-Freeman (2017).

7 Raúl later says that he has no neighbors next door to him on either side, so perhaps the Black neighbors he refers to early on are not immediately next door, but nearby. He only mentions them when I ask about the racial composition of his street.

8 While Carthage was home to different ethnic whites (German immigrants, English settlers, Appalachians), Sue is likely referring to how Carthage used to be an exclusively white community.

9 This is not to say that the police never address resident complaints in Carthage, but rather that the overall assessment Carthage residents give of police efficacy is more critical than in Creekridge Park. For example, white renter Ben said, "This is the laziest police district I've lived in."

10 After strict curfews and a police–community agreement facilitated in part by the US Department of Justice, Over-the-Rhine has been gentrified and rebranded. Over-the-Rhine's new status is perhaps best captured by a recent New York Times article on visiting the Queen City: "Cincinnati is experiencing a boom, especially in the Over-the-Rhine district where rich cultural offerings and breweries thrive" (Glusac, 2017).

References

Alexander, M. (2010). *The New Jim Crow: Mass incarceration in the age of colorblindness.* New York, NY: The New Press.

Anderson, E. (2011). *The cosmopolitan canopy: Race and civility in everyday life.* New York, NY: WW Norton.

Aptekar, S. (2015). Visions of public space: Reproducing and resisting social hierarchies in a community garden. *Sociological Forum, 30*(1), 209–227.

Berrey, E. (2005). Divided over diversity: Political discourse in a Chicago neighborhood. *City and Community, 4*(2), 143–170.

Bonilla-Silva, E. (2017). *Racism without Racists: Color-blind racism and the persistence of racial inequality in America.* Lanham, MD: Rowman and Littlefield. (Original work published 2003)

Ellen, I. G., Horn, K., & O'Regan, K. (2012). Pathways to integration: Examining changes in the prevalence of racially integrated neighborhoods. *Cityscape, 14*(3), 33–53.

Fong, E., & Shibuya, K. (2005). Multiethnic cities in North America. *Annual Review of Sociology, 31*, 285–304.

Frey, W. (2001). *Melting pot suburbs: A census 2000 study of Suburban diversity.* The Brookings Institution. Retrieved from https://www.brookings.edu/wp-content/uploads/2016/06/frey.pdf

Frey, W. (2014, November 26). Glimpses of a ghetto-free future. *The New Republic.* Retrieved from https://newrepublic.com/article/120385/black-white-segregation-steadily-declining

Glusac, E. (2017, August 17). 36 hours in Cincinnati. *New York Times.* Retrieved from https://www.nytimes.com/interactive/2017/08/17/travel/what-to-do-36-hours-in-cincinnati-ohio.html

Hyra, D. S. (2017). *Race, class, and politics in the cappuccino city.* Chicago, IL: University of Chicago Press.

Ingraham, C. (2014, August 25). Three quarters of whites don't have any non-white friends. *Washington Post.* Retrieved from https://www.washingtonpost.com/news/wonk/wp/2014/08/25/three-quarters-of-whites-dont-have-any-non-white-friends/?utm_term=.0e074d50d9d9

Jones-Correa, M. (2011). Commonalities, competition, and linked fate. In E. Telles, M. Sawyer & G. Rivera-Salgado (Eds.), *Just neighbors? Research on African American and Latino relations in the United States* (pp. 63–95). New York, NY: Russell Sage Foundation.

Leip, D. (2012). *David Leip's Atlas of U.S. presidential elections.* Retrieved from http://uselectionatlas.org/

Ley, D. (2003). Artists, aestheticisation and the field of gentrification. *Urban Studies, 40*(12), 2527–2544.

Maly, M. T. (2005). *Beyond segregation: Multiracial and multiethnic neighborhoods in the United States.* Philadelphia, PA: Temple University Press.

Massey, D. S., & Denton, N. (1993). *American apartheid: Segregation and the making of the underclass.* Cambridge, MA: Harvard University Press.

Mayorga-Gallo, S. (2014). *Behind the white picket fence: Power and privilege in a multiethnic neighborhood.* Chapel Hill, NC: University of North Carolina Press.

Mayorga-Gallo, S., & Hordge-Freeman, E. (2017). Between marginality and privilege: Gaining access and navigating the field in multiethnic settings. *Qualitative Research, 17*(4), 377–394.

Nteta, T. M. (2014). The past is prologue: African American opinion toward undocumented immigration. *Social Science History, 38*(3-4), 389–410.

NYT/CBS News Poll. (2010, April 28–May 2). *The New York Times/CBS News.* Retrieved from http://s3.amazonaws.com/nytdocs/docs/330/330.pdf

Oliver, M. L., & Shapiro, T. M. (1995–2006). *Black wealth/white wealth: A new perspective on racial inequality.* New York, NY: Routledge.

Powell, W. (2012, June 1). The question. *Cincinnati Magazine.* Retrieved from http://www.cincinnatimagazine.com/features/the-question3/

Putnam, R. (2000). *Bowling alone: The collapse and revival of American community.* New York, NY: Simon and Schuster.

Putnam, R. (2007). E pluribus unum: Diversity and community in the twenty-first century, the 2006 Johan Skytte prize lecture. *Scandinavian Political Studies, 30*(2), 137–174.

Smith, T. W., Marsden, P., Hout, M., & Kim, J. (2011). *General social surveys, 1972–2010.* Chicago, IL: National Opinion Research Center and Storrs, CT: The Roper Center for Public Opinion Research, University of Connecticut.

Swartsell, N. (2015, August 26). That which divides us. *CityBeat.* Retrieved from http://www.citybeat.com/home/article/13001852/that-which-divides-us

Tach, L. M. (2014). Diversity, inequality, and microsegregation: Dynamics of inclusion and exclusion in a racially and economically diverse community. *Cityscape, 16*(3), 13–45.

Wellman, D. T. (1977). *Portraits of white racism.* Cambridge, England: Cambridge University Press.

Wilson, W. J. (1987–2012). *The truly disadvantaged: The inner city, the underclass, and public policy.* Chicago, IL: University of Chicago Press.

CONCLUSION

Where Do We Go from Here?

Christina M. Greer

Almost all Americans can agree that the outcome of the 2016 presidential election will have reverberating effects for Black communities, cities, and immigrants for generations to come. The rippling effects of defunded and underfunded public resources, mass deportations of undocumented Black and Latinx immigrants, and the overall destruction of the social safety net will adversely affect marginalized groups in hard-hitting and racially targeted ways. Generations from now, Americans will look at this moment as a pivotal shift in how race, ethnicity, and immigrant status were redefined. We will also see this moment as a critical turning point in how cities and suburbs serve as focal points for scholars to better understand the effects of shifting Black demographics, especially as they relate to new or evolving challenges to Black politics and political leadership.

Together, Trump and his administration have been a catalyst for excavating a particular brand of racial animus in the United States, one rooted in white supremacy. However, as vocal and insidious as this presidential administration has been, most illuminating has been the complicit role of the federal government in aiding and abetting draconian policies that affect local and state level politics. For example, this administration has consistently nominated unqualified candidates for various cabinet positions with the support and subsequent confirmation by the Republican-led Senate. Education Secretary Betsy DeVos and Housing and Urban Development Secretary Ben Carson are just two of the most glaring examples of individuals unqualified for and uneducated about the positions they hold. Philanthropist and businesswoman DeVos has held no positions in higher education, and neurosurgeon Dr. Carson has had no experience in urban planning, development, or housing. Ultimately, their lack of expertise (and eagerness to defund their respective institutions) adversely affects local governments and their services to urban populations.

Overall, the administration and/or defunding of healthcare and reducing social welfare programs and creating additional barriers for those who need services will negatively affect all Americans, and marginalized populations in particular. The complex relationship between and among administrations at the local, state, and federal levels in this particular political moment has created grave concerns, especially for mayors' ability to lead and implement policy. For example, the financial independence of a mayor is often limited and tied to state-level budgets. Therefore, with over two-thirds of all state houses and governorships controlled by the Republican party for nearly a decade, many Black and Latinx mayors have found themselves attempting to negotiate with less than welcoming state-level parties who often view cities—which are implicitly associated with the most negative stereotypes of populations of color—as a drain on state level resources. The fiscal fate of local governments is intertwined with state and federal level leadership, which makes the late twentieth and early twenty-first century conservative wave in state houses and in the federal government especially disconcerting for Black (and Latinx) populations at the local level.

What's more, the redistribution of US House of Representative delegates after the 2010 US Census count coupled with the subsequent racial and partisanship gerrymandering of historically underrepresented communities and the fallout of the Supreme Court's decision to gut the Voting Rights Act has opened Pandora's box. Black and Latinx communities have been packed into districts leaving groups battling for scarce resources and diluted political strength. In addition, state-level laws pertaining to increased obstacles to vote or even attempting to register to vote have also contributed to a weakened Black political power at the local level. Consequently, the Republican Party has been able to reign supreme even in places where state partisan demographics are by no means predictive of the partisan composition of state legislative houses. Republicans' conservative agenda, in turn, has been put into full effect across the US, and it has had crippling effects for Black and Latinx Americans at the local level.

To some, state versus local tensions have been cause for great concern. However, even with political and partisan infighting, cities are seeing a resurgence with population increases and white migration back into urban spaces. What are the political, economic, and social costs and benefits of "resurgence" and "revitalization"? As Black mayors and leaders of majority–minority cities, suburbs, and towns attempt to negotiate the effects of crumbling infrastructure, weed out "bad apples" in police departments, grapple with the sociopolitical effects of shifting population demographics, and negotiate rapid gentrification and overall affordability issues, the complexities of descriptive versus substantive representation as well as the limitations of local leaders are often laid bare. Is a Black female mayor best for a majority–minority city if her agenda primarily placates corporate interests? Is a Latinx mayor of a changing city of use to families of mixed-immigration status if s/he does not overtly fight for the rights of immigrants, both documented and undocumented, and their children?

Perhaps the most glaring new phenomenon with the uptick in revitalization processes of cities is that the possibilities for Black leadership have actually begun to decline at the mayoral level. Black and brown constituencies elected Black mayors during an era when cities were in economic decline, thus providing a so-called "empty prize," but nowadays major cities like Philadelphia and Detroit no longer have Blacks at the helm. Meanwhile cities like New York, Chicago, and Los Angeles seem to be "one and done" for the foreseeable future. That is, each of the three largest US cities has had one elected Black mayor in their city's history—David Dinkins, Harold Washington, and Tom Bradley—with no real contenders being groomed for the future. Currently, of the top 15 largest US cities, only one has a Black mayor: Houston.

Needless to say, rapidly changing demographics in cities have other potentially troubling effects. First, now that some cities are seeing influxes of younger, wealthier, and whiter migrants, Blacks are being pushed out of their homes, neighborhoods, and sometimes the entire city altogether. There are some places where Blacks are more vulnerable to these processes, but the twenty-first century push-pull factors seem to be disproportionately aimed at pushing Blacks out of cities into surrounding and sometimes declining suburbs, while pulling in corporations, wealthier individuals, and even immigrant populations to satisfy the needs of a growing or rebuilding city. One need only to look at New Orleans post-Hurricane Katrina. After the 2005 storm, the city lost roughly half of its population, dropping the city's population to a mere roughly 255,000 residents. However, as of the 2015 recounting, the city has regained almost 80% of its pre-Katrina population, but many of the new residents are neither Black nor are they former residents of the city. This type of "disaster capitalism", as Naomi Klien calls it, has particular adverse effects on Black communities as much of the economic redevelopment after a disaster often excludes marginalized groups or the groups who were initially displaced by the disaster.

Second, as cities seek to replenish their populations from the drastic losses due to white- and middle-class flight during the 1980s and 1990s era of crack-cocaine and widespread institutional disinvestment of urban centers, many cities are now actively recruiting immigrants into their ranks with the promise of affordable housing, small business opportunities and loans, and a recommitment to providing goods and services one should expect from an urban center. Not to put too fine a point on it, but when white- and middle-class flight occurred almost 30 years ago, cities and the Black populations that remained were neglected, underserved, and often ignored. The Black residents who were "left behind" are often blamed for the woes that befell their respective cities, even though, at times, poor Black populations were one of the primary sources of any revenue generated in dilapidated and underpopulated locales.

Thus, the promise of revitalization is not only bittersweet for many Blacks but also a poignant reminder of the racialized policies that initially led to the urban neglect in the first place. To be sure, contemporary revitalization plans are often steeped in modern, racialized policies (as were the previous plans which built up the suburbs many decades ago). On the one hand, new city planning processes and incoming capital are contributing to many cities' revitalization, but on the other hand, these plans often do not consider the needs of the Black citizens who already live there; indeed, many of these plans rely on the removal of Black, Latinx, and in some cases, Asian American bodies in order to come to fruition.

Third, as the country begins to incorporate a more inclusive political understanding of racial and ethnic groups beyond the Black–white paradigm, the perception of ostensibly scarce resources has the potential to erode substantive coalition-building across racial, ethnic, and class lines. Although many Blacks see the narratives surrounding "Black versus Latinx" competition as a racialized attempt at economic distraction and racist scapegoating, declines in economic mobility (exacerbated by the Great Recession) coupled with the loss of descriptive representation could contribute to growing dissent and distrust among traditionally underrepresented and marginalized groups. Future scholarship ought to grow the literature that dissects the relationship between Black groups, other groups of color, and liberal whites in order to best chronicle the shifting demands for new leadership and political incorporation.

As Blacks are pushed out of urban centers and into suburbs (and as many willingly choose to migrate to suburbs across the country), new questions surrounding representation and the urbanization of the suburbs arise. Lest we forget, Mike Brown was not murdered by a St. Louis police officer, but instead, he and his family were living in the majority Black suburb of Ferguson, Missouri. The continued geographic expansion of Black populations raises new and interesting questions surrounding the future of second-, third-, and fourth-tier city mayors and electoral leadership, as well as the ways in which racial and partisan gerrymandering will affect the political outcomes and prospects of Black citizens. How will newly located Black and immigrant populations adjust, become politically active, and negotiate the racial and sometimes racist norms of American suburbs? Will suburban areas merely become mini-cities with paralleled economic disparities and imbalanced opportunities? With increased Black migration, will American suburbs ultimately become neglected areas mirroring the institutional and economic neglect witnessed in the latter part of the twentieth century in majority Black cities?

Finally, as our contributors noted, Black communities continue to diversify geographically in part due to the flow and dispersal of Black immigrants across the United States. Black immigrants are contributing to the economic vitality of cities as well as running for state and local office, as they seek to simultaneously represent the interests of members of their ethnic group, their racial group, and their non-Black constituents. Though there are several clearly positive aspects of increased Black ethnic diversity, the coupling of Black racial and ethnic identities has created complex and sometimes complicated discussions pertaining to representation, inclusion, stereotypes, and in-group verses out-group status. Consequently, as the definition of Black identity is complicated by candidates, so are the nuances of particular issues within the increasingly diverse group of Blacks living in urban centers and suburbs throughout the country. A more robust discussion of the needs and wants of Black groups can only better assist in our understanding of Black political participation and inclusion moving forward.

The concepts of suburbanization, gentrification, and immigration affect Black communities in specific ways. It is our hope that this text has illuminated some of the themes, theories, and scholarship that help us to better understand the ways in which Black politics and political identity are redefined and negotiated in the twenty-first century.

INDEX

CPSIA information can be obtained
at www.ICGtesting.com
Printed in the USA
LVHW081753110919
630734LV00012B/234/P